John Heffernan, actor

'Really wonderful. The clear-sightedness, wit and depth of knowledge and insight into the plays and their worlds is unparalleled. It brought back so many happy memories of sitting in the audience at the Tobacco Factory over the years, the psychological detailing as thrilling on the page as it is on stage. The only downside was I ended up on several occasions kicking myself for the productions I have missed! The chapter on the "seriousness" of comedy and granting *As You Like It* and *The Comedy of Errors* the compliment of a fully complex reality should be required reading for everyone approaching those plays. The discussion of Leontes' jealousy and the fracturing of his focus as he tries to speak to Mamillius is completely fascinating. I kept wanting to jump up and shout "Yes!" that Andrew had found the key to unlock so many of these plays and it was now being passed on. It's a fabulous book, brimful of wisdom and revelations and a gift to anyone interested in Shakespeare or, quite frankly, in people.'

Susannah Clapp, theatre critic of the Observer

'Andrew Hilton's Tobacco Factory Shakespeares were an inspiration. A small area, an ensemble; no stars, just all-out talent. Above all, a determination to find the truth of each speech: what he calls "mining the text". What audiences saw and heard was not a display but an uncovering. His productions did not add to the drama: they revealed it. In *Shakespeare on the Factory Floor*, Hilton shows how he penetrates to the heart of a scene. And then projects it. His examination of individual lines is exact, minute and illuminating – but never merely academic. This is spoken and embodied Shakespeare. Strategic observations help to explain why his productions were so buoyant: one underlying belief is that seriousness is not to do with resisting comedy but depends on taking seriously the inner lives of characters; one fundamental resistance is to the "warping" of plays by the hierarchy of stars; one settled dislike is of the idea that Shakespeare had a fixed moral scheme – a "recipe for deadly theatre". Once again Hilton has lit up Shakespeare: lucid and penetrating on the page and on the stage.'

Andrew Hilton

Shakespeare
on the Factory Floor

A Handbook
for Actors, Directors & Designers

NICK HERN BOOKS
London
www.nickhernbooks.co.uk

A Nick Hern Book

Shakespeare on the Factory Floor
first published in Great Britain in 2022
by Nick Hern Books Limited,
The Glasshouse, 49a Goldhawk Road, London W12 8QP

Cover photograph: Natalia Dobryanskaya/Shutterstock.com

Designed and typeset by Nick Hern Books, London
Printed and bound in Great Britain by TJ Books Limited

A CIP catalogue record for this book is available from the British Library

ISBN 978 1 84842 893 5

MIX
Paper from
responsible sources
FSC
www.fsc.org   FSC® C013056

For Diana and Jim

&

*in fond memory of
Carrie*

Contents

Preface

Over eighteen spring seasons, from 2000 to 2017, I directed twenty-seven Shakespeare productions for Shakespeare at the Tobacco Factory, the company that I created for the new studio theatre in South Bristol. That added up to 5,000 hours or more spent putting the plays on their feet on the Tobacco Factory floor, a process that required that every line, every relationship, every feeling, every motive, every entrance and exit was questioned and understood; one that constantly threw up new problems and new possibilities. It was a truly collaborative process that, year by year, deepened our understanding, overturned many of our preconceptions, and confirmed me in my own belief that in tackling Shakespeare we should start with questions, not with answers.

While I hope theatre study students and a general audience might find food for thought here, this is a book principally for practitioners – for directors, actors and designers. I am a passionate believer in the collaborative approach to production, that there should be crossover between all three disciplines; most specifically, that actors should be allowed an interpretative head, a voice on the development of the whole. It is a matter of mutual respect, but also of stimulus. In my many years of teaching Shakespeare acting, at the Bristol Old Vic School and elsewhere, I have found that the intense pleasure in getting to grips with Shakespeare's purpose – intellectually as well as instinctively and emotionally – has a profoundly liberating effect on young actors' work; a release from exacting self-analysis about their technique; about their voice, their movement and their stagecraft. And at the Tobacco Factory the same collective sharing and focus fostered a degree of unselfishness I had never encountered in the theatre before.

At the Factory ours was that now rare thing, an ensemble company. We gathered for about sixteen weeks each January to put on two plays, mainly Shakespeare, but also Chekhov, Middleton and Rowley, Molière, Sheridan and Stoppard. Despite no public funding we were able – by keeping administration to a minimum, with a team of never more than three multi-talented managers and publicists – to afford an acting company of between fifteen and twenty-two. In our improvised space we worked in the round, with little more than actors in costume, and a few sticks of furniture, on a part-tiled floor bare but for four structural iron pillars. These we learned to dress as stone or wooden columns, as stove chimneys or as trees; we hung hammocks from them, built seats round them, or bolted ladders to them for fairies to hang from in the Athenian woods.

The space was intimate without being poky; it made for Shakespeare in close-up, with no member of the 300-strong audience sitting more than twenty feet away. The glories of the plays – and sometimes their shortcomings – were laid bare, as were the actors' immersion in their roles; for them there was no hiding place, and nothing to be gained from grandstanding or rhetorical booming; Shakespeare need only be spoken 'trippingly on the tongue', as the great man prescribed, with a complete understanding – instinctive, emotional and intellectual – of the dramatic moment.

This book is just one fruit of that process, and is likewise an attempt to understand and explore.

*

Shakespeare Text: All the quoted text I use – allowing for some generally accepted emendations – is from the First Folio collected edition, except where noted. But the punctuation throughout is my own, as is my choice not to capitalise the first letter of every verse line. I find almost all Shakespeare texts too heavily punctuated, and the formality of the traditional typography at variance with the light and rapid flow of Shakespeare's words.

Of the two conventions used to denote whether or not the final 'ed' in a past tense verb is sounded – by replacing the 'e' with an apostrophe when it is *not*, or marking it with an accent when it *is* – I use the former. And for consistency's sake – and because Shakespeare's prose is almost as rhythmic as his verse – I follow this through in the prose sections (as does the Folio, on the whole).

I follow many editors in attempting to show when a verse line is shared between two speakers, as in this passage from Act 3 Scene 2 of *The Comedy of Errors*:

LUCIANA. Why call you me love? Call my sister so.

SYR. ANTIPH. Thy sister's sister.

LUCIANA.   That's my sister.

SYR. ANTIPH.   No.

– the second, third and fourth speeches sharing an iambic pentameter. The Folio texts do not do this, and there are many instances when the sharing is uncertain, owing to the frequent irregularity of Shakespeare's verse, but as the sharing implies a continuity in the rhythm it can be an illuminating practice. I will point to one such instance in the great scene between Isabella and Claudio – Act 3 Scene 1 – in *Measure for Measure*.

I also risk interpreting a missing syllable or two in the pentameter pattern as a *break*, a momentary hiatus in the flow; this is always speculative, but always worthy of consideration.

I quote extensively, so that – although a broad knowledge of the plays in question is assumed – readers will not have to have copies of the texts open as they progress through the book.

Glosses on obscure words and phrases are my own. My production practice has been to substitute current usages in those relatively few instances where I believe an audience might be baffled, but here I use Shakespeare's words only, again unless otherwise noted.

'Shadow text': I use this term of my own to describe an implied meaning – expressed in imagery or metaphor – that is not the intended meaning of the speaker and may even contradict that meaning, as in a Camillo speech in the opening scene of *The Winter's Tale* (see page 109). This is distinct from a 'subtext', the term we use to describe an underlying intent or feeling of the speaker that generates – and can occasionally be masked by – the surface text. There are times, however, when the distinction between the two is blurred. The 'shadow' meaning may be registered by the onstage hearer(s), or not.

Production Notes: Completing each section, I detail a number of choices we made – including some radical edits and additions – in the Tobacco Factory productions.

Sources: the study of Shakespeare's transformations is always enlightening, and a number of the key source texts I refer to are available (see the notes at the end of each chapter) to download in modern spelling versions from my own website: www.andrewhilton.online

References: I am not an academic, and this is not an academic book; as far as possible I restrict my references to commentaries easily accessed by the general reader – for example, to such works as *Will in the World* by Stephen Greenblatt, *The Genius of Shakespeare* by Jonathan Bate, *1599* by James Shapiro and *Women of Will* by Tina Packer, all of which have figured in good High Street bookshops. I also refer to some older critical works that still have currency, such as John Dover Wilson's *What Happens in Hamlet* and T.S. Eliot's *Essays*. There are references to some more testingly academic works, mostly from America's fecund university presses, but these are few.

Introduction

Image and Word

Theatre now, following in the footsteps of film, so often foregrounds the image. In the Elizabethan theatre it was the word. Words were deemed sufficient in themselves; beyond the record of entrances and exits, and the odd 'stabs him' or 'she dies', there was little or no need to supply producers with ancillary instructions. On a largely unchanging stage, language alone transported the audience from Rome to Alexandria, from palace to prison, and from giddy excitement to the depths of despair.

Shakespeare is, and will always remain, that theatre's greatest expositor. This is a book about staging his words; exploring them, relishing them, trusting them; and inhabiting the characters who speak them. It is about mining the text: for feeling, for the tones and intents Shakespeare so precisely articulates, for truth.

Opening Our Minds

While there are, and should be, no absolute rights and wrongs in Shakespeare production, we should never forget that it is Shakespeare's imagination that is the real matter in hand and that it is – forgive me – vastly more interesting, challenging and profound than yours or mine. So we should explore the plays in as open-minded a fashion as we can, rather than attempt to annex them to our own preoccupations. To some degree such annexation will happen anyway; Shakespeare's account of the human experience is so wide, rich and robust that every generation will be drawn instinctively to contrasting emphases, will 'read' Shakespeare differently. As Peter Hall once said of *Hamlet*, 'it turns a new face to every decade'.

The obstacles to open-mindedness are of two varieties. The first is our own vanity – and directors' vanity has outstripped that of actors by a large margin in recent decades – and the second, to which all involved are victim, is the lumber of memory we carry about with us: ineradicable images of star performances, inherited character judgements, performance tricks and traditions both large and small, and – most of all – our gross over-familiarity with Shakespeare's plots. But the task to renew and refresh is endlessly exciting, providing we strive to be guided by the language and are at ease in spending time in rehearsal in creative muddle, in not knowing where our journeys will end.

I present not a single thesis, but pursue a number of issues: emotional truth in Shakespeare comedy, the usefulness of source material, the importance of the plays' social dynamics, the choice of settings and periods, making and withholding moral judgements, a technique for creative ignorance and more; all in the course of tracking twenty individual character stories. I am concerned to resist easy theatrical notions of identity – of defining Leontes as the type of the jealous man, Lady Macbeth the type of the manipulative, or Orsino the type of the narcissistic – since such pigeonholing stifles the possibility of change and development, and fixes characters in ways that exclude them from the continuum of human experience; it allows us to 'place' them and spare us the realisation that we all have the potential for a Leontes, a Lady Macbeth or an Orsino within us.

These people live in action and intention, in thought and emotion, all elements that are capable of a wide spectrum of behaviour and – most excitingly for the actor – of radical change. It is as if all Shakespeare's major characters, within their inescapable roles as prince, general, duchess, shepherd or counsellor, have access to a wide spectrum of states of being, and of possibility; that the plays are more about *living*, than about *lives*.

Step by Step

To keep those possibilities in play, I will advocate a step-by-step approach. To begin with an example: in *King Lear* there is no escaping the fact that Regan's husband, the Duke of Cornwall, has a fiery temperament and that it is wise not to cross him. This is a defined personality trait that he has brought with him to the action:

> You know the fiery quality of the Duke,
> how unremoveable and fix'd he is
> in his own course.
>
> Act 2 Scene 4

And we see this exemplified when he commits an emissary from the King to a night in the stocks. But it does not mean that he should be defined from the start as a practised tyrant, let alone a sadist. In the RSC's powerful and moving 2016 production of the play, directed by Gregory Doran and designed by Niki Turner, with Antony Sher as Lear, James Clyde as Cornwall and David Troughton as Gloucester, we were introduced to the Gloucester-blinding scene (Act 3 Scene 7) with a stark image: a perspex cell containing a single chair. The reference was immediate, the all too familiar setting for extra-judicial torture. (To anyone familiar with the play, the perspex screening also suggested the likelihood of a spectacular but controlled bloodletting – we were not disappointed.) Now it is true that some extreme violence is in Cornwall's mind from the start:

> Edmond, keep you our sister company. The revenges we
> are bound to take upon your traitorous father are not fit
> for your beholding.

But there is no evidence in the text that he has a specific plan, though at the beginning of the scene Regan advocates hanging and Goneril – who will not be present at the event itself – plants a seed by saying 'Pluck out his eyes'. Far from being a man coldly inured to the kind of action he intends, Cornwall is uncomfortably aware that he is being led by rage rather than by policy:

> Go seek the traitor Gloucester,
> pinion him like a thief, bring him before us.
> Though well we may not pass upon his life
> without the form of justice, yet our power
> shall do a curtsy to our wrath, which men
> may blame, but not control.

That 'curtsy to our wrath' is tellingly fastidious, a form of apology that suggests a man entering unfamiliar territory.

Gloucester is brought in and Cornwall orders that his servants 'bind fast his corky arms'. Then comes the order that no doubt provoked the RSC's chilling setting:

> To this chair bind him.

But is this really a cell, and has the chair been specifically placed? There needs to be one ready to hand, certainly, but that would hardly be by special order in the hall or great chamber of a great house. And the next beat is not the eye-gouging, but the interrogation – 'Come, sir, what letters had you late from France?' – when the furious Cornwall overbears the nervous old man and Regan plucks hairs from his beard. When the real cruelty comes, far better that it does so as a shock, that it is improvised, the setting *unprepared*. Each step in this appalling scene is as one taken in new snow, and it is at its most interesting if Cornwall does not know what the revenges unfit for Edmond's beholding will be until the cornered Gloucester tires of evasion and in the most courageous speech he may ever have voiced, gives this justification for the help he has extended to Lear:

> Because I would not see thy cruel nails
> pluck out his poor old eyes, nor thy fierce sister
> in his anointed flesh stick boarish fangs.
> The sea, with such a storm as his bare head
> in hell-black night endur'd, would have buoy'd up
> and quench'd the stelled fires,
> yet, poor old heart, he holp the heavens to rain.
> If wolves had at thy gate howl'd that stern time,
> thou shouldst have said 'Good porter, turn the key,
> all cruels else subscribe'. But I shall see
> the winged vengeance overtake such children.

With these words Gloucester himself determines his punishment. For it is his eyes' witness to the cruelty of the children, the older generation overseeing and censuring the behaviour of the younger, that – more than the treason of which he is unarguably guilty – cannot be borne. He offers up the remedy, to pluck those witnesses out, and Cornwall seizes on it:

> See't shalt thou never. Fellows, hold the chair.
> Upon these eyes of thine I'll set my foot.

But his 'curtsy to wrath' is the error of a beginner in tyranny and risks consequences a more practised hand would have foreseen, as Regan will reflect later in the play:

> It was great ignorance, Gloucester's eyes being out,
> to let him live. Where he arrives he moves
> all hearts against us.

Act 4 Scene 4

New-felt, chaotic passions drive Cornwall's actions, not premeditated strategy. If we set out on the scene knowing exactly how it will end – as the RSC's setting signalled so heavily – we lose much of its interest, and engage merely in the longstanding theatrical competition in graphic nastiness. We lose the sense of newness, the possibility of alternative outcomes, and the element of surprise.

Much of this book will be about trying to take scenes like this step by step, putting our foreknowledge as best we can to one side and living in the moment, while listening as acutely as we can to the varying tunes of the human mind.

Acknowledgements

Many friends, family and colleagues have contributed to the work described in this book. I am grateful first to my parents for introducing me to Shakespeare theatre when I was a very young child; to teachers Jim Garbett, Neil Gill, Norma Wardle and Michael Long; to Jonathan Miller for promoting me both as actor and director; to Richard Cottrell and Adrian Noble for taking me to Bristol to play my first season there at the Old Vic; to the Old Vic Theatre School for employing me to teach Shakespeare acting to many wonderfully talented young students; to George Ferguson for allowing me to create a Shakespeare company in his inspirational Tobacco Factory; to my wife, Diana Favell, without whose practical, moral and financial support I could never have started or sustained a new company; and to my associate, Dominic Power, and the 500-strong army of Actors, Designers, Composers, Administrators, Technicians, Trustees, Patrons and Volunteers who contributed so much to the success of Shakespeare at the Tobacco Factory (stf) during my eighteen-year tenure as Artistic Director.

Specifically in the preparation of the book, I am hugely indebted to Lesel Dawson of the University of Bristol (and an stf Trustee) for close analyses of early drafts; and to her colleague, Laurence Publicover; to Susannah Clapp, Alan Coveney, Christopher Frayling, John Heffernan and Jim Hilton, who all read an early draft and gave it enthusiastic endorsement; to Christina Shewell and Nick de Somogyi who examined a late draft (any surviving howlers are entirely my own); and lastly to Matt Applewhite and John O'Donovan of Nick Hern Books for taking the book on and requiring me to make it a better one.

Chapter One

Serious Comedy

It seems to have come about – or perhaps it was ever so in the theatre – that comedy and tragedy are assumed to work to very different rules. The characters of tragedy are to be probed as deeply as they are capable, while their counterparts in comedy may be reached down from a severely circumscribed library of comic and romantic types. But Shakespeare's comedies are very much more complex than that, and in this chapter I make an argument for them to be taken seriously, and in no area more so than in their exploration of sexual love, which is their common theme.

So I am going to look at romantic relationships in three of Shakespeare greatest serious comedies: first, and briefly, at Antipholus of Syracuse and Luciana in *The Comedy of Errors*; then at greater length at Rosalind and Orlando in *As You Like It*; and finally at Viola and Orsino in *Twelfth Night*. *The Comedy of Errors* I directed for stf in 2011, *As You Like It* in 2003 and again in 2014, and *Twelfth Night* in 2002.

Seriousness is not a matter of *resisting* comedy – of choosing, for example, that Malvolio's yellow stockings should be of such a subtle shade that they will not look ridiculous against his puritanical black. It is a matter of how we choose to present characters' inner lives, how seriously we take what they do and what they say. Again and again in the production of these plays we see disparities between language and presentation, words floating by unexamined and unheeded, all in the cause of what is considered to be Shakespeare's simple intention, to entertain.

Love is his subject, and he repeatedly refers to it – seriously, I suggest – as a madness, or a fever. It attacks suddenly and without warning. It expresses itself in hyperbolic praise of the loved object, in impossibly infinite qualities of beauty, virtue, courage, manners. It is immensely volatile; a new madness may expel an old in seconds; or the green-eyed monster, jealousy, may turn the hyperbole of praise into the hyperbole of hate almost as quickly.

It is a madness because love is all-consuming, because it enslaves the mind and heart, turning rational beings into Cupid's playthings. It is fundamental to the greater part of human joy, but is also instrumental in terrible tragedy, as we see particularly in *Othello* and *The Winter's Tale*. In dealing with love, the comedies and tragedies are not of different worlds, but a continuum, each bearing within them the seeds of the other.

1. Antipholus of Syracuse and Luciana

The Comedy of Errors has been considered by some to have been Shakespeare's first play. I doubt that myself, but if it was, and despite a structural problem – the late introduction of both Antipholus of Ephesus and the Courtesan – it was an extraordinarily assured debut. It has also been widely thought of as a knockabout farce and frequently produced as such.

The opening scene, where the Syracusean Egeon faces execution by sundown in the enemy city of Ephesus, is particularly difficult, containing as it does the lengthy exposition of Egeon's tragic history; but by staging it simply and quietly it can serve well to set the play in motion, and on anything but a comic note. In our intimate space at the Tobacco Factory we sat David Collins' Egeon on a simple wooden chair, and Paul Currier's Duke behind his office desk; a stenographer, Nicky Goldie (later to double as the Abbess), took shorthand notes, and a single officer (Craig Fuller) stood by an entrance; there were no others present. To aid the audience to listen – and to listen hard – the Duke himself must listen, and *want* to listen. The sympathy he would like to extend to the prisoner, but which Ephesian law forbids, is crucial to our own comprehension.

Egeon's story is a particularly moving one and it should alert us to the fact that this is no farce, but a drama in which profound attachments are at stake. But if Egeon's predicament is not enough, then listen to one of his lost sons, Antipholus of Syracuse. He has coincidentally arrived at Ephesus by ship on the same day and his imagination is full of the sea and of what seems to be a hopeless quest, the search for his identical twin brother from whom he was parted at sea when a baby:

I to the world am like a drop of water
that in the ocean seeks another drop,
who, falling there to find his fellow forth,
unseen, inquisitive, confounds himself.
So I, to find a mother and a brother,
in quest of them unhappy, lose myself.

Act 1 Scene 2

The vastness of the ocean, and its capacity to absorb flesh and blood like so many drops of water is a repeated trope in Shakespeare, together with magical survivals; in *Measure for Measure* Mariana's brother has been lost at sea (together with Mariana's dowry), while in *Twelfth Night* Sebastian will be presumed lost in a storm, and yet be found; in *Pericles* Thaisa will be cast overboard as a corpse, yet discovered with still a spark of life on the shore of Ephesus. In this play as many as five souls are feared erased by the ocean, and yet all will be found.

Antipholus' search is not only for a twin. He is looking also for his mother, just as his luckless father has spent seven summers combing the Mediterranean for all five of his lost family. Towards the end of his career, in *The Winter's Tale*, Leontes will lose and then find a wife and a daughter; and in *Pericles* a child believed murdered and buried will be found to have survived. *The Comedy of Errors* marks the beginning of a career-long theme.

Interrogating the Moment

So I, to find a mother and a brother,
in quest of them, unhappy, lose myself.

This notion of a loss of self takes us straight into both the comedy and the beating heart of this wonderful play. If we take this speech seriously, give space to its emotional moment, what might we make of Antipholus' feeling? How incomplete is he without his mother and without his twin? We know of levels of empathy between identical twins that go far beyond that between ordinary siblings, so are the two Antipholuses almost one and the same? Or are the two Dromios? Actually, it would seem not. Shakespeare would have been abundantly aware that the actors who would be shaved and dressed to look as alike as possible would still have different personalities, different voices. And that is how he portrays them: Antipholus of Syracuse 'abhors' his sister-in-law, Adriana, for a wife and 'inclines' instead to her sister, Luciana. Dromio of Ephesus is married, or promised to Nell, the greasy kitchen wench, from whom his brother will run for his life, 'as from a bear'. Dromio of Syracuse can run riddling circles round his master, yet his brother is sometimes as bewildered by language as all the characters are by circumstance.

Could these be merely differences of nurture? The two Syracusans have been brought up in the knowledge that their twins are lost but may yet be found. In contrast, the two Ephesians are completely ignorant of their natural families, ignorant of the full nature of their loss, ignorant of their *twinhood*. Has this made them different people – the first pair into wanderers, forever bonded by their shared sense of incompleteness, the second comfortably embedded within the social structure of Ephesus, very much wealthy master and exploited servant? Or is there even a possibility that a completely unrecognised incompleteness within Antipholus of Ephesus has functioned unconsciously as a barrier to him realising a full marital relationship with Adriana – for their marriage is clearly in trouble? That is almost certainly a step too far, and there may be no answers to any of these questions to be gleaned from the text, yet in rehearsal it is important that we ask them; the psychological consequences of the tragedy that befell them all as infants should be explored. The 'drop of water' speech demands that much from us.

Attention to such possibilities always pays dividends; even when we explore avenues that lead nowhere the discipline of questioning lends us access to the fullest humanity a play can offer. This play's genesis is in the Plautine comedy *Menaechmi*, which Shakespeare may have studied (in Latin) at Stratford's free Grammar School, and it may account, in part, for the play's mistaken characterisation as farce, for *Menaechmi* makes little room for psychological depth and none at all for romantic interest. But Shakespeare is already adept at modifying his stolen vehicle to carry a much richer tonal load than his Roman master, and we should give it credit for that.

To take just one scene, Act 3 Scene 2: in this Antipholus of Syracuse attempts to woo his twin's sister-in-law, Luciana. He has evidently distressed his twin's wife, Adriana, who has taken him for her erring husband, by ignoring her and paying rapt attention to Luciana instead. Entering together from their uncomfortable dinner scene, Luciana takes Antipholus to task for his apparently callous cruelty:

> LUCIANA. And may it be that you have quite forgot
> a husband's office? Shall, Antipholus,
> even in the spring of love, thy love-springs rot?
> Shall love, in building, grow so ruinate?

If you did wed my sister for her wealth
then for her wealth's sake use her with more kindness…

Dan Winter as Antipholus of Syracuse and Ffion Jolly as Luciana, photo © Hide the Shark 2011

She expresses her protectiveness towards her sister, and a worldly-wise acknowledgement that not all marriages are love-matches. She is inventively eloquent – 'be not thy tongue thy own shame's orator', 'though others have the arm, show us the sleeve'. It is completely bewildering to Antipholus who has met both sisters for the first time only a matter of an hour or so ago, but we must not allow the comedy of bewilderment to overwhelm the scene; Luciana's words have their own validity, their profound feeling, and Antipholus is affected as well as bewildered. In fact he is entranced, and inclined to doubt his own self-knowledge rather than Luciana's sanity:

> SYR. ANTIPH. Sweet mistress – what your name is else, I know not,
> nor by what wonder you do hit of mine.
> Less in your knowledge and your grace you show not
> than our earth's wonder, more than earth divine.
> Teach me, dear creature, how to think and speak.
> Lay open to my earthy gross conceit,
> smother'd in errors, feeble, shallow, weak,
> the folded meaning of your words' deceit.
> Against my soul's pure truth why labour you

to make it wander in an unknown field?
Are you a god? Would you create me new?
Transform me then and to your power I'll yield.
But if that I am I, then well I know
your weeping sister is no wife of mine,
nor to her bed no homage do I owe.
Far more, far more to you do I incline.[1]
O, train me not, sweet mermaid, with thy note,
to drown me in thy sister's flood of tears.
Sing, siren, for thyself and I will dote,
spread o'er the silver waves thy golden hairs
and as a bed I'll take thee and there lie,
and in that glorious supposition think
he gains by death that hath such means to die.
Let Love, being light, be drowned if she sink!

This is a love poem – six quatrains long – almost worthy of the mature sonneteer, or of John Donne. Antipholus is no longer lost in the ocean, but would be found, completed, in Luciana's love. It is persuasive; observe the sudden change in Luciana's expression from her own flowing quatrains into single questions and statements as she struggles to hold her purpose. Antipholus' certainty in reply Shakespeare emphasises with answering rhyme:

LUCIANA. What, are you mad, that you do reason so?

SYR. ANTIPH. Not mad, but mated, how I do not know.

LUCIANA. It is a fault that springeth from your eye.

SYR. ANTIPH. For gazing on your beams, fair sun, being by.

LUCIANA. Gaze where you should, and that will clear your sight.

SYR. ANTIPH. As good to wink, sweet love, as look on night.

LUCIANA. Why call you me 'love'? Call my sister so.

SYR. ANTIPH. Thy sister's sister.

LUCIANA.   That's my sister.

SYR. ANTIPH.   No,
        it is thyself, mine own self's better part,
        mine eye's clear eye, my dear heart's dearer heart,
        my food, my fortune and my sweet hope's aim,
        my sole earth's heaven and my heaven's claim.

LUCIANA. All this my sister is, or else should be.

SYR. ANTIPH. Call thyself sister, sweet, for I am thee.
        Thee will I love and with thee lead my life.
        Thou hast no husband yet nor I no wife.
        Give me thy hand.

Only now can Luciana's own thought be again expressed by completing a rhyming couplet:

> LUCIANA.   O, soft, sir, hold you still.
> I'll fetch my sister, to get her good will.

She leaves, not to escape this madman, but to 'get [*Adriana's*] good will' to take her husband for herself. It is an extraordinary journey for her from the start of the scene; but she is won.

If the words get in the way...

This is often played for pure comedy, with a touch of frenzy on the Antipholus actor's part that renders his wooing as laughable as the competitive wooing of Helena by Lysander and Demetrius, both under the influence of a mind-bending drug, in *A Midsummer Night's Dream.* That way the intended focus of our attention is not Antipholus' passion, but Luciana's comic confusion, chased round the stage perhaps by her bewilderingly importunate wooer. And all those words get in the way. *If the words get in the way, think again! Contrary to popular belief, Shakespeare is rarely verbose.* The better choice is to recognise that Antipholus is not only sincere, but that in his growing bewilderment as to his own identity, he believes he has found in Luciana a saving reality.

But a resolution now – to this amour, or to the identity-confusion – would cut the play short. So, in what is a mirroring, and certainly a highly comic one, of the wooing we have just seen, Shakespeare radically shifts the tone with the entrance of Dromio of Syracuse from the kitchen:

> SYR. ANTIPH. Why, how now, Dromio, where runn'st thou so fast?
>
> SYR. DROM. Do you know me, sir? Am I Dromio? Am I your man? Am I myself?
>
> SYR. ANTIPH. Thou art Dromio, thou art my man, thou art thyself.
>
> SYR. DROM. I am an ass, I am a woman's man and besides myself.
>
> SYR. ANTIPH. What woman's man? And how besides thyself?
>
> SYR. DROM. Marry, sir, besides myself, I am due to a woman, one that claims me, one that haunts me, one that will have me... she's the kitchen wench and all grease, and I know not what use to put her to but to make a lamp of her and run from her by her own light... She is spherical, like a globe. I could find out countries in her...

The lewd anatomisation of the spherical Nell readies us for the panic that overcomes Antipholus when Dromio reveals Nell's apparently supernatural knowledge of the marks on his body:

> … this drudge, or diviner, laid claim to me, call'd me
> Dromio, swore I was assur'd to her, told me what privy
> marks I had about me, as the mark of my shoulder, the
> mole in my neck, the great wart on my left arm, that I
> amaz'd ran from her as a witch.

This enables Antipholus to leave the house quickly. An early resolution is avoided, Antipholus apparently rejecting Luciana almost as suddenly as he has declared his passion for her:

> SYR. ANTIPH. There's none but witches do inhabit here,
> and therefore 'tis high time that I were hence…
> She that doth call me husband, even my soul
> doth for a wife abhor. But her fair sister,
> possess'd with such a gentle sovereign grace,
> of such enchanting presence and discourse,
> hath almost made me traitor to myself…

He fears that the spirit that was 'mine own self's better part, mine eye's clear eye' was a witch, a siren, luring him to his destruction.

In very quick time we have a plausible motive for Antipholus to prepare to depart the town, at the same time leaving – *if we have given it its due* – a true emotional thread that can be taken up in the last scene, a strong element of plausibility in his infatuation, and an equally strong hint that Luciana has been won by him.

The daring of this necessary manipulation of tone is one of the glories of this play. We are pitched into a thrilling switchback of emotion, in a Pirandellian world that repeatedly explores, then threatens to depart from, reality, but is masterful enough to keep all its elements in play, and to bring them together to give real emotional substance to the happy resolution at the end.

The lesson of this early masterpiece is that the greater the emotional truth we mine out of its characters' experiences, the richer the play becomes – and very probably the funnier too. In a five-star review of our own production John Peter wrote:

> This production is a revelation. This early play is more than a
> comedy. Voltaire announced that Shakespeare was a barbarian
> because his tragedies had comic scenes; the great Gallic sage

would have been appalled to see a shadow of fear hung over this improbable story... unmissable. (*The Sunday Times*, 3 April 2011)

Production Notes

A New Scene: A new scene, by my associate Dominic Power, inserted as a continuation of Act 1 Scene 2, provided an early introduction to both Antipholus of Ephesus (Matthew Thomas) and the Courtesan (Kate Kordel) – in her case avoiding the need for a hurried, and slightly clumsy, backstory in Act 4 Scene 3. Uncomfortably delayed exposition is not unique to this play (see also *Measure for Measure*) and highlights how Shakespeare lacked the time – let alone the cut-and-paste technology we now enjoy – to go back and adjust his plotting.

The Courtesan, Antipholus of Ephesus and Angelo, photo © Hide the Shark 2011

The scene, of fifty-four lines, shows Antipholus of Ephesus and his friend, the merchant Balthasar (David Collins, doubling), and the goldsmith, Angelo (Alan Coveney), out on the town. Angelo is asked about the progress of the gold chain that Antipholus has commissioned in an attempt to repair his relationship with Adriana, but they are intercepted by the

Courtesan who tempts the men into her house to dine, thus delaying Antipholus' return home to his wife.

The awkwardness in Act 4 Scene 3 is thus avoided – and the ripe *double entendres* Dominic gave the Courtesan were happily credited to Shakespeare by a national critic.

Four Songs: Dominic Power also interpolated four songs, set by our composer, Elizabeth Purnell. The first was for Dromio of Syracuse, on his arrival in Ephesus, the second a rowdy piece for Antipholus, arriving home with Angelo and Balthasar from their dinner with the Courtesan, and the fourth for Dromio of Ephesus at the beginning of Act 4 Scene 1. The third was this one, for Dromio of Syracuse, placed between Act 3 Scene 1 and Act 3 Scene 2:

> Mistress, thou doth love in error,
> when thou endeavour Love to know.
> We may not understand nor measure
> the aching heart, nor yet the treasure
> love at hazard doth bestow.
>
> Thy image study in the mirror,
> the glass will show the changes wrought
> by Love that we would make a minion,
> that o'er mankind hath dominion,
> so our confusion is Love's sport.

As Richard Neale sang, a light picked out Dorothea Myer-Bennett's Adriana *en déshabillé*, and in tears. Her attempt to woo her husband (as she believed him to be) back to her bed had failed, and she is both distressed and humiliated.

Setting: We brought the setting forward to the Edwardian period, which the play seemed to accept without a squeak; swordsticks replaced swords, and light linen suits and white cotton frocks evoked the warm Aegean climate.

Dominic's full production text is published on my website.

2. Rosalind and Orlando

Much academic commentary, and the focus of many productions of *As You Like It*, is on the play's metatheatricality – its self-consciousness that it is theatre, its performances within the performance, with their onstage observers and commentators – and its latent homoeroticism; Rosalind as 'Ganymede' (who in the Middle Ages typified homosexual love) would, in Shakespeare's theatre, have been a boy-player playing a woman playing a man. These are rich topics, but they are often explored to the exclusion of narrative tension; what happens in the play – and in particular what happens to Rosalind, so often assumed invulnerable – can be overlooked.

Here I offer a counter to that; that amid its cross-dressing, its wrestling match, its show-stopping songs, Touchstone's clowning and Jaques' oratory, the comedy of *As You Like It* encompasses a high seriousness; in the story of Rosalind and Orlando sanity, self-esteem and the human heart are at risk.

Using the Source

Shakespeare found his narrative for *As You Like It* in Thomas Lodge's *Rosalynde*, a lengthy pastoral romance that Lodge wrote to stave off boredom on a long voyage he made to the Canaries in about 1586. It was published in 1590, nearly a decade before Shakespeare adapted it into his play.[2] Attention to a play's source(s) often pays dividends, the choices and transformations made by the playwright offering keys to his own concerns. *As You Like It* is no exception.

Lodge's story, set in Paris and in the Forest of the Ardennes, has its own seriousness and moral purpose, focused on the disaster that threatens the de Boys family when the eldest son ignores his father's dying wish and treats his youngest brother very much as Oliver treats Orlando in the play. But its pastoral world is a particularly fanciful one. His love-lorn shepherd, Montanus (Shakespeare's Silvius), is able to express his unrequited love in highly wrought verse of his own invention, in both English and French; and he shares elements of the classical education that Lodge would have acquired at Merchant Taylors' School and Trinity College, Oxford, and Shakespeare more humbly at Stratford Grammar, but is unlikely to have been accessed by a hard-worked shepherd in the Ardennes or anywhere else. Montanus is a shepherd in name, but in action and behaviour he is a lover, a poet and a musician.

There are elements of fancy in Shakespeare's more English Arden, too; he retains the 'hungry lioness' that he found in *Rosalynde*, and places Corin's sheepcote among olive trees; but he fashions a greater connection to reality. His Arden, like Lodge's, is a blessed refuge from 'the envious court', a world 'sweeter than that of painted pomp', but at the same time – *unlike* Lodge's – it is subject to the 'season's difference, the icy fang and churlish chiding of the winter's wind', and to the darker tones associated with the five characters he introduces to the story: Jaques, Touchstone, Sir Oliver Martext, Audrey and William. In broadening the cast-list Shakespeare introduces realities of class: Audrey, the illiterate goatherd at the bottom of the social scale, is deceived into believing Touchstone a gentleman and therefore her route to become 'a woman of the world'. In William we do get the slow wit of the archetypal country bumpkin, but in Shakespeare's reimagining of the elderly shepherd, Corin, we find a completely individual countryman; his spat with Touchstone in Act 3 Scene 3 reveals a sharp wit, dignity and self-knowledge. Phebe, another character Shakespeare takes from Lodge, finds her own place in this adjusted scenario. She is literate, can even turn her pen to verse, and has the sharp and expressive intelligence to counter Silvius' charge that there is 'murder' in her eye:

> 'Tis pretty, sure, and very probable
> that eyes, that are the frail'st and softest things,
> who shut their coward gates on atomies,
> should be call'd tyrants, butchers, murderers!

Act 3 Scene 6

But she belongs, plausibly enough, to a rural community that is by no means immune to bourgeois values or to romantic cliché. While no one in *Rosalynde* seems to have any real connection with the soil, instead all sharing a common language of pastoral romance, Shakespeare's Arden is necessarily rooted in the real world – a world it is imperative we realise.

The Hyperbole of Love

As You Like It flows with the hyperbole of love. This is problematic – intentionally so – because it is so difficult to read from hyperbole the true value of the feeling it purports to express. Orlando, who has fallen in love with Rosalind at first sight, adorns the trees in the Forest of Arden with verses that extol her perfection in every conceivable respect. She is:

The quintessence of every sprite
Heaven would in little show…
Nature presently distill'd
Helen's cheek, but not her heart,
Cleopatra's majesty,
Atalanta's better part,
sad Lucretia's modesty.
Thus Rosalind of many parts
by heavenly synod was devis'd
of many faces, eyes and hearts,
to have the touches dearest priz'd.

Act 3 Scene 3

Rosalind, who finds these derivative scrawlings as she wanders through the forest, is quite properly embarrassed by them:

O most gentle pulpiter,[3] what tedious homily of love have you wearied your parishioners withal, and never cried 'Have patience, good people!'

Act 3 Scene 3

She knows that she is flesh and blood and no goddess. She is troubled, profoundly so, by the whole matter of the idealisation of the lover and of love itself. In her love-game with Orlando – disguised from him as the boy, Ganymede, pretending only to *play* Rosalind – she will declare:

Well, in her person I say I will not have you.

to which Orlando will offer the utterly clichéd response:

ORLANDO. Then in mine own person I die.

Rosalind's riposte is famous:

ROSALIND. No, faith, die by attorney. The poor world is almost six thousand years old and in all this time there was not any man died in his own person, videlicet in a love-cause. Troilus had his brains dash'd out with a Grecian club, yet he did what he could to die before, and he is one of the patterns of love. Leander, he would have liv'd many a fair year, though Hero had turn'd nun, if it had not been for a hot midsummer night. For, good youth, he went but forth to wash him in the Hellespont and being taken with the cramp was drown'd. Yet the foolish chroniclers of that age found it was [for] 'Hero of Sestos.' But these are all lies.

> Men have died from time to time and worms have eaten
> them, but not for love.
>
> Act 4 Scene 1

That scene is so often played as one between a thoroughly sorted young woman and a naively idealistic young man; as the sentimental education of Orlando, you might say, or the testing of Orlando by a prudently circumspect prospective wife. Indeed this approach is taken as a given, unquestioned and unexamined in much of the academic commentary on the play. James Shapiro remarks of Rosalind:

> We would expect Rosalind to shed her doublet and hose once
> secure in the knowledge of Orlando's love for her; but she won't
> until Orlando's education and transformation are complete.[4]

For Michael Hattaway, the editor of the New Cambridge edition of the play,[5] Rosalind is a therapist:

> ... in [Orlando's] courtship lesson with Rosalind, we have the
> feeling that she is preparing him to be her 'child's father' – the
> thought had come to her mind as early as 1.3. Unpunctual
> writers of trite verse are not made for such a role, and Rosalind
> initiates the therapy her lover seems to require, fashioning him
> according to her needs as well as her desires.

This idea of Rosalind in supreme control is, I believe, a grave mistake that has historically misjudged Rosalind, and delivered a play far less passionate and dramatic than the one Shakespeare wrote. For Rosalind is responding to the perils of sexual love as she apprehends them within herself, trying to master her own all-consuming adoration of Orlando, which is quite as boundless as Orlando's adoration of her. She is experiencing an involuntary loss of self in her own passion; and the absurd mismatch between Orlando's hyperbolic image of her and her felt reality – so much less than an ideal, less than divine – is the subject for her urgent enquiry, not for the amused and ironic commentary we so often see portrayed.

This misreading has been compounded, possibly even led, by the workings of the theatrical star system, warping a play to its own hierarchy, allowing the leading players to dominate the play's interactions, even to the point that they stand outside the contingent world of the text. In Rosalind's case, this seems to have led at least one academic commentator to fall in love with her; Harold C. Goddard writes:

> she supplies [the Forest] with an internal light... like the sun...
> she attracts everything that comes within her sphere and sheds

a radiance over it. She is the pure gold that needs no
touchstone.[6]

There have been others likewise in awe of Rosalind – or besotted by her –
and focused as all such are on Rosalind's agency within the play ('her play'
they often call it), they pay scant attention to what *happens to her.* Yet, I will
argue, what happens to her is the real issue and the real event. She is the
play's chief subject, not its author.

Meanwhile, in contrast to the adoration accorded to Rosalind, the play's
plotting provokes anything from a wry smile to outright scorn: Orlando's
failure to see through Rosalind's disguise; Oliver's sudden, Damascene,
change of heart in the forest; the second 'conversion', of bad Duke Frederick,
upon a chance encounter with 'a religious man'; and, to cap it all, the news
of that delivered by the 'second son' (unhelpfully named 'Jaques') of Sir
Roland de Boys, a man about whom we know little and care less, who we
had been told was kept 'at school' in France, but has somehow just
happened upon Frederick in what now seems a very English Arden. All
these things have put the play beyond the pale for at least one director of my
acquaintance, and beyond consideration of serious intent for many more.

For most of my life I shared some of that feeling. I had found the play
fairly silly, having seen – I realise now – only fairly silly and rather camp
productions of it, set in worlds bearing scant relation to any reality, either
Shakespeare's or our own. But some years ago, to put my scepticism to the
test, I chose it for a text exercise I was conducting at the Bristol Old Vic
Theatre School. I don't think I found it a completely well-made play, but I
did find a piece full of a lightly worn seriousness about one of the most
delightful but also problematic areas of human experience.

Putting Rosalind at Risk

What must surely have caught Shakespeare's eye was Lodge's central
notion: two young aristocrats who have fallen for each other, are exiled,
separately, and potentially permanently, from their urban and upper-class
milieu. They are exiled, and disinherited, but they are also *free*; at the end
of Act 1 Scene 3 the third escapee, Celia, declares:

> Now go we in content
> to liberty and not to banishment.

In Shakespeare they take into the wilderness the education and sensibility
that in Lodge's less credible imagining is already there, but at the same

time they cast off the duties and obligations of their class. This is particularly the case in respect of love and marriage; no one is now measuring their wealth, for they have lost all they had; inheritance will no more determine their future; parents will no more plan their alliances. They are – unusually, for their class – their own masters.

It is an exciting scenario, full of promise. But 'liberty' is also full of danger.

To return to the basics of the story for a moment:

Orlando: No sooner has he fallen for Rosalind after the wrestling match – he has only a token, a chain, from her to indicate her feelings for him – than he returns home to be warned about his brother's plan to burn him alive. He and Adam leave Oliver's house, they assume never to return. After a long and exhausting journey into the Forest they encounter Duke Senior and his group of exiles and join them. This gives Orlando space to express his love for Rosalind, but with no inkling that it can ever be reciprocated.

Rosalind: No sooner has she fallen for Orlando – she has even less to go on, his tongue-tied silence – than she is banished, on pain of death, by her uncle Frederick. She, Celia and Touchstone escape to Arden, unaware of Orlando's parallel fate. While still impersonating a boy, Rosalind suddenly finds herself in possession of a sheep farm. With a base established, and hunger assuaged, Arden seems to be a welcoming place. But as for love:

> Alas, poor shepherd,

she says of Silvius,

> searching of thy wound, I have by hard adventure found
> mine own.

Act 2 Scene 4

Shakespeare doesn't dwell on the apparent hopelessness of Orlando's and Rosalind's romantic fates. Orlando, in particular, seems full of zest and spirit in expressing a love that should seem impossible on two fronts – his own, possibly irreversible, exile from aristocratic society, and his position in the hierarchy that scarcely merits union with the daughter and niece of the ruling House:[7]

> … O Rosalind, these trees shall be my books
> and in their barks my thoughts I'll character,
> that every eye which in this forest looks
> shall see thy virtue witness'd everywhere.

Run, run, Orlando, carve on every tree
the fair, the chaste, the unexpressive she.

Act 3 Scene 2

What would happen next, if... ?

But we should pause in rehearsal to ask an important question, one we should ask repeatedly, but in my experience rarely do: 'What would happen next, if what *does* happen next *didn't*?' In this case, 'What would happen to Rosalind and Orlando if they were never to meet, and if Duke Frederick were to hold on to power?' For how long could Rosalind and Celia be happy as sheep-farmers? Could they marry the likes of Silvius and William to make a complete transition to the rural life? How long could Orlando's burning passion survive on mere imagining? There are more pressing reasons to ask 'what would happen next?' elsewhere in Shakespeare – I shall come to particularly critical instances in *Measure for Measure* and *Macbeth* – but it is necessary here too. It is part of that discipline of inhabiting an ignorance of what *will* happen, the better to understand the true significance of what *does*.

Certainly the play moves swiftly on to the discovery, by both Rosalind and Celia, of the poems on the trees, to Celia's first sighting of Orlando, and then to Orlando's approach to them, in sparring conversation with Jaques, a contest that makes it abundantly clear that Orlando, far from being the amiable dunce of tradition, can easily better his not-inconsiderable adversary in wit:

> JAQUES. I thank you for your company. But, good faith, I had as
> lief have been myself alone.
>
> ORLANDO. And so had I. But yet, for fashion sake, I thank you
> too for your society.
>
> JAQUES. God be wi' you. Let's meet as little as we can.
>
> ORLANDO. I do desire we may be better strangers.
>
> JAQUES. I pray you, mar no more trees with writing love-songs
> in their barks.
>
> ORLANDO. I pray you, mar no more of my verses with reading
> them ill-favour'dly.
>
> JAQUES. 'Rosalind' is your love's name?
>
> ORLANDO. Yes, just.
>
> JAQUES. I do not like her name.

> ORLANDO. There was no thought of pleasing you when she was
> christen'd…
>
> Act 3 Scene 3

In *Rosalynde* it is 'Aliena', not 'Ganymede', who proposes the game of love
– and will go on to initiate the mock marriage between Orlando and
Ganymede. But Shakespeare has something much more interesting and
exploratory in mind. With Jaques fairly routed, Rosalind tackles Orlando:

> (*To Celia.*) I will speak to him like a saucy lackey and under
> that habit play the knave with him. – Do you hear, forester?

In this moment she intends a game – to 'play the knave with him'. And if
we know the play, we know precisely how the game will play out. But does
Rosalind? Does she already intend her pretence of Rosalind-as-
Ganymede-as-Rosalind? Tradition has it so. But more probably, she is
making it up as she goes along, acting *and* reacting. This almost too-good-
to-be-true opportunity, to rip off her doublet and fall into Orlando's arms,
has caught her unawares and, in the exchange over the varying paces of
time, she is perhaps *playing* for time:

> Do you hear, forester?
>
> ORLANDO. Very well. What would you?
>
> ROSALIND. I pray you, what is't o'clock? –

– then, as now, the commonest pretext for getting a stranger's attention –

> ORLANDO. You should ask me what time o' day. There's no
> clock in the forest.
>
> ROSALIND. Then there is no true lover in the forest. Else
> sighing every minute and groaning every hour would
> measure the lazy foot of Time as well as a clock.
>
> ORLANDO. And why not the swift foot of Time? Had not that
> been as proper?
>
> ROSALIND. By no means, sir. Time travels in divers paces with
> divers persons.

This is just one of several moments when Rosalind could follow up on her
'then there is no true lover in the forest' and cut to the matter of the poems
on the trees, but she prolongs the relatively inconsequential, elaborating at
length on 'who Time ambles withal, who Time trots withal, who Time
gallops withal and who he stands still withal'. Orlando is the first to tire of
it, but the youth has intrigued and attracted him and he cuts in with:

Where dwell you, pretty youth?

ROSALIND. With this shepherdess, my sister, here in the skirts
    of the forest, like fringe upon a petticoat.

ORLANDO. Are you native of this place?

She could simply say 'no'. She has so many choices in this sequence, and it
is crucial the actor makes them, moment by moment:

ROSALIND. As the cony that you see dwell where she is kindl'd.

ORLANDO. Your accent is something finer than you could
    purchase in so remov'd a dwelling.

This provokes first an invention, to steer the conversation away from her
identity; then a use of that invention to bring the conversation around to
love and women's worth:

ROSALIND. I have been told so of many. But indeed an old
    religious uncle of mine taught me to speak, who was in
    his youth an inland man [*meaning a city man*]. One that
    knew courtship too well, for there he fell in love. I have
    heard him read many lectures against it and I thank God
    I am not a woman, to be touch'd with so many giddy
    offences as he hath generally tax'd their whole sex withal.

Is she feeling giddy herself at this moment? Is she finding ways of holding
herself back? Orlando is further intrigued:

ORLANDO. Can you remember any of the principal evils that he
    laid to the charge of women?

ROSALIND. There were none principal. They were all like one
    another as half-pence are, every one fault seeming
    monstrous till his fellow fault came to match it.

ORLANDO. I prithee, recount some of them.

ROSALIND. No, I will not cast away my physic but on those that
    are sick.

Then comes the choice to address the all-important matter of the quality
of Orlando's love for her; what, if any, reality lies behind the hyperbole?

There is a man haunts the forest, that abuses our young
plants with carving 'Rosalind' on their barks, hangs odes
upon hawthorns and elegies on brambles, all, forsooth,
deifying the name of Rosalind. If I could meet that fancy-
monger I would give him some good counsel, for he
seems to have the fever of love upon him.

> ORLANDO. I am he that is so love-shak'd. I pray you tell me
> your remedy.
>
> ROSALIND. There is none of my uncle's marks upon you. He
> taught me how to know a man in love, in which cage of
> rushes I am sure you are not prisoner.

The prison of love is made of soft bars, easily pushed aside, but Orlando seems not to be constrained even to that degree; he shows none of the conventional signs of the languishing lover:

> ORLANDO. What were his marks?
>
> ROSALIND. A lean cheek, which you have not, a blue eye and
> sunken, which you have not, an impatient spirit, which
> you have not, a beard neglected, which you have not...
> Then should your hose be ungarter'd, your bonnet
> unbanded, your sleeve unbutton'd, your boot untied and
> everything about you demonstrating a careless
> desolation. But you are no such man. You are rather
> point-device in your accoutrements, as loving yourself
> than seeming the lover of any other.

What *are* the signs of sincerity in passion? How can one distinguish self-loving infatuation from real love? We must remember that Rosalind – who has lost her heart to this man – has nothing more to go on than his tongue-tied silence after the wrestling and a sheaf of poor, hyperbolic poetry, to give her hope that her love is reciprocated. It is too easy – and our over-familiarity with the story conspires with us in this – to assume that Rosalind is already confident of Orlando's love and is merely continuing to 'play the knave' with him. If that were so, we should conclude that, far from being the transcendent intelligence of stage tradition, she is stupidly complacent.

Looking ahead for a moment, to the play-within-the-play that is the Silvius/Phebe scene (Act 3 Scene 6) we might add to that charge an unattractively patronising sense of superiority, if we are to read Rosalind's startlingly sudden intervention in that scene as just another example of her patrician confidence:

> And why, I pray you? Who might be your mother
> that you insult, exult and all at once
> over the wretched? What though you have no beauty –
> as, by my faith, I see no more in you
> than without candle may go dark to bed –
> must you be therefore proud and pitiless?

But this should alert us to the fact that Silvius' wretchedness has hit a nerve in her; she could yet be rejected herself, and she feels in that moment an apprehension of loss and the insupportability of humiliation – a humiliation Silvius seems only too prepared to bear. This is vulnerability, not regal confidence.

But to return to her encounter with Orlando...

> ORLANDO. Fair youth, I would I could make thee believe I love.

She is so very tempted to do so:

> Me believe it? You may as soon make her that you love
> believe it. Which, I warrant, she is apter to do than to
> confess she does. That is one of the points in the which
> women still give the lie to their consciences. But, in good
> sooth, are you he that hangs the verses on the trees,
> wherein 'Rosalind' is so admir'd?
>
> ORLANDO. I swear to thee, youth, by the white hand of
> Rosalind I am that he, that unfortunate he.

And now comes the question she has longed – but perhaps feared? – to ask:

> But are you so much in love as your rhymes speak?

and it is met with Orlando's guileless answer:

> Neither rhyme nor reason can express how much.

This is as simply sincere and straightforward as a declaration of love can be; and a recognition, despite its apparent wealth, of the actual poverty of the hyperbole of love.

Love as a Madness

Rosalind's response (if only it wasn't so famous) should be against all our expectations:

> Love is merely a madness and, I tell you, deserves as well a dark
> house and a whip as madmen do. And the reason why they are
> not so punish'd and cur'd is that the lunacy is so ordinary that
> the whippers are in love too.

These are lines that, incomprehensibly, get no mention in a standard guide, *The Shakespeare Handbooks'* scene-by-scene analysis;[8] for wherever we set this play – in France or England; in 1599, 1750 (as I did in my 2003 production) or 1930 (as I did in 2014), or even in the present day – we must be mindful of Elizabethan perceptions of madness – at best mockable, at worst devilish – and, in London's 'Bedlam', of the cruelty meted out to the insane: the chainings, the whippings and the ogling, paying public.

Is the reference *contrived* by Rosalind to usher in the game of love? Is it mocking, playful, thoroughly cool and collected? I cannot hear it except as the fulcrum of the play, as Rosalind's panicked retreat from the opportunity that she is offered in that moment. Isn't this the moment she has dreamt of – and Celia has dreamt of for her – much in the way that we look forward to the happy resolution of a fictional love story, when by some extraordinary twist of fate what has seemed hopeless is suddenly made possible?

But in real life there is terror in such hope; that the 'happy ending' that is promised will dissolve in one's hands as soon as it is grasped. Shakespeare is the master of this particular fear – in the so delicately managed reunion of Viola and Sebastian in *Twelfth Night*, and of father and daughter at the end of *Pericles*. This is quite enough to give Rosalind pause, but there is a second dimension: madness involves the loss of self. And this, I think, is the greater part of her panic. The game of love is not her controlled and rational plan. It is hardly a plan at all. Cupid, not Rosalind, is in charge – Cupid,

> that same wicked bastard of Venus [*she will call him later*] that
> was begot of thought, conceiv'd of spleen and born of madness.
>
> Act 4 Scene 2

The victim is not so much Orlando, as Rosalind herself. Yes, Orlando is deceived; when he says he'll die if Rosalind refuses him, he's talking nonsense; likewise when he declares that he will love her 'for ever and a day'. Such protestations are the common currency of romantic love, and they often prove hollow. To the dispassionate observer that is transparent. But to the engaged participant these feelings are sincere, and we know that rejection can lead to black despair.

It is only when we recognise that Rosalind, although she pretends to be that dispassionate observer, is as much in thrall to Orlando as Orlando is to her, and that she is at risk of rejection herself, that the play's narrative finds its motive tension and Rosalind's 'game of love' becomes urgent and necessary.

Dorothea Myer-Bennett as Rosalind and Jack Wharrier as Orlando, photo © Mark Douet 2014

Tina Packer, the founding artistic director of Shakespeare & Company in Massachusetts, writes:

> [Rosalind] lives underground. Her disguise gives her the ability to find out about herself, what she really thinks and feels. *It also* [my emphasis] allows her to teach Orlando what Rosalind thinks and feels, and to guide him from his romantic version of love into an honest, tough love that will endure. And she can do all this freely, without having anyone in power to tell her how women should or should not behave.[9]

Though Packer may not find quite the urgency that I do, her emphasis is surely correct: Rosalind's love-game *begins* in a need, not to educate Orlando, but to understand herself.

At the end of the great scene between the lovers in Corin's cottage (Act 4 Scene 1), Orlando cuts their meeting short. He claims this is because he is required to wait upon the Duke, but we may sense he has an emotional need to leave at that moment. Celia's comment at the beginning of Act 4 Scene 3 –

> I warrant you, with pure love and troubl'd brain, he hath ta'en his bow and arrows and is gone forth to sleep.

– will suggest he left the cottage in a disturbed state of mind. This is corroborated later by Oliver's account of a man who clearly needs to be on his own –

> pacing through the forest, chewing the food of sweet and bitter fancy...

His mood is hardly surprising; the last element of Ganymede's 'lesson', that perhaps provoked it, is this:

> ROSALIND. Nay, you might keep that check for it till you met
>   your wife's wit going to your neighbour's bed.
> ORLANDO. And what wit could wit have to excuse that?
> ROSALIND. Marry, to say she came to seek you there. You shall
>   never take her without her answer unless you take her
>   without her tongue. O, that woman that cannot make her
>   fault her husband's occasion, let her never nurse her child
>   herself for she will breed it like a fool.

This is a cynical and reductive verdict on womanhood: faithless, dishonest and manipulative, qualities Orlando's 'pure love' cannot stomach. This is neither wise nor considered on Rosalind's part; her wit, released by the twin liberties of Arden and her male persona, is running away with her. Celia's protest when Orlando is gone is well deserved:

> You have simply misus'd our sex in your love-prate. We must
> have your waistcoat and shirt pluck'd o'er your head and show
> the world what the bird hath done to her own nest.

But Rosalind's response to his departure –

> Alas, dear love, I cannot lack thee two hours.

– even if played teasingly, cannot entirely conceal a truth:

> O coz, coz, coz, my pretty little coz, that thou didst know how
> many fathom deep I am in love!

'Fathom deep' is a hyperbolic description of the intensity of her love, perhaps a commonplace one, but it is also an image – and Shakespeare doesn't use images casually – of drowning. Moments later, her 'I'll tell thee, Aliena, I cannot be out of the sight of Orlando' is another fairly commonplace expression of the intensity of her love. But if that line is broken momentarily, as its rhythm suggests, like this:

> I tell thee, Aliena, I cannot *be* | out of the sight of Orlando.

– then the commonplace recovers its full meaning; there is a recognition of the loss of self, and the urgent, vulnerable need for the presence of Orlando to complete her. Read this way, her line bears a startling equivalence to Orlando's 'Then in mine own person, I die', the claim she has just mocked so passionately.

The whole of Act 4 Scene 1 should reek of self-doubt. In Rosalind's imagining of how irrationally she might behave as a married woman she could almost have in mind Cleopatra's volatile contrariness:

> I will be more jealous of thee than a Barbary cock-pigeon over
> his hen, more clamorous than a parrot against rain, more new-
> fangl'd than an ape, more giddy in my desires than a monkey. I
> will weep for nothing like Diana in the fountain, and I will do
> that when you are dispos'd to be merry. I will laugh like a
> hyena, and that when thou art inclin'd to sleep.

If this were a coolly considered warning to men of the common personality of women – irrational, changeable, jealous, deceitful – a feminist might suggest that this play be permanently shelved alongside *The Taming of the Shrew*. But it's neither cool nor considered; it arises entirely from Rosalind's panic at losing a grasp of herself, and her instinct that once the die is cast – the moment she reveals her true identity, here in the forest, where there are no controlling conventions of courtly behaviour – that at that moment she will be Cupid's plaything, not his heroine. What lengths she goes to, towards the end of the play, to secure Orlando's promise that he will marry her when that moment comes! Just when we expect to see her finally reveal herself as Rosalind, she returns again as Ganymede:

> Patience once more, whiles our compact is urg'd.
> You say, if I bring in your Rosalind,
> you will bestow her on Orlando here?
>
> SENIOR. That would I, had I kingdoms to give with her.
>
> ROSALIND. And you say, you will have her, when I bring her?
>
> ORLANDO. That would I, were I of all kingdoms king.
>
> Act 5 Scene 4

Her disguise has been her defence against the loss of self; it has provided a safe area in which she can play at being in love, withholding express commitment. But disguise is, in itself, a loss of self, as we shall see again in Viola's disguise as the boy Cesario.

Rosalind's change back from Ganymede into Rosalind has to be prepared for. It is a defining moment and one which will at last confront

Orlando with the actuality of Rosalind, and no longer that dangerously hyperbolised idea. As the audience we are meant, I think, to be ahead of Rosalind here, not to share her nervousness, but to know that the transition from trousers to frock will be a smooth and uncomplicated completion:

If there be truth in sight, you are *my Rosalind*

says Orlando. Or maybe (and the better choice, I think):

If there be truth in sight, you *are* my Rosalind.

In that moment, for him, Rosalind and Ganymede are not in opposition, but are one and the same. And – though occasionally late for an appointment – Orlando has loved and been faithful to them both.

The hyperbole of love has been interrogated and mocked, and yet it has survived. Before the conclusion of the play, the real shepherdess, Phebe, has asked her devoted lover, the real shepherd Silvius, to declare what it is to love. Unembarrassedly, he has declared:

> It is to be all made of sighs and tears…
> it is to be all made of faith and service…
> it is to be all made of fantasy,
> all made of passion and all made of wishes,
> all adoration, duty, and observance,
> all humbleness, all patience and impatience,
> all purity, all trial, all obedience.

Act 5 Scene 2

Faith, fantasy, adoration – all complete and boundless. This from the simple shepherd who has followed the contemptuous Phebe around like a dog. Yet his sentiments are echoed – literally so – by Orlando and Phebe, and by clear implication by Rosalind herself. Far from the confident controller of events she has so often been thought to be, Rosalind has hesitatingly and nervously – step by step – *achieved* a confidence in her own capacity to give and receive unqualified love and in Orlando's capacity and determination to do the same. It is a commitment to a mutual future, with no reservation, but no safety net.

The Recognition Hypothesis

My argument here runs counter to a widely accepted notion – I will call it the 'recognition hypothesis' – that at some point in the love-game between Orlando and Rosalind, perhaps at the moment of the mock marriage in Act 4 Scene 1, Orlando realises (privately) that Ganymede is truly Rosalind. (Some commentators go further by claiming that '*she* knows that *he* knows', which renders Rosalind's later anxiety about the moment of revelation redundant.) One motive for this argument is the desire to rescue Orlando from Bernard Shaw's dismissive judgement that he is 'a safely stupid and totally unobservant young man',[10] echoed more recently by Stephen Greenblatt, who calls him 'earnest, decent, slightly dim Orlando';[11] but if we can accept the convention of successful disguise – as we are asked to do unequivocally in *The Two Gentlemen of Verona* where Proteus unknowingly employs his jilted lover as a boy-servant, or in *The Winter's Tale* where, through an extended face-to-face dialogue, Florizel fails to recognise his own father behind a false beard,[12] and in this play, too, where Rosalind goes unrecognised by *her* own father – Orlando needs no rescuing. One could say that his love for Rosalind, first expressed in silence, then in unremarkable, hyperbolic poetry that *could* imply that he is merely in love with being in love, is indeed *tested* by Rosalind's love-game – tested for authenticity and stamina – but is not essentially changed by it; it provokes puzzles in his mind about the behaviour of others, but no doubts, no second thoughts about his own feelings. His love for the Rosalind he met so briefly in Duke Frederick's court remains as simple and complete as the love that his brother Oliver and Celia will conceive for each other in one of the most rapid courtships in drama:

> ROSALIND.... your brother and my sister no sooner met but
> they look'd, no sooner look'd but they lov'd, no sooner
> lov'd but they sigh'd, no sooner sigh'd but they ask'd one
> another the reason, no sooner knew the reason but they
> sought the remedy.
>
> Act 5 Scene 2

Rosalind seems to feel no urge to counsel *them*.

The recognition hypothesis is well articulated by James Shapiro, who – echoing Shaw – maintains that to exclude recognition turns 'Orlando into a cloddish figure, unworthy of Rosalind's affections'.[13] But what of the way he follows up on that assertion? –

> Paradoxically, the only way that Shakespeare can show that
> Orlando has matured in his understanding of love is to show

him masking what he's learned, having him playing and lying
in love, learning to appreciate Rosalind's deception.

Shapiro's underlying assumption – which I have repeatedly questioned –
that Rosalind is the all-knowing teacher and Orlando the needy pupil,
demands that some form of learning on Orlando's part be identified.
Convoluted though it is, Shapiro's might be the answer, if the right question
has been asked. But while the text will bend to a production determined
on the Rosalind-as-teacher and Orlando-as-pupil reading, and to the
recognition hypothesis, I can find no substantial textual authority for
either. The true power of the play lies in Rosalind's attempt to confront
and survive the madness of love within herself; an extended tutorial on
the risks and realities of marriage is an altogether flatter affair. Later
instances called in support of recognition are more potent without it.
Oliver's 'fair sister' that he addresses to Ganymede in Act 5 Scene 2
emerges perfectly credibly from his earlier assessment of the fainting
Ganymede as effeminate, and his amusement at the love-game his brother
has been playing; and later in the same scene Orlando's 'I can live no longer
by thinking', when played as a knowing 'Isn't it time we stopped this,
Rosalind?' renders Rosalind's response – her claim to have magical powers
– even more ridiculous. His hopelessness at this point is affecting and has
already been expressed in the previous speech:

> But, O, how bitter a thing it is to look into happiness through
> another man's eyes! By so much the more shall I tomorrow be
> at the height of heart-heaviness, by how much I shall think my
> brother happy in having what he wishes for.

And in the later declarations of love, led by Silvius, the notion that, again,
Orlando looks *knowingly* at Rosalind in this exchange –

> If this be so, why blame you me to love you?
>
> ROSALIND. Who do you speak to 'Why blame you me to love
> you?'
>
> ORLANDO. To her that is not here, nor doth not hear.

– is a poor substitute for the truth, which is that in that moment, in
Orlando's imagination, Rosalind and Ganymede have merged. He is yet
to realise it, but he has come to know, and love, Rosalind in the person of
Ganymede.

The completeness of disguise is a theatrical convention that
Shakespeare has used before and will again. In our over-familiarity with a
Shakespeare play we often feel the urge to discover hidden truths, to find

a key that no one has found before. The recognition key can be intriguing for a while, and we can throw it around in rehearsal with great relish, but it actually diminishes the play. And in our two productions, both Rupert Ward-Lewis in 2003 and Jack Wharrier in 2014 had no difficulty whatever in burying Shaw's dismissive judgement of Orlando without any need to play a conscious recognition that 'Ganymede' was not what 'he' seemed.

Production Notes

Rebecca Smart as Celia, Saskia Portway as Rosalind, and Rupert Ward-Lewis as Orlando in 2003, photo © Alan Moore

Settings: For our first *As You Like It* in 2003, our designer, Andrea Montag, and I wanted to escape the 'Jacobethan' moment, while at the same time highlighting the pastoral background to the story of Rosalind and Orlando. So we looked forward just a century or two to the Arcadian enthusiasms of the eighteenth century, those years when great men built dairies close to their great houses so that their wives and daughters could don aprons and mob caps and pretend to be milkmaids. We felt the disjunction between sophistication and simplicity, between the urban and the bucolic – and particularly its provenance in classical myth and literature, so woven into the text of *As You Like It* – would sing out more vividly in the world of 1780 than of 1580. One has to think only of the paintings of Gainsborough, Boucher and Fragonard. But in 2014 Harriet de Winton and I chose to put that priority aside and opted instead for the most modern setting we felt the play could bear, the 1930s. Moving the plays across periods – including into our own time – is an important issue and I will have more to say about it later.

Scene Order: In 2014, we altered the scene order early in the play, bringing forward Act 2 Scene 3 – when Orlando arrives home from the wrestling – so that it preceded the first scene in the forest with Duke Senior (Act 2 Scene 1) and the short Act 2 Scene 2 where Duke Frederick is told that Rosalind and Celia have disappeared. It seemed to make a better narrative. Again, the edited text is available on my website.

The Dukes: Also in 2014 we followed the fairly common practice of doubling the roles of Frederick and Senior. Often chosen simply to save on a salary it has a double benefit in that it focuses the difference between the two men entirely on the cast of their minds, their respective 'tunes'; they are both under stress, but while Frederick is brittle, jealous and defensive, Senior is warm, generous and expansive. They vividly encapsulate the contrast between the two worlds of the play. Christopher Bianchi achieved the switching between the two with great precision and economy, requiring only the donning and doffing of a military greatcoat to mark the change.

Hymen: In both productions we chose to present Hymen, not as a god literally descending from the heavens, but as one represented by a mortal; in 2003 by Jonathan Nibbs' Amiens, and in 2014 by Offue Okegbe (seen here) in the same role. Both carried a burning torch, one of Hymen's traditional symbols.

The Folio is ambiguous on the matter, saying only 'Enter Hymen, Rosalind, and Celia. Still Music' and then marking no exit for the god when the ceremony is done. The English literary critic A.D. Nuttall notes wryly that Hymen descends 'in a curiously unobtrusive manner'.[14] Though a descent from the heavens would anyway be tricky to pull off on a factory floor with only twelve feet of headroom, and the in-the-round format is not the ideal context for masque-style scenic effects, I find a sudden switch from the material to the metaphysical risible rather than magical, and likely to recall the 'walkdown' at the end of a British pantomime, rather than a truly transfiguring moment.

Dorothea Myer-Bennett as Rosalind and Offue Okegbe as Hymen, photo © Mark Douet 2014

Jaques de Boys: As I noted earlier, in *Rosalynde*, which begins with Sir Rowland de Boys' dying testament, Lodge is particularly interested in the fate of the de Boys family, so the reunion and reconciliation of the three brothers at the end of his narrative is particularly important. For Shakespeare it is less so, and by Act 5 Scene 4 we have probably completely forgotten the existence of Jaques de Boys. I have often merged smaller roles to make more substantial, single characters. Here I had become fascinated by Le Beau, who in his warning to Orlando after the wrestling reveals a thoroughly decent man previously hidden behind a camply pretentious exterior – itself an implicit criticism of the culture of Frederick's court. Played this way, he becomes a character of far greater interest than Jaques de Boys; so at the end of the play (in 2014) we brought Vincenzo Pellegrino's Le Beau back in de Boys' place. We imagined he had gone into Arden with Frederick's army, but was relieved at his conversion and abdication and only too happy to bring the glad tidings to Senior and his men.

3. Orsino and Viola

Perhaps half a decade or more after he wrote *The Comedy of Errors*, *Twelfth Night* picks up from it in a tonally even richer comedy whose 'bittersweet' seriousness has long been recognised (though by no means always enacted; silliness has invaded this play too). Its title has always intrigued me: the twelve days of Christmas, culminating in the Feast of the Epiphany, was a period Elizabethans devoted to 'misrule', a heady release of energy and sanctioned rule-breaking that made for necessary punctuation in a severely authoritarian society. Another period was, of course, midsummer, and references to the time of year in this play suggest that its misrule belongs more to midsummer than to midwinter:

> ORSINO. Away before me to sweet beds of flowers.
> Love-thoughts lie rich when canopied with bowers.
>
> Act 1 Scene 1

> FESTE. Many a good hanging prevents a bad marriage. And, for turning away, let summer bear it out.
>
> Act 1 Scene 5

> OLIVIA. Why, this is very midsummer madness.
>
> Act 3 Scene 4

> FABIAN. More matter for a May morning!
>
> Act 3 Scene 4

And there is also the placing of two crucial scenes – Act 2 Scene 5 (the Malvolio 'gulling' scene) and Act 3 Scene 1 (the second Olivia/Cesario scene) – outside in Olivia's garden.

Though we know of a 1602 performance in the Middle Temple on 2nd February, the Feast of Candlemass, there is no record of a 6th January performance that might have provoked an opportunistic 'Twelfth Night' titling. At the same time, the subtitle 'What You Will' seems very much of a piece with 'As You Like It', 'Much Ado About Nothing' and 'All's Well That Ends Well', which suggests it could have been Shakespeare's first thought. It may also, like the other three, enjoy the fun of a sexual pun: 'it' possibly referring to intercourse, 'nothing' to the vagina, 'end' to the penis, and 'will' to strong sexual desire. The unruly power of sexuality is at the heart of all these plays.

Realising the Social Dynamics

Again, some background research is vital, this time to discover the play's social dynamics. The cast – probably for the same commercial reasons that limit us now – is small. Duke Orsino has perhaps three or four attendants (I have once seen him reduced to one); the Lady Olivia seems to have one gentlewoman, Maria (the 'gentle' part is sometimes forgotten, Maria appearing as a plainly dressed maid), and a male attendant, Malvolio, who appears to have little to do except answer the door and return gifts. But we should not be deceived by these short theatrical rations; these are aristocrats of immense power and wealth, a fact that would have been well understood by Shakespeare's audience from their own observation and experience. In his classic study, *Life in the English Country House*[15] – highly recommended – Mark Girouard describes the life of the super-rich from the medieval period through and beyond Shakespeare's own time: the wealth earned from their vast estates, more often from rental income from farmers than from farming itself; the make-up of their huge households, predominantly of men, who fulfilled almost every function except personal attendance on the lady of the house and her young children; the strict hierarchy among these which Girouard likens to the ranks in a modern army; and, importantly for this play, the positions of the leading officers. Of the household of the Earl of Derby, for instance, in the 1580s, he says:

> Its size, exclusive of the family, varied from 115 to 140 people (and the women in it from three to six)… The hierarchy of gentlemen, yeomen and grooms was firmly based on the Stanley power-base of Lancashire and Cheshire. The earl's treasurer was Sir Richard Sherborne, who built his own great house at Stonyhurst and was one of the biggest landowners in Lancashire. The earl's steward, William Farington of Worden, was a member of a well-established Lancashire family, a substantial property owner, a magistrate and deputy-lieutenant of the county…

Though great households were shrinking, under financial pressure, towards the end of the sixteenth century, Londoners could still have seen such great men ride into London, accompanied by their liveried retinues. The Steward we might liken to the Executive Director of the great estate, a task to which he would devote most of his year, entrusting his own estate to his own steward in a microcosm of his lord's.

Where Orsino and Olivia belong on this great ladder of wealth is a matter of speculation. Orsino, clearly Illyria's ruler, is first entitled 'Duke' (by the Captain in Act 1 Scene 2), in England the highest status below royalty, but thereafter as 'Count', except in the Folio speech prefixes which retain 'Duke' throughout. 'Count' is not formally an English title, though 'Countess' describes the wife of an Earl, the degree below a Duke. But *Twelfth Night* is set not in England but in Illyria, in antiquity a specific region in the western Balkans, but by 1600 having perhaps a more loosely mythical resonance. I speculate that Shakespeare may have been attracted to it as his far-flung location for one passage alone –

> VIOLA. What country, friends, is this?
>
> CAPTAIN. This is Illyria, Lady.
>
> VIOLA. And what should I do in Illyria?
> My brother he is in Elysium.
>
> Act 1 Scene 2

– exploiting the irony Viola feels that she should be lost and grieving in an earthly paradise, when her brother has been carried off to a heavenly one.

Late in the play we learn of Orsino's military history, including a reference to his fleet of galleys, suggesting a power-base of truly Duke-like proportions. But for Olivia there are few clues. She is lower in status than Orsino, though referred to once by Malvolio as 'Countess', and once, flatteringly by Cesario, as 'fair Princess'.

These definitions seem loose enough, and the severe formality of life in the great houses described by Girouard, seems to fall away in this play. When Sir Andrew refers to Maria as a 'wench' we could even be in the bourgeois world of *The Merry Wives of Windsor*, in which Maria would deserve plain attire and Malvolio would be very far from being a knight of the realm or a magistrate, or have responsibility for a grand estate. But I would counsel against going too far down that path; Malvolio is a Steward, not a doorman or a butler, and Shakespeare's audience would have had some cognisance of the crucial relationship between him and his mistress, particularly as responsibility for her house and lands has fallen so suddenly and unexpectedly on her young shoulders. I say 'young' deliberately, though I have seen many more mature Olivias than young ones. It is as if the very phrase 'the Lady Olivia' implies a *grande dame*, fully at ease in her position and power. But Olivia is to marry Sebastian, who (putting biological impossibility aside) as the identical twin of the girl who can impersonate a boy, is necessarily a boy himself. Is then Olivia to marry a man fifteen or twenty years her junior? I see every reason for Olivia to be an eighteen- or twenty-year-old, pitched into a role she had never expected, and falling in love with all the headiness of youth. Such was Lucy Black's luminous performance for stf in 2002, which rightly won her a nomination for the 2003 Ian Charleson Award.[16]

Elizabethans would have had some sense of the time Lady and Steward would have to spend together, and might have been less surprised than we are when Malvolio dreams of marriage to her. His reference to an even more unlikely coupling –

The Lady o' the Strachy married the yeoman of the wardrobe.

– is a mystery; we don't know if it is a topical reference, or Shakespeare's invention, but there certainly had been precedents. Girouard records that in 1553 the widowed Duchess of Suffolk married her Gentleman Usher, and later her successor as Duchess, also widowed, married her Master of the Horse. Such cross-class liaisons were severely censured, but the fact was that these wealthy single women lived in an almost exclusively male environment, and had sexual and emotional needs that men almost constantly in their company might have been happy to meet, either completely reciprocally or merely as a means to advance their positions in society.

The looseness of Shakespeare's imagining is, however, a danger for us, lacking as we do much of his known frame of reference. We must always realise a world for a Shakespeare play, one that allows all the fundamentals of its action to make sense. In this case those fundamentals must involve immense wealth and political power, including Orsino's absolute power over life and death. For this reason my decision in 2002 was to set the play in the time of its composition, identifying Orsino as an archetypal Renaissance prince – scholar, lover, soldier and ruler.

Another Heroine in Drag

But to the plot: after our brief introduction to Orsino's court (in 2002 I cast an actor in his early twenties, Tom Espiner, as the Duke), the play's narrative begins, like *The Comedy of Errors*, with an apparent tragedy involving identical twins, and with an arrival from a sea voyage. In this case the storm that appears to have taken Viola's brother Sebastian is only just abating, and Viola is cast upon the shore of Illyria in grief and shock. Where she and Sebastian were sailing to or from, or for what purpose, is not addressed, perhaps because Shakespeare wants us to see Viola as an orphaned castaway with no option beyond what she can make of herself by her own initiative. Reaching for a disguise that is both a practical tool for survival, but also – at least as far as dressing as a boy goes – an unconscious immersion in the persona of her lost twin, she determines to get access to Orsino's court by impersonating a eunuch:

> Thou shall present me as an eunuch to him.
> It may be worth thy pains, for I can sing
> and speak to him in many sorts of music
> that will allow me very worth his service.
> What else may hap to time I will commit.
> Only shape thou thy silence to my wit.
>
> CAPTAIN. Be you his eunuch and your mute I'll be.
> When my tongue blabs then let mine eyes not see.

Act 1 Scene 2

The Captain's vow will not be tested in our view, as we shall not see him again, and the idea of Viola as a musical eunuch will be dropped as she is accepted into the court, not as an entertainer, but as a youth – 'Cesario' – who has quickly caught Orsino's fancy as a confidant:

> ORSINO.   …Cesario,
> thou know'st no less but all. I have unclasp'd
> to thee the book even of my secret soul.

We might well smile at this 'secret soul', since Orsino seems to have shared his infatuation with the world at large; just one example of a fevered mind, full of sensual longing, losing its purchase on reality. Cesario must take over Valentine's role of go-between:

> Therefore, good youth, address thy gait unto her.
> Be not denied access, stand at her doors
> and tell them there thy fixed foot shall grow
> till thou have audience.
>
> VIOLA.   Sure, my noble lord,
> if she be so abandon'd to her sorrow
> as it is spoke, she never will admit me.

Orsino brushes mourning aside:

> Be clamorous and leap all civil bounds
> rather than make unprofited return.

The risk to him in this – of ultimate humiliation – again points to an unprincely loss of proportion, and to a potential for the ugly consequences threatened in the final scene. But Viola has no choice but to comply:

I'll do my best

to woo your lady. [*Aside*] Yet, a barful strife,
whoe'er I woo, myself would be his wife.

Act 1 Scene 4

Identifying Orsino

Here we meet what is for some a stumbling block in the plausibility of this play. How can we possibly empathise with Viola in her sudden passion for a young man capable of the laughable self-indulgence of the play's opening lines:

> ORSINO. If music be the food of love, play on.
>   Give me excess of it, that surfeiting
>   the appetite may sicken and so die.
>   That strain again. It had a dying fall.
>   O, it came o'er my ear like the sweet sound
>   that breathes upon a bank of violets,
>   stealing and giving odour. Enough – no more.
>   'Tis not so sweet now as it was before.
>   O spirit of love, how quick and fresh art thou,
>   that notwithstanding thy capacity
>   receiveth as the sea. Nought enters there
>   of what validity and pitch soe'er
>   but falls into abatement and low price
>   even in a minute. So full of shapes is fancy
>   that it alone is high fantastical.

Act 1 Scene 1

What is immediately clear – Orsino seems to know it himself – is that these lines are not about Olivia, but about the delicious sensation of infatuation. It is a pastime, an indulgence by a young man who can command live music to start, stop, and repeat at his whim. His authority is absolute, he is the centre of attention and the court must attend to his fancy. Directors would love to afford a court of a dozen or more, obliged to listen in formal silence to a recital by a substantial consort, yet be prevented from hearing a delightful tune through to its end. The nearest these men can come to criticise or protest is to suggest an alternative pastime in which all their youthful energies would find release:

> CURIO. Will you go hunt, my lord?
> ORSINO.   What, Curio?
> CURIO.   The hart.

37

But Orsino can turn anything to feed his own preoccupation:

> ORSINO. Why, so I do, the noblest that I have.
> O, when mine eyes did see Olivia first
> methought she purg'd the air of pestilence!
> That instant was I turn'd into a hart
> and my desires, like fell and cruel hounds,
> e'er since pursue me.

('Pestilence' will be a reference to the bubonic plague, an almost constant threat to Shakespeare and his contemporaries. It was commonly invoked as a curse – 'A plague on you!' – and used more widely as a metaphor. In Act 1 Scene 5 Olivia will use it herself to express her sense of helplessness – and perhaps dread – in her sudden passion for Cesario:

> How now,
> even so quickly may one catch the plague?

– a striking image about love, given that the plague delivered a quick, though appallingly painful, death. We have now experienced our own pandemic and, as well as perhaps losing friends and loved ones to it, shared Shakespeare's experience of the closure of the theatres; but even so I suspect that these references – however acutely the actor feels them – will retain little of their original power.)

Orsino's reference to Olivia purging the air is hyperbolic, suggesting she has godlike powers. And then comes the sudden change to the dramatisation of himself as a victim pursued by 'fell' – meaning killer – hounds. Shakespeare affords the court no spoken reaction to all this; it is in thrall to him, and cannot be seen to demur. In such unreadable silences autocratic courts are well practised.

Briefly Shakespeare now shifts our focus to the Lady Olivia, offering a companion sketch of a mind and heart indulging itself; this time in what King Claudius would no doubt censure as 'obstinate condolement'. Valentine has returned from Olivia's estate empty-handed:

> So please my lord, I might not be admitted,
> but from her handmaid do return this answer:
> the element itself, till seven years' heat,
> shall not behold her face at ample view
> but, like a cloistress, she will veiled walk
> and water once a day her chamber round
> with eye-offending brine. All this to season
> a brother's dead love which she would keep fresh
> and lasting in her sad remembrance.

This echoing self-engrossment is telling, but we should be even kinder to Olivia; her brother's death has followed quickly after their father's, leaving her unexpectedly mistress of the family's great estate without paternal or fraternal guidance. Her performance of her grief may be self-dramatising, but it also serves as a defence against Orsino, whose importunate embassies are unwelcome. Whatever the truth of it, Valentine's account is yet more food for Orsino's masturbatory imagination:

> O, she that hath a heart of that fine frame
> to pay this debt of love but to a brother,
> how will she love, when the rich golden shaft
> hath kill'd the flock of all affections else
> that live in her. When liver, brain and heart,
> these sovereign thrones, are all supplied and fill'd –
> her sweet perfections – with one self king!
> Away before me to sweet beds of flowers.
> Love-thoughts lie rich when canopied with bowers.

This is all richly comic, and what experienced connoisseur of Shakespeare theatre has not seen these speeches define Orsino irrevocably as a limp-wristed narcissist? A.D. Nuttall characterises Orsino as 'a dreamy, etiolated figure, an Aubrey Beardsley decadent'.[17] A Victorian, and even more a 1920s or 1930s *Twelfth Night* has tempted many a director and designer, with all sense of power and authority drained from Orsino's world in which, in complete contrast to an Elizabethan scenario, he and his friends lounge about together, inviting us to mock them all as if they were a bunch of Wodehousian drones. In such contexts the fact of Viola's devotion – for all that in real life admirable people do occasionally fall for fools – does become problematic; as does the wordlessness of Orsino's friends.

However, there is another definition of Orsino, offered by Olivia herself in Act 1 Scene 5:

> … I suppose him virtuous, know him noble,
> of great estate, of fresh and stainless youth,
> in voices well divulg'd, free, learned and valiant,
> and in dimension and the shape of nature
> a gracious person. But yet I cannot love him.

Again, I must petition for Orsino to be cast as described here – a 'youth'. The older Orsino is, the more his behaviour borders on the pathological, and the more unequal his eventual marriage to the young Viola will be. It might be better to think of his passion for Olivia as his first, a heady new experience. Very powerful, very young men were far from uncommon in

Shakespeare's time. Robert Devereux, the Earl of Essex, distinguished himself at the Battle of Zutphen at the age of twenty and became the Queen's Master of the Horse only a year later.

Say what you mean, mean what you say!

But there is more that we should heed in Olivia's speech. It is my belief that Shakespeare's characters, unless they actually tell us that they are dissembling, should always be taken at their word – that they say what they mean and mean what they say (words in Shakespeare matter that much). If we do so here, and we are prepared to credit Olivia with a measure of good judgement, we have to recognise that this 'learned', 'valiant' and 'gracious' 'youth' is the very same that we have found, on first acquaintance, comically self-indulgent. An 'etiolated, Aubrey Beardsley decadent' does not fit Olivia's description.

It is perfectly possible, and dramatically necessary, to allow Orsino to be capable of both Olivia's judgement and the comedy of his self-absorbed infatuation for her. In Shakespeare's imagination, where a great man is as emotionally vulnerable, and as capable of idiocy, as any other, it is wholly comprehensible. It is also volatile, exciting, and because of the power Orsino wields as an absolute ruler, dangerous. Orsino need not, should not, be defined as a narcissistic fool; but as a perfectly decent young man, precisely as described by Olivia, *behaving like a fool* because he is in thrall to the madness of love.

Not character, but Love itself – Orsino's for Olivia, Viola's for Orsino, Olivia's for Cesario, Malvolio's for Olivia, Aguecheek's for Olivia, Antonio's for Sebastian, Maria's for Sir Toby, Sir Toby's, perhaps, for himself – is then allowed full credit as the dominant and chaotic agent within the play; the power that changes lives and brings the story very close to tragedy, but is ultimately – in this festive-comic moment – shown to be largely benign. Not entirely so, of course, as Antonio, Malvolio and Aguecheek will all be excluded from the happy outcome.

Though we feel instinctively that Orsino's passion for Olivia is essentially specious, we know that Shakespeare is asking us to accept that Viola's passion for Orsino is sincere and substantial. In which case his promise to her that, if she helps him to win Olivia –

> thou shalt live as freely as thy lord
> to call his fortunes thine.

> Act 1 Scene 4

– is one that will, ironically, confound, not fulfil, her hopes.

It quickly becomes apparent that Viola's too quickly conceived strategy to 'preserve' herself in Illyria has become her prison. And, following her realisation that Olivia is smitten with her alter-ego, Cesario, she expresses the profound, moral unease with which the Elizabethans regarded disguising:

> Disguise, I see thou art a wickedness
> wherein the pregnant enemy does much –

– the 'enemy' being the Devil, pregnant with malice –

> What will become of this? As I am man,
> my state is desperate for my master's love.
> As I am woman – now alas the day –
> what thriftless sighs shall poor Olivia breathe!
> O Time, thou must untangle this, not I.
> It is too hard a knot for me to untie!

Act 2 Scene 2

This discomfort, quite lightly held in its rhyming conclusion is followed up, in rather darker mood, in her next scene with Orsino – one of the very greatest in the play – Act 2 Scene 4. Orsino is in musical mood again:

> ORSINO. Now good Cesario, but that piece of song,
>   that old and antic song we heard last night.
>   Methought it did relieve my passion much,
>   more than light airs and recollected terms
>   of these most brisk and giddy-paced times.
>   Come, but one verse.

Here we may suspect that the change of intention in Viola/Cesario's role in Orsino's court is not Viola's but Shakespeare's. A great song of deep melancholy, of a true lover 'slain' by his lover's rejection, is in Shakespeare's conception, but who is to sing it? Was his first idea that it should be by the eunuch, Cesario, fulfilling Viola's stated ambition on the seashore? And did it then occur to him that the scene would be so much more powerful if the unhappy Viola were to be obliged to sit alongside Orsino, *listening to* the song with him? The first lines of the scene (above) do suggest that Cesario should sing it, and the provision of a substitute performer, Feste, seems an unlikely convenience:

> CURIO. He is not here, so please your lordship, that should sing it.
> ORSINO. Who was it?

CURIO. Feste, the jester, my lord. A fool that the lady Olivia's
    father took much delight in. He is about the house.

Surely Feste should be too busy repairing his fractured relationship with
Olivia to be moonlighting at Orsino's; but the excellence of what Shakespeare
achieves more than makes up for the crudity of this manipulation:

ORSINO. Seek him out and play the tune the while.

Tom Espiner as Orsino and Esther Ruth Elliott as Viola/Cesario, photo © Alan Moore 2002

Sitting together, Orsino and Cesario now enjoy the intimacy one can enjoy
within a crowd, as the musicians 'play the tune':

ORSINO. Come hither, boy. If ever thou shalt love
    in the sweet pangs of it remember me,
    for such as I am all true lovers are,
    unstaid and skittish in all motions else
    save in the constant image of the creature
    that is belov'd. How dost thou like this tune?

VIOLA. It gives a very echo to the seat
    where Love is thron'd.

ORSINO.   Thou dost speak masterly.
    My life upon't, young though thou art thine eye
    hath stay'd upon some favour that it loves,
    hath it not, boy?

It is to Viola's credit – and to Orsino's too – that her 'masterly' response can allow Orsino's focus to swing, if only momentarily, away from himself…

> VIOLA.   A little, by your favour.
> ORSINO. What kind of woman is't?
> VIOLA.   Of your complexion.
> ORSINO. She is not worth thee, then. What years, i' faith?
> VIOLA. About your years, my lord.

His judgement is also swinging, perhaps prompted by a real concern for Cesario, from his 'constant image of the creature that is beloved' to this more cynical assessment of male passion:

> ORSINO. Too old by heaven! Let still the woman take
>   an elder than herself. So wears she to him,
>   so sways she level in her husband's heart.
>   For, boy, however we do praise ourselves
>   our fancies are more giddy and unfirm,
>   more longing, wavering, sooner lost and worn
>   than women's are.

And he goes even further, crisply defining what all but he can see is the fickle basis for his own declared devotion to Olivia :

> Then let thy love be younger than thyself,
> or thy affection cannot hold the bent.
> For women are as roses whose fair flower,
> being once display'd, doth fall that very hour.

In her growing misery Viola accepts that lamentable notion:

> And so they are. Alas, that they are so;
> to die, even when they to perfection grow!

Then Feste enters:

> ORSINO. O, fellow, come, the song we had last night.
>   Mark it, Cesario, it is old and plain.
>   The spinsters and the knitters in the sun
>   and the free maids that weave their thread with bones
>   do use to chant it. It is silly sooth
>   and dallies with the innocence of love
>   like the old age.

This is an oddly inappropriate introduction to the song we are about to hear, one of Shakespeare's finest, and a song for a man, not for 'spinsters and knitters in the sun'; perhaps (though this hardly answers the charge) Shakespeare mis-sells it deliberately, wanting its grave power to hit Viola, and the play's audience, with unexpected force:

> *Come away, come away, death,*
> *and in sad cypress let me be laid.*
> *Fly away, fly away breath,*
> *I am slain by a fair cruel maid.*
> *My shroud of white, stuck all with yew,*
> *O, prepare it!*
> *My part of death, no one so true*
> *did share it.*
>
> *Not a flower, not a flower sweet*
> *on my black coffin let there be strown.*
> *Not a friend, not a friend greet*
> *my poor corpse, where my bones shall be thrown.*
> *A thousand thousand sighs to save,*
> *lay me, O where*
> *sad true lover never find my grave*
> *to weep there!*

There is an implicit silence, before Orsino pays the piper:

> There's for thy pains.
> FESTE. No pains, sir. I take pleasure in singing, sir.
> ORSINO. I'll pay thy pleasure then.
> FESTE. Truly, sir, and pleasure will be paid, one time or another.

Orsino is now impatient to return to his main theme:

> Give me now leave to leave thee.

But Feste is not to be hurried:

> Now, the melancholy god protect thee and the tailor
> make thy doublet of changeable taffeta, for thy mind is a
> very opal. I would have men of such constancy put to sea
> that their business might be every thing and their intent
> every where…

Feste's clear-eyed assessment of Orsino's state of mind Orsino seems too self-engrossed even to hear. Far from finding the song 'silly sooth' and a relief from his passion, it has worked powerfully on his damaged ego; he is re-energised, determined not to become the cruelly rejected figure of the song:

> Once more, Cesario,
> get thee to yond same sovereign cruelty.
> Tell her, my love, more noble than the world,
> prizes not quantity of dirty lands…
> but 'tis that miracle and queen of gems
> that nature pranks her in attracts my soul.

Now Viola is the would-be teacher, full of care for Orsino, informed by her own hopeless love for him (as she sees it) –

> But if she cannot love you, sir?
>
> ORSINO. I cannot be so answer'd.
>
> VIOLA.   Sooth, but you must.
> Say that some lady, as perhaps there is,
> hath for your love as great a pang of heart
> as you have for Olivia. You cannot love her,
> you tell her so. Must she not then be answer'd?

– but her lesson provokes in him a contempt now for the shallowness of *women's* passion, so poor in value beside his own:

> There is no woman's sides
> can bide the beating of so strong a passion
> as love doth give my heart. No woman's heart
> so big, to hold so much, they lack retention…
>   Make no compare
> between that love a woman can bear me
> and that I owe Olivia.
>
> VIOLA. Ay, but I know –

Here the trap that is her disguise provokes Viola's most difficult and moving negotiation between truth and falsehood, as she is forced to talk of herself in the third person:

> ORSINO.   What dost thou know?
>
> VIOLA. Too well what love women to men may owe.
> In faith, they are as true of heart as we.
> My father had a daughter loved a man,
> as it might be, perhaps, were I a woman
> I should your lordship.
>
> ORSINO.   And what's her history?
>
> VIOLA. A blank, my lord. She never told her love
> but let concealment, like a worm i' the bud,
> feed on her damask cheek. She pin'd in thought,

and with a green and yellow melancholy
she sat like patience on a monument,
smiling at grief. Was not this love indeed?…

Again, the enigmatic power of Viola's thought allows Orsino's focus to move from himself:

ORSINO. But died thy sister of her love, my boy?

Tom Espiner's Orsino felt real shock here; the commissioner of Feste's self-dramatising song brought up short by a supposedly real-life death:

VIOLA. I am all the daughters of my father's house
and all the brothers too. And yet I know not.

Her misery at being trapped rather than emancipated by her disguise has segued from her misery at the loss of her brother, a part of herself. There is another momentary silence; Orsino is for once without words. Viola, unable to endure this painful intimacy a moment longer, reaches blindly for her only means of escape – ironically, to pursue the petition she has so argued against, and the second interview with Olivia that she had so hoped to avoid:

Sir, shall I to this lady?

ORSINO.   Ay, that's the theme.
To her in haste. Give her this jewel. Say
my love can give no place, bide no denay.

This has been a scene of high seriousness, Shakespeare picking apart male attitudes to women that make it a little hard for us to like Orsino; and it ends with him all but issuing an order to Olivia to accept him. But we should reserve our censure. Viola's own concern for him, her understanding that they are both to be disappointed, goes some way to soften us; more, we take into account the 'giddy and unfirm' condition of his mind, in which all sense of proportion and grace fall away under the chaotic powers of pride and libido – his complete surrender to what you will. We recognise the madness of Love.

In contrast to the febrile showiness of his passion for Olivia, Orsino's growing attachment to Viola works at a much quieter level. Though other directors see it otherwise – in Christopher Luscombe's RSC production in 2017 Orsino and Viola fell into a clinch following Feste's song – I believe it is unacknowledged on Orsino's part at this stage. But it is there in her sudden adoption into intimacy and in the concern for her (and her supposed sister) that we have seen can wrest Orsino, albeit briefly, from his self-absorption. It will finally emerge into the light – though in the ugliest of ways – in the final scene when he finds Olivia is already married (apparently to Cesario):

> … since you to non-regardance cast my faith
> and that I partly know the instrument
> that screws me from my true place in your favour
> live you the marble-breasted tyrant still.
> But this your minion, whom I know you love,
> and whom, by heaven, I swear I tender dearly,
> him will I tear out of that cruel eye
> where he sits crowned in his master's spite.
> Come, boy, with me. My thoughts are ripe in mischief.
> I'll sacrifice the lamb that I do love
> to spite a raven's heart within a dove.

– a threat, and a declaration, that brings Viola's own passion into the light –

> VIOLA. And I, most jocund, apt and willingly
>   to do you rest, a thousand deaths would die.
>
> OLIVIA. Where goes Cesario?
>
> VIOLA.   After him I love
>   more than I love these eyes, more than my life,
>   more, by all mores, than e'er I shall love wife.
>
> Act 5 Scene 1

We must not pull our punches on Orsino's violence here; but Shakespeare is asking that even the threat of murder be costed to Cupid's 'insanity' account.

The Dénouement

The entrance of Sebastian, and the revelation of the mistake that has almost resulted in this deadly outcome allows for the bridging change of tone necessary to take us through to the festive conclusion. This is no quick 'Oh, thank God!' moment. Though ultimately joyful, the great recognition scene between the twins involves its own apprehension of peril, that what appears to be promised is but a cruel illusion. Though they stand face to face, they require corroboration of their eyes' witness before they can permit belief. The long, thirty-line sequence that begins –

> SEBASTIAN. Do I stand there? I never had a brother,
>   nor can there be that deity in my nature

> of here and every where. I had a sister,
> whom the blind waves and surges have devour'd...

– has to be handled with the greatest delicacy. Again, if the words seem to get in the way, or if the actors want to rush them, then the peril their characters feel in this extraordinary moment has been undervalued.

In such ways, a potential for tragedy – the threatened murder of Viola – or the recognition of the proximity of loss and heartbreak that Viola and Sebastian envision here, are ever present in Shakespearean comedy; in the threat to Hermia if she refuses to marry Demetrius in *A Midsummer Night's Dream*, in Beatrice's injunction to Benedick to 'kill Claudio' in *Much Ado About Nothing*, in Marcade's entrance with the news of the King's death in *Love's Labours Lost*. We must never shirk these things. The potential for tragedy validates and enriches the joy. And, though occasionally allowing for far-fetched strokes of fortune, like Sebastian's marriage to Olivia, we should not assume a qualitative difference in the reality of human experience between the characters of a comedy and those of a tragedy.

The conclusion of this play is etched with shadows: with the 'notoriously abus'd' Malvolio, and his threat to 'be reveng'd on the whole pack of you'; with the question mark that must hang over the marriage between Maria and Sir Toby; with the rejected Sir Andrew and the forgotten Antonio (what is to be his fate?); and the final, subversively sceptical song from Feste:

> *When that I was and a little tiny boy*
> *with hey, ho, the wind and the rain,*
> *a foolish thing was but a toy*
> *for the rain it raineth every day...*

If, as seems likely, the composition of this play followed that of *As You Like It*, it could well mark Shakespeare's farewell to festive comedy. He is already turning his attention to *Hamlet* and the darker comic worlds of *Troilus and Cressida*, *All's Well That Ends Well* and *Measure for Measure*. Is there perhaps in Orsino's murderous threats the germ of a harsher judgement on human cupidity, that a capricious classical god cannot carry all the blame?

I have sometimes been asked 'Are you not taking these comedies *too* seriously?' but I believe I have never done so. My company has certainly never succeeded in banishing laughter, had that been our aim. But, somewhere – seen or unseen – Adriana is in floods of tears at her husband's cruelty (as she perceives it); and surely Viola is sincere when she declares she will die at Orsino's hand for love of him. Are we not to value these states of mind as humanly real, as if they might be our own? And if

Rosalind, who is clearly at the very centre of *As You Like It*, is not seriously at risk to its events, then do we not have a sort of pastoral cabaret – Jaques' anthologised monologues, Amiens' beautiful songs, a wrestling bout, and a handful of sketches on the theme of love – rather than a play?

We must not *import* seriousness, but we must never avoid it; just look for the precise human value in every line, every scene – step by step. And it is certainly the case that, while it is possible in the final stages of rehearsal to lighten a production that has become positively ponderous with meaning and lost its bounce, at that point it is far too late to deepen a too-trivial reading; seriousness must begin on Rehearsal Day 1.

Production Notes

Fabian: 'Why Fabian?' is a frequently asked question, to which I can offer no answer, except an instinct that his sudden and unexplained introduction in Act 2 Scene 5 for the 'box tree' gulling of Malvolio may have had as much to do with company administration or politics as with artistic need. In conceiving the plot in Act 2 Scene 3 Maria has said, 'and let the fool make a third', so the substitution of Fabian is clearly yet another change of mind on Shakespeare's part, and a more questionable one. In our 2002 production I followed a number of other directors in excising Fabian completely, and giving Feste his promised role in the box tree as well as most of Fabian's lines elsewhere.

Maria: I also removed the reference to a hasty marriage ceremony between Sir Toby and Maria, preferring to have Maria onstage at the finale, making her own apology (in place of Fabian's) for the cruel treatment meted out to Malvolio.

The Box Tree Scene: One element of the production we had to re-think mid-rehearsal was the design of the box tree scene. Our assumption had been that as we were to play in the round, Sir Toby, Aguecheek and Feste would hide, widely spread, among the audience, leaving the whole stage for their strutting victim, but in rehearsal this seemed to make communication between them difficult to realise with any degree of reality. Reality is often scanted in Shakespeare's physical comedy, and particularly in this sequence; the trio ape stone statues that constantly strike new poses and shift their ground, or hide behind plant pots that are barely large enough to cover a knee or a crotch. Our 2002 solution was to ask for a circular box hedge to be placed centre stage. While neatly suggesting a formal Elizabethan garden, it provided a cramped but credible hide for Toby and friends (Jeremy Kingston in *The Times* described it as 'a green stewpot'[18]) and Roland Oliver (Toby), John Mackay (Aguecheek) and Jonathan Nibbs (Feste) quickly matured the choreography of heads and limbs to make the scene as funny as every audience hopes it will be.

But Malvolio (David Collins) saw only a hedge.

Jonathan Nibbs as Feste, photo © Alan Moore 2002

1. 'Incline' is my own emendation from 'decline'.

2. The full text of *Rosalynde*, in modern spelling, is available on my website.

3. 'Pulpiter' is a popular emendation from the Folio's 'Jupiter'. It is certainly more comprehensible to us now.

4. *1599 : A Year in the Life of William Shakespeare* (Faber and Faber, 2005).

5. Cambridge University Press, 2000.

6. *The Meaning of Shakespeare, Volume 1* (University of Chicago Press, 1951).

7. It is true that Orlando is now a member of Senior's Court in Exile; but with no prospect of an end to that exile and (in Orlando's view) no likelihood of Rosalind joining the outlaw band, he can hardly believe himself much closer to gaining her. Shakespeare avoids possible conversations about Rosalind between Orlando and her father. It is important that the parent remains out of the loop.

8. A Palgrave Macmillan series, the *As You Like It* volume is edited by Lesley Wade Soule (2005).

9. In *Women of Will* (Vintage Books, 2016).

10. *The Saturday Review*, 2 May 1896.

11. In *Will in the World* (Jonathan Cape, 2004).

12. A false beard, or some other signifier of disguise that can be rapidly cast aside at the critical moment.

13. *1599 : A Year in the Life of William Shakespeare*.

14. *Shakespeare the Thinker* (Yale University Press, 2007).

15. Yale University Press, 1978.

16. The Ian Charleson Award is run annually by *The Sunday Times* and National Theatre. It commemorates the life of an outstanding actor who died of AIDS at the age of forty. Charleson is best remembered as Eric Liddell in the film, *Chariots of Fire*, and as Sky Masterson in *Guys and Dolls*, and the title role in *Hamlet* at the National Theatre. The award recognises an outstanding achievement in a classical role by an actor under thirty, and is the only national award of its kind. At the time of writing, six stf actors have been nominated.

17. *Shakespeare the Thinker*.

18. 28 March 2002.

Chapter Two

The Word as Deed

When we speak, we *do*; at least some of the time. When we say for the first time 'I love you', we change the relationship we have with the auditor, whether or not he or she can reciprocate; the consequence is likely to be a marked intensification of the relationship, or the beginning of its end. The three words cannot be recalled, even if on a later occasion they can be denied (as in Hamlet's 'I lov'd you not'); they have such an echoing permanence that we might as well have carved them in stone. Plays are almost always about moments of change – of war or death, or falling in or out of love – where what is said is often as momentously life-changing as what is done. As actors and directors we need to be acutely alive to the word as deed, to be able to feel the frisson on the tongue, the ear and the eye as we speak or hear the word that changes everything.

In this chapter I am going to look at three passages – a single scene from *Hamlet,* all the central character journeys in *Measure for Measure,* and the crucial contrast between court and country in *The Winter's Tale* – in all of which language so characterises thought that one sometimes wonders how much power the shared language of a specific milieu has to dictate behaviour. My plea this time is for the most scrupulous listening and obedience to the text. Shakespeare's language is not always easy, but the modern actor can inhabit it comfortably and completely, and if s/he does so, audiences will lose their fears, listen and understand.

1. Ophelia

I delayed directing *Hamlet* until 2016, very near the end of my time with stf, though Jonathan Miller had directed a hugely successful production for the company in 2008, with Jamie Ballard in the title role and Annabel Scholey as Ophelia. But there were a number of scenes I had worked on with students many times, among them Act 1 Scene 3, the domestic trio for the Polonius family.[1] That might seem an odd focus, as it lacks the Prince himself, and while it is 135 lines long, almost twice the length of a momentous scene between the Macbeths (Act 1 Scene 5 in that play), it seems to concern merely the departure of Laertes to France, an intention we are already aware of, and one last piece of exposition, namely that Hamlet has recently – though we may assume before his father's sudden death – sent Ophelia many tokens of his love for her and that they have spent 'private time' together.

Though the clouds of state mourning are yet to be entirely banished, we may assume that, as the scene opens, Ophelia is enjoying the unmatchable excitement of a first love. But, though her relationship with Hamlet will be of central importance to the plot, the mere fact of it could have been communicated in a matter of moments. So what possible reason can there be for so many words, except to characterise, verbosely, the verbosity of Polonius and to suggest that the son is fast developing the same disease? Does anything of any real significance actually *happen* in this scene? If not, and given that the play is almost impossibly long, should we not shorten it by half or more? I believe that we should not, that in it Shakespeare offers a guide to the world in which Hamlet's tragedy will unfold. For actors and directors it also raises once again that important question: how should we value statement in these plays?

Casting Her

The casting of Ophelia is a particularly crucial choice. As with so many of Shakespeare's central characters there are almost as many Ophelias as there are actors to play her; the text is, at least at first sight, so bare of specific instructions. But the traditional image of her, as an innocent young virgin, so beautifully encapsulated by Anastasiya Vertinskaya in Kozintsev's Russian film, has fallen out of favour in recent decades.

In casting Isabella Marshall, I chose to set the clock back to some degree, in that Isabella was young (she came over as perhaps sixteen or seventeen), pale and delicate, while having reserves of energy and passion that she would tap into with explosive effect in Act Four. I felt that the text – far from being silent on the matter – clearly demands such a choice, that the scene only makes sense, and only earns its place in the play, if Ophelia is young and vulnerable.

Anastasiya Vertinskaya as Ophelia in Hamlet (*dir. Grigori Kozintsev, 1964*) © *Alamy*

Laertes is the first to warn her of the dangers of losing her heart to a man of Hamlet's eminence:

> For Hamlet and the trifling of his favour,
> hold it a fashion and a toy in blood,
> a violet in the youth of primy nature,
> forward, not permanent, sweet, not lasting,
> the perfume and suppliance of a minute,
> no more.
> OPHELIA.   No more but so?
> LAERTES.   Think it no more,
>   for nature crescent does not grow alone
>   in thews and bulks, but as this temple waxes
>   the inward service of the mind and soul
>   grows wide withal. Perhaps he loves you now
>   and now no soil nor cautel doth besmirch
>   the virtue of his will, but you must fear –

> his greatness weigh'd – his will is not his own.
> He may not, as unvalu'd persons do,
> carve for himself, for on his choice depends
> the safety and health of this whole state.
> And therefore must his choice be circumscrib'd
> unto the voice and yielding of that body
> whereof he is the head. Then if he says he loves you
> it fits your wisdom so far to believe it
> as he in his particular act and place
> may give his saying deed, which is no further
> than the main voice of Denmark goes withal.

Despite the uncorroborated presumption that Hamlet is 'trifling' with Ophelia, a brother might well be forgiven for an anxiety that his sister will be used as a plaything by a privileged young man who is far more likely to wed for reasons of political alliance than for love. And we might attribute the formal tone and diction of 'and therefore must his choice be circumscrib'd unto the voice and yielding of that body whereof he is the head' more to Laertes' nervousness in addressing the sex question with his sister than to any natural pomposity. But he goes on:

> Then weigh what loss your honour may sustain
> if with too credent ear you list his songs,
> or lose your heart, or your chaste treasure open
> to his unmaster'd importunity.

'Chaste treasure' is a commonplace of the time, but sustains its unpleasant strains of euphemistic prissiness on the one hand and the ugliness of the price upper class Elizabethans put on the maidenhead on the other. 'Trifling' has hardened (forgive the pun) into 'unmaster'd importunity', Hamlet's will now clearly located in his crotch. And then Laertes casts wider – to the battlefield – to enlarge on the threat to Ophelia's defences:

> Fear it, Ophelia, fear it, my dear sister,
> and keep you in the rear of your affection,
> out of the shot and danger of desire.

Though the shot may be Cupid's dart, it has none of Cupid's playfulness. This is a real battlefield where a virgin should shelter in the rearguard or pay a mortal price. Fear is the best strategy, and fear is Laertes' theme. To press his message home, he seeks to alarm Ophelia further with a possibly commonplace ragbag of truisms (the Second Quarto gives them the inverted commas I include here):

> 'The chariest maid[2] is prodigal enough
> if she unmask her beauty to the moon.'

– that is, even if she displays herself only to the moon, the emblem of chastity –

> 'Virtue itself 'scapes not calumnious strokes.'

– from the proverbial 'Envy [calumny] shoots at the fairest mark' –

> 'The canker galls the infants of the spring
> too oft before their buttons[3] be disclos'd'
> and in the morn and liquid dew of youth
> contagious blastments[4] are most imminent.
> Be wary then. Best safety lies in fear.

Finally, with an apparent logic reinforced by the rhyme, but in fact with none –

> Youth to itself rebels, though none else near.

– he casts all proportion and sense aside and warns Ophelia that she may be corrupted autonomously, merely by being a youthful creature of flesh and blood.

From a practical warning about Hamlet's intentions, and the parameters within which his personal life must be framed, Laertes has journeyed on the rails of panic – and in the dominant cultural language of sexual disgust – to a destination that, when confirmed by her father, will act on Ophelia's imagination as forcefully as a physical blow. It is a sermon he offers, and it should be felt as shocking in a man of his young age, and potentially emotionally disabling to a young woman.

There is now a break in this theme for the famous advice of father to son. Then Laertes departs with these words spoken (we assume privately) to his sister:

> Farewell Ophelia, and remember well
> what I have said to you.
> OPHELIA.   'Tis in my memory lock'd
> and you yourself shall keep the key of it.

Polonius – eavesdropping, as ever – hears it and demands the secret be revealed:

> What is't, Ophelia, he hath said to you?
> OPHELIA. So please you, something touching the Lord Hamlet.

POLONIUS. Marry, well bethought.
'Tis told me, he hath very oft of late
given private time to you. And you yourself
have of your audience been most free and bounteous.
If it be so – as so 'tis put on me,
and that in way of caution – I must tell you
you do not understand yourself so clearly
as it behoves my daughter and your honour.
What is between you? Give me up the truth.

– 'You do not understand yourself'; the preamble to a lesson that will prove
fatal to Ophelia, all her instincts and intuitions scorned and discredited –

OPHELIA. He hath, my lord, of late made many tenders
of his affection to me.

We might well feel here the tenderness of Hamlet's expressions of love to
which Ophelia will refer later – his letters and gifts, his 'remembrances'.
But Polonius will have none of it; he is contemptuous, derisive:

Affection? Puh, you speak like a green girl,
unsifted in such perilous circumstance.
Do you believe his 'tenders', as you call them?

The 'tender' here is a dishonest proposal, the illusion of a genuine love
proffered only to deceive and dishonour.

Say what you mean, mean what you say! (again)

Interpretatively, this is a crucial moment. The actor playing Ophelia has a
choice: to retreat into a truculent avoidance – she knows what is coming
and decides to let it happen, closing her ears and heart to her father's all-
too familiar cynicism – or to be genuinely rattled by her father's attitude
in a way rather foreign to our modern sensibility, handing her mind and
heart over to him to write on as he wishes:

I do not know, my lord, what I should think.

Again we should accept that the character says what she means and means
what she says. The word is Shakespeare's medium and its integrity is vital.
In this moment, unhappily, tragically, Ophelia loses trust in her own
instinct. So it was with Isabella Marshall's Ophelia, who was bewildered
and helpless. Ian Barritt's Polonius seized the moment:

> Marry, I will teach you. Think yourself a baby
> that you have ta'en these tenders for true pay
> which are not sterling. Tender yourself more dearly
> or – not to crack the wind of the poor phrase,
> running it thus – you'll tender me a fool.[5]

For the virgin Ophelia – as I rather unfashionably believe her next line confirms she is – this is an accusation too far; her instinct is rekindled and she fights back:

> My lord, he hath importun'd me with love
> in honourable fashion!
>
> POLONIUS. Ay, 'fashion' you may call it. Go to, go to.
>
> OPHELIA. And hath given countenance to his speech, my lord,
> with almost all the holy vows of heaven.

This is meat and drink to Polonius, for whom little in this world is honourable or holy:

> POLONIUS. Ay, springes to catch woodcocks. I do know
> when the blood burns how prodigal the soul
> lends the tongue vows… From this time
> be something scanter of your maiden presence.
> Set your entreatments at a higher rate
> than a command to parle. For Lord Hamlet,
> believe so much in him that he is young
> and with a larger tether –

– Hamlet as goat –

> – may he walk
> than may be given you. In few, Ophelia,
> do not believe his vows for they are brokers,
> not of that dye which their investments show,
> but mere implorators of unholy suits,
> breathing like sanctifi'd and pious bawds,
> the better to beguile.

Like his son, he has an instinct for a telling conclusion, but likewise, while it is presented as logical it has less to do with logic than with terror:

> This is for all:
> I would not, in plain terms, from this time forth
> have you so slander any moment leisure
> as to give words or talk with the Lord Hamlet.
> Look to't, I charge you. Come your ways.

Slander of the powerful was a dangerous crime in Shakespeare's world, as it remains in autocracies the world over. Here Polonius uses it as a very blunt rhetorical weapon, but by implication slanders Hamlet himself, something that in a more rational, and less fearful mood the super-conformist and ultra-cautious Polonius would never dream of doing.

Ophelia has now no spirit to contradict him. Her response has all the defeated compliance of the puppet she will become until Hamlet's sword-thrust through the curtain cuts her puppeteer's strings:

> I shall obey, my lord.

Again – and though this can be, and frequently is, played with a sullen disingenuousness that will indicate how little the whole episode has touched her in her heart – if Ophelia really means this, then the scene has a real journey to travel and a real reason to be. If one objects that the young woman who, earlier in the scene, has countered her brother's sermon with:

> But, good my brother,
> do not, as some ungracious pastors do,
> show me the steep and thorny way to heaven
> whiles, like a puff'd and reckless libertine,
> himself the primrose path of dalliance treads
> and recks not his own rede.

– if one objects that this is a young woman of wit and spirit, then of course this is so. This is the very flame that Polonius' bullying will suffocate. This is the magnitude of Ophelia's journey within the scene – from excitement and confidence to bewilderment and defeat – and it is appalling to witness. Here, as so often in Shakespeare, these journeys of the mind and heart are extreme – *they are events* – and they happen before our eyes. If this one is fully travelled then Act 1 Scene 3 is not verbose but pithy and compact.

Is Ophelia Portable?

Can we export this scene to a modern setting? It is very difficult, and I have seen at least one fine young actress struggle to make sense of Ophelia in a late twentieth-century court. Referencing Girouard again, Shakespeare's Elsinore – as a high status dwelling – seems to be typical of the period, with women few and far between. Gertrude must have one or two ladies-in-waiting, but there is no evidence that Ophelia has any. Her mother we must conclude is dead;[6] and if, Juliet-like, she had a wet-nurse as a baby, she has been long ago retired. There is no reference to any female friend or helpmate of any kind. This is not just theatrical economy; it is a very likely scenario. Her virginity is (to put it crudely) bankable; her education limited; her access to society at large, and the freedoms of the town, nil. She is lonely while being fiercely protected.

This is the soil in which the chaos of her madness springs; naivety, grief and unmediated sexuality woven together in lethal combination. It is also a representative soil; representative of a fearful and puritanical society, one in which – in the higher echelons at least – unmarried men and women are kept apart, and a young woman's sexual awakening is expected to begin after marriage, not before it.

Is there a parallel for this in the western world in the twenty-first century? I think not, and here – as elsewhere in this book – I must demur from Juliet Stevenson's recent call for all future Shakespeare productions to be in modern dress.[7] Social dynamics matter; and they change over time, impinging radically differently on interpersonal relationships and the sense of self. Our experience of politics, law, religion, work, love and marriage, poverty and wealth, disease and death all change. The extent to which these changes matter varies hugely from one Shakespeare play to the next, and I have as often felt able to escape the traditional 'Jacobethan' moment in design as felt compelled to stick with it. At the same time, I think we must credit our audience with the capacity to recognise themselves through the prism of an earlier period; that the past is not such 'another country' that it cannot live vibrantly and potently in our imagination.

Ophelia's tragic journey, in the particular circumstances of a life lived in Shakespeare's own time, was one of my main reasons for locating my 2016 production in 1600.

2. The Duke, Angelo, Isabella and Claudio

The Quality of Listening

Measure for Measure is, linguistically, one of Shakespeare's more challenging texts, for in its great central scenes it demands that we listen with intense concentration. Even its opening lines are a test:

> DUKE. Escalus.
> ESCALUS. My lord.

DUKE. Of government the properties to unfold
    would seem in me to t'affect speech and discourse
    since I am put to know that your own science
    exceeds in that the lists of all advice
    my strength can give you. Then no more remains
    but that, to your sufficiency, as your worth is able,
    and let them work. The nature of our people,
    our city's institutions and the terms
    for common justice y'are as pregnant in
    as art and practice hath enriched any
    that we remember. There is our commission
    from which we would not have you warp.

                                                    Act 1 Scene 1

Easy enough to grasp in a reading, but hard for a modern audience to take in as they settle in their seats and begin the task of attuning to the language of Shakespeare's London. In my 2001 production Dominic Power and I made one small adjustment, and one cut to ease that process just a little:

DUKE. Escalus.

ESCALUS. My lord.

DUKE. Of government the properties to unfold
    would seem in me to *waste both* speech and discourse
    since I am put to know that your own science
    exceeds in that the lists of all advice
    my strength can give you. [*Cut*] The nature of our people,
    our city's institutions and the terms...[*etc.*]

Cutting Shakespeare texts has rarely raised eyebrows – some are impracticably long – and editors from Nicholas Rowe in 1709 onwards have ventured minor changes to words and phrases where corruption has been suspected and the sense deficient. But emendations to make the sense transparent to the modern ear have only recently become generally acceptable. Where will it all end, we ask – in a general modernisation, deemed as necessary as a modern rendering of Chaucer? In 2008, in a talk he gave at the Rose Theatre in Kingston, Sir Peter Hall ventured that Shakespeare had only one more decade to survive in the original language. That decade is now up, and his prediction is yet to be realised, at least in wholesale form. I am far more sanguine than Hall on this, though I challenge the notion, still held in some quarters, that every word Shakespeare wrote should be sacrosanct.

My overriding concern, and it applies as much to *Measure for Measure* as to any play, is that the text should be fully comprehensible. Audiences must not feel that to 'get the gist' will be enough; and I believe that in the way it presents language, particularly in its opening minutes, a production suggests to the audience the quality of attention – of listening – that it will demand. Working in an intimate space like the Tobacco Factory is a huge advantage; text that is not loudly projected, but spoken quietly, supported by all the additional signifiers in the human face, can be so much more comprehensible than that experienced at a distance on a large conventional stage.[8] But no degree of intimacy, or actor-skill, can help audiences to an understanding of statements that even academic editors cannot explain, or of words that over four centuries have lost their meanings, or even worse, *changed*[9] their meanings. In these cases I believe interventions *must* be made, so that the real and intended difficulties in a Shakespeare text can be laid before the audience in the reasonable expectation that they will be grasped.

But another problem with Shakespeare's language, which cannot be resolved by emendation resides in the wider problem of the insulating effect of historical distance. Here the argument for modern dress has some force. There is a danger of a general response that *that is how people were, that is how they spoke and behaved in those far-off days*, leading to a suspension of the critical faculty, of the normal process of discrimination between one mode of thought, language, or behaviour and another. It is a huge danger in rehearsal, that we do not ask the questions of a sixteenth- or seventeenth-century character that we would instinctively ask of a modern one. My argument would always be that this is essentially an *acting*, rather than a *setting* issue, that it is up to us – as actors and directors – to ask those questions, to identify every urgent reality, to fully inhabit lives that operate in environments very different from our own, rather than to drag those lives crudely into our own world.

The Duke

In the case of *Measure for Measure*, it seems extraordinary to me that the central figure of the Duke can have been regarded, both in the theatre and by some academic commentators, to be invulnerable to that questioning, to be a device rather than a character; or even that he impersonates King James I,[10] or Christ.[11] In such scenarios – even more than the idea of Rosalind transcending the more earth-bound life around her – he is an omnipresent *deus ex machina*, setting a moral test for Angelo, and further ones for Isabella and Claudio, rather than, like them, a subject of the play. I would suggest that this is a gross error that could not happen were it not for that insulating blanket woven over four centuries. Geoffrey Bullough, editor of the invaluable series *Narrative and Dramatic Sources of Shakespeare*, encapsulates this error:

> The Duke is an ambiguous figure and it is easy by over-minute examination to make him seem unlikeable, an *agent provocateur*, and the tormentor of those he befriends, indeed the 'old fantastical duke of dark corners' that Lucio calls him. But Lucio is the *advocatus diaboli* throughout, a spirit of false report, and we should not believe his slanders.[12]

It is inconceivable that such an argument could be advanced about a character in a modern drama. And this goes to the heart of what we are about in bringing Shakespeare's words to life on stage. There can be no 'over-minute examination' of a character's behaviour; no putting aside of a single tone or feeling. It is not to see only with Lucio's eyes to be critical of the Duke; we have only to be human, and to recognise him as human, to be that.

The Schematic Play

There is another factor here, a common rationale behind judgements such as Bullough's: that Shakespeare had a moral or political scheme in mind as he sat down to write; and that his characters are, first and foremost, the agents of that scheme. That is a recipe for deadly theatre, and were it true we would not now value Shakespeare as we do; he would have shrivelled to a figure of literary-historical interest, not remained the most vital and commanding voice in world drama. *We cannot be sure what Shakespeare thought*, because his characters speak for themselves, not for him. Though we often feel we recognise his sympathies and antipathies, he offers not a single truth, but captures a multiplicity of voices and perspectives.

This is not to say that the plays do not provoke moral judgements. We will inevitably make them here, in responding to Angelo's actions and – with greater difficulty – to Isabella's, Claudio's and the Duke's; but we must proceed with care; our task is to identify and inhabit what George Eliot described as the 'equivalent centre of self'[13] in each protagonist, not to dictate moral judgements to the audience, or to banish ambiguity. There is no consistency in this; over the years, *Measure for Measure* has provoked rather strident moral judgements, and divided both company and audience into ardently pro- and anti-Isabella factions, while moral judgements I believe we should be prompted to in *Hamlet* have so often been lost in our instinct to identify with its charismatic hero.

Sex and the Duke's Law

But I shall come to Elsinore's play later. The first thing to observe about Shakespeare's Vienna – apart from its curiously Italian and English population – is that its 'biting laws' against fornication were not those of early Jacobean England. There was the less severe punishment of penance, in which the offender had to wear a white sheet and proclaim their sin in church, in the market place, or both; but pre-marital sex, even adultery, were not to be made capital offences until the time of Cromwell's commonwealth,[14] though perhaps the fiercest Puritan voices in the government of Shakespeare's London – the same voices that railed against the theatre – would have introduced such laws had they been able. The pamphleteer Philip Stubbes in his *Anatomie of Abuses* (1583) looked to the animal kingdom for a pattern for the treatment of adulterers:

> It is said… that (almost) all unreasonable beasts and flying
> fowls after they have once linked and united themselves
> together to any one of the same kind and after they have once
> espoused themselves the one to the other, will never after join
> themselves with any other, til the one be dissolved from the
> other by death. And thus they keep the knot of matrimony
> inviolable to the end. And if any one chance to revolt and go
> together with any other during the life of his first mate, all the
> rest of the same kind assemble together, as it were in a counsel
> or parliament, and either kill or grievously punish the adulterer
> or adulteress whosoever it be, which law I would God were
> amongst Christians established.

Shakespeare's choice in Vienna's 'biting laws' suggests that his play concerns more than questions of how to balance justice and mercy; that he is fascinated by the psychology of puritanical attitudes to sex and authority. His Vienna is, perhaps, his London as imagined and projected by the new puritanism.

But to begin with the Duke: what – the question Peter Clifford and I asked ourselves in January 2001 – is this extraordinary man up to? It is one of the most difficult of all questions in the interpretation of Shakespeare, and though I will express trenchant opinions about the detail of his behaviour, I cannot be confident of an entirely satisfactory answer.

Peter Clifford as the Duke, photo © Alan Moore
2001

On the pretence of going on a journey to Poland, for some unspecified purpose, the Duke hands his authority over to Angelo. He then adopts the disguise of a friar and remains in Vienna. The narrative of the ruler adopting disguise to observe the realities of life within his own jurisdiction is a time-honoured one. But what, in this case, is the motive? The Duke's focus of enquiry seems not to be the people at large, but a single man among the elite, his chosen deputy, Angelo. He asks Escalus:

> What figure of us think you he will bear?
> For you must know, we have with special soul
> elected him our absence to supply,
> lent him our terror, dress'd him with our love,
> and given his deputation all the organs
> of our own power. What think you of it?

> Act 1 Scene 1

When Angelo enters there is almost no reference to the task of government that he is to assume; the focus is on Angelo himself:

> Angelo,
> there is a kind of character in thy life
> that to th'observer doth thy history
> fully unfold. Thyself and thy belongings

> are not thine own so proper as to waste
> thyself upon thy virtues, they on thee.
> Heaven doth with us as we with torches do,
> not light them for themselves, for if our virtues
> did not go forth of us, 'twere all alike
> as if we had them not.

This tribute to Angelo's virtues, his potential as a beacon for others, becomes in its final sentence extremely dense:

> Spirits are not finely touch'd
> but to fine issues, nor Nature never lends
> the smallest scruple of her excellence
> but, like a thrifty goddess, she determines
> herself the glory of a creditor,
> both thanks and use.

It seems to translate as 'Spirits are finely endowed only to address fine issues; and Nature never lends such a spirit the tiniest amount of her excellence (a *scruple* is a unit of weight equal to 1.2 grams), without ordaining both the thanks and the interest (*use* referring to usury) that are due to her'. In the cause of good listening a cut is tempting, but we would lose the sense that the Duke is 'laying it on thick' here, which brings the speech close to an overt challenge to Angelo to practise as he preaches, perhaps even with an edge of sarcasm. He then cuts off any modest rebuttal:

> But I do bend my speech
> to one that can my part in him advertise.
> Hold therefore, Angelo:
> in our remove be thou at full ourself,
> mortality and mercy in Vienna
> live in thy tongue and heart. Old Escalus,
> though first in question, is thy secondary.

The reference to Escalus as the more likely choice and then Angelo's response –

> ANGELO.   Now, good my lord,
>   let there be some more test made of my metal,
>   before so noble and so great a figure
>   be stamp'd upon it.

– make abundantly clear how sudden and surprising the Duke's action appears; but he shuts down further questioning:

> No more evasion:
> we have with a leaven'd and prepared choice
> proceeded to you; therefore take your honours.
> Our haste from hence is of so quick condition
> that it prefers itself and leaves unquestion'd
> matters of needful value.

He then reiterates the test:

> Your scope is as mine own,
> so to enforce or qualify the laws
> as to your soul seems good.

and then offers a questionable excuse for what we might feel is a rather furtive exit:

> I'll privily away. I love the people
> but do not like to stage me to their eyes.
> Though it do well, I do not relish well
> their loud applause and Aves vehement,
> nor do I think the man of safe discretion
> that does affect it. Once more, fare you well.

If we remember these last six lines at the dénouement, when the Duke's return to power is accomplished in full public view at the gates of the city – a thoroughly stage-managed event – we may wonder at either the quality of his self-knowledge or his honesty.

Guarded and mysterious with Escalus and Angelo, for our benefit he opens up to lowly Friar Thomas in Act 1 Scene 3:

> No, holy father; throw away that thought.
> Believe not that the dribbling dart of love
> can pierce a complete bosom. Why I desire thee
> to give me secret harbour hath a purpose
> more grave and wrinkl'd than the aims and ends
> of burning youth.

Do we not recognise immediately that this man has a problem? There is a defensiveness in both the 'dribbling dart of love' and 'complete bosom'; only the insecure proclaim how secure they are. The Friar helpfully asks him to explain and the defensive, self-justifying tone continues:

> My holy sir, none better knows than you
> how I have ever loved the life remov'd
> and held in idle price to haunt assemblies
> where youth, and cost – witless bravery – keeps.

A second reference to youth, as antithetical to himself, begs the question of how old the Duke is. Though Lucio will later declare him sexually 'past it' (Act 3 Scene 1) there is no definitive textual answer, beyond the reference below to his nineteen years of neglect, which suggests he can hardly be much less than forty. But is he an elderly man, now challenged and affronted by youth, or is it his own still 'burning' impulses that trouble him?

He justifies his stratagem:

> We have strict statutes and most biting laws,
> the needful bits and curbs to headstrong weeds,
> which for this nineteen years we have let slip –
> even like an o'ergrown lion in a cave
> that goes not out to prey. Now, as fond fathers,
> having bound up the threatening twigs of birch
> only to stick it in their children's sight
> for terror, not to use – in time the rod
> more mock'd than fear'd – so our decrees,
> dead to infliction, to themselves are dead,
> and liberty plucks justice by the nose,
> the baby beats the nurse, and quite athwart
> goes all decorum.

This characterisation of the law as a wild animal is extraordinary. Violence infects almost every line: the 'biting laws', the 'bits and curbs'; in the twigs of birch we might hear a shadow meaning – an alarming one – of them being quite literally stuck into the children's eyes; and finally the nonsense notion of the baby rising from its cradle to 'beat' its nurse.

I shall return to this speech shortly. But, briefly, we have here the Duke's personal assessment of the condition of Vienna: the law stands in contempt. This verdict has often been read, both in commentary and production, as a statement of fact: Vienna is rife with prostitution and all kinds of disorder, and anarchy threatens. Yet when Angelo's crackdown comes, what do we have but the sentencing to death of a high-born young man for getting his contracted fiancée pregnant, and the gloriously comic scene (Act 2 Scene 1) of the prosecution of Froth, a silly young ass caught visiting a brothel, and Pompey, a common bawd with a drily realistic eye.

Turning to that court scene, however simply we set it – and simplicity in setting in Shakespeare is invariably the best choice – we should bear in mind that Angelo's presence implies an element of grandeur (perhaps his own Great Hall), not some poky magistrates' court. There is size and scale to the occasion, the first 'show' trial – at least the first we shall witness – under Angelo's new order. As Shakespeare cuts into it, Escalus has evidently challenged Angelo on the fate that awaits Claudio:

ANGELO. We must not make a scarecrow of the law,
    setting it up to fear[15] the birds of prey,
    and let it keep one shape, till custom make it
    their perch and not their terror.
ESCALUS.   Ay, but yet
    let us be keen, and rather cut a little,
    than fall, and bruise to death. Alas, this gentleman
    whom I would save, had a most noble father.

Escalus offers us one of several touchstones for normality (the Provost, Pompey, Lucio and Barnadine provide others). He is an establishment figure, a Cavalier, perhaps, to Angelo's Roundhead, warmly human but willing to conform to authority, even – as we see it at the very end of this scene – to defend Angelo's strategy before a junior, where we might suspect he would prefer to censure it; and he is protective of his class, here urging leniency for the son of 'a most noble father'. His query as to Angelo's own blamelessness in the matter of lechery is long-windedly guarded:

Let but your honour know,
whom I believe to be most strait in virtue,
that, in the working of your own affections –
had time coher'd with place or place with wishing,
or that the resolute acting of your blood
could have attain'd the effect of your own purpose –
whether you had not sometime in your life
err'd in this point which now you censure him,
and pull'd the law upon you.

But it provokes the clearest position-statement from Angelo, one that will set him up for his fall:

'Tis one thing to be tempted, Escalus,
another thing to fall…
You may not so extenuate his offence
for I have had such faults, but rather tell me,
when I, that censure him, do so offend,
let mine own judgement pattern out my death
and nothing come in partial. Sir, he must die.

In this context, of a young man brutally condemned to death, and the full panoply of the law – the Duke-Deputy himself, the First Minister, a Justice, the Prison Provost and others – brought to bear on the supposed chaotic lawlessness of Vienna, there now enter an illiterate and incompetent Constable, the young ass and the common bawd:

ELBOW. Come, bring them away. If these be good people in a
commonweal that do nothing but use their abuses in
common houses, I know no law. Bring them away.

ANGELO. How now, sir? What's your name? And what's the
matter?

ELBOW. If it please your honour, I am the poor Duke's
constable, and my name is Elbow. I do lean upon justice,
sir, and do bring in here before your good honour two
notorious benefactors.

ANGELO. Benefactors? Well, what benefactors are they? Are they
not malefactors?

ELBOW. If it please your honour, I know not well what they are.
But precise villains they are, that I am sure of; and void of
all profanation in the world that good Christians ought to
have.

ESCALUS. This comes off well; here's a wise officer.

ANGELO. Go to: what quality are they of? Elbow is your name?
why dost thou not speak, Elbow?

POMPEY. He cannot, sir; he's out at elbow... [*etc.*]

This is broad comedy, but not alone for comedy's sake. Angelo's new
beginning is the loser here. Pompey feels none of the 'terror' the law should
exert, and coolly undermines the occasion. It is no wonder that Angelo
eventually finds such a masterly command of the courtroom a challenge
to his own dignity and makes for the door:

> This will last out a night in Russia,
> when nights are longest there. I'll take my leave...

But the scene goes on – quite gloriously on – with Escalus showing a practised
capacity to manage a situation of actually very little import, while protecting
his own dignity with a few more sardonic remarks. This Vienna is not Sodom
and Gomorrah. The chaos that threatens is in the mind, not on the streets.

Going back now to the Duke's confession – as I think we might
characterise it, though he might not – to Friar Thomas, we can see how
personally felt it was, how much it was about his own sense of self-worth.
The final phrase, 'and quite athwart goes all decorum' is so redolent of this;
not of morality itself, but authority, standing, respect. The characterisation
of the law as a violent predator, an analogy the Friar takes up –

> It rested in your grace
> to unloose this tied-up justice when you pleas'd,

> and it in you more dreadful would have seem'd
> than in Lord Angelo.

– connects the Duke with the age-old strain of ferocity in law-making that is rooted not in morality, but in control. But the Duke wants it every way. He wants the control but not to have to wield the rod himself –

> I do fear, too dreadful.
> Sith 'twas my fault to give the people scope,
> 'twould be my tyranny to strike and gall them
> for what I bid them do...

His 'too dreadful' might be arguable, but the disarmingly frank follow-up reveals just how utterly self-centred this whole strategy is:

> Therefore indeed, my father,
> I have on Angelo impos'd the office
> who may, in th'ambush of my name

– 'ambush' having the shadow meaning, perhaps, of a lawless attack –

> strike home
> and yet my nature never in the fight
> to do in slander.

'The job will be done and I won't get the blame!' To add to this is further confirmation that the Duke's focus of difficulty is the intolerable certainty of the (one assumes) younger man, not the chaos of Vienna:

> Lord Angelo is precise,
> stands at a guard with envy, scarce confesses
> that his blood flows, or that his appetite
> is more to bread than stone. Hence shall we see,
> if power change purpose, what our seemers be.

If we are able to judge the Duke's language as if it were our own we will sense that he is deeply fearful, and that he can be vain, authoritarian and devious (isn't Lucio's the 'old fantastical duke of dark corners' actually rather apt?). In his first recorded meeting with Mariana we learn that his fears extend to the unruly power of music, which 'oft hath such a charm to make bad good, and good provoke to harm'. All these elements are absent from Shakespeare's chief sources in Cinthio's Italian *Hecatommithi* (1565) and George Whetstone's play, *Promos and Cassandra* (1578), where the Emperor Maximian (Cinthio), and King Corvinus of Hungary (Whetstone) appear only at the end to deliver justice tempered with mercy.

Shakespeare's Duke, in contrast, occupies more of his play than any other character. So once again, the transformations Shakespeare works must point to some new and radical purpose; to maintain that the Duke is merely an agent of the plot in a play that is about the morality and psychology of others is unsustainable.

Angelo and Isabella

But let me put him aside for a moment and turn to Angelo and Isabella.

Angelo is clearly a bad thing, a hypocrite and a would-be rapist (though there will be much more to say of him than that); but there has been a long-running dispute about Isabella. Should she accede to her brother's request to save his life by having sex with Angelo? This question has long divided readers and audiences.

She is evidently an upper-class young woman, but she has chosen to turn her back on her privileged life to become a nun; and she has chosen an Order that she believes will provide a life of extreme self-denial:

> ISABELLA. And have you nuns no farther privileges?
>
> FRANCISCA. Are not these large enough?
>
> ISABELLA. Yes, truly; I speak not as desiring more,
>   but rather wishing a more strict restraint
>   upon the sisterhood, the votarists of Saint Clare.
>
> Act 1 Scene 4

The sisterhood that was eventually to be named 'The Order of Poor Ladies to the Order of Saint Clare' was founded in the early thirteenth century by the high-born Chiara Offreduccio, the eldest daughter of Favorino Sciffi, Count of Sasso-Rosso and his wife Ortolana. Sciffi owned a large palace in Assisi and a castle on the slope of Mount Subasio, and the devout Ortolana was also from the Italian aristocracy.

The Order was inspired, promoted and protected by St Francis of Assisi and has ever since been seen as the sister organisation to the Franciscan Friars. Unlike the men, however, the St Clares lived in seclusion, walked barefoot, slept on the floor, rarely spoke and ate no meat. Chiara had defied her father to become a nun, something that Shakespeare – if he was aware of that fact – did not replicate in Isabella, though this may only have been because he chose that both her parents should have died before the action of the play. Like Viola and Sebastian, Isabella and Claudio must have no powerful relatives to enlist in aid.

Lucy Black as Isabella, photo © Alan Moore 2001

Shakespeare has a little fun with Isabella's enthusiasm, obliging the nun who is introducing her to the convent to negotiate the arrival of a male of the species at the door:

LUCIO. [*Within*] Ho! Peace be in this place!

ISABELLA. Who's that which calls?

FRANCISCA. It is a man's voice. Gentle Isabella,
    turn you the key, and know his business of him.
    You may, I may not. You are yet unsworn.
    When you have vow'd, you must not speak with men
    but in the presence of the prioress.
    Then, if you speak, you must not show your face,
    or, if you show your face, you must not speak.

In what follows Shakespeare brings into close collision the contrasting states of mind that will provoke the comedy and the near-tragedy of the play. Though Lucio is sometimes teasingly tongue-in-cheek, sometimes derisive, sometimes expansive, sometimes blunt – and here we sense him thoroughly enjoying privileged access to an all-female environment – his characterisations of both Juliet's pregnancy and Angelo's temperament will resonate through the play:

      … Fewness and truth, 'tis thus:
    your brother and his lover have embrac'd.

74

> As those that feed grow full, as blossoming time
> that from the seedness the bare fallow brings
> to teeming foison, even so her plenteous womb
> expresseth his full tilth and husbandry…

Indulgent at this point to her brother, Isabella is simply practical, and perhaps unconcerned by Juliet's shame:

> O, let him marry her.
>
> LUCIO.   This is the point.
> The Duke is very strangely gone from hence…
>   Upon his place,
> and with full line of his authority,
> governs Lord Angelo, a man whose blood
> is very snow-broth, one who never feels
> the wanton stings and motions of the sense
> but doth rebate and blunt his natural edge
> with profits of the mind, study and fast.

– exactly the profits to which Isabella is now dedicating herself. Lucio urges Isabella to appeal to Angelo, and to employ a classic, female strategy:

> Go to Lord Angelo
> and let him learn to know, when maidens sue,
> men give like gods, but when they weep and kneel
> all their petitions are as freely theirs
> as they themselves would owe them.
>
> ISABELLA. I'll see what I can do.

Isabella gives little away here, though we may already suspect that kneeling and weeping before a mere mortal is not her preferred posture.

With both Claudio and Juliet now in prison, the scene is set for three of the greatest scenes in all Shakespeare, scenes that are accomplished almost entirely in language. They require great stillness and concentration. The first is Act 2 Scene 2. The Provost, whose duty it will be to cut off Claudio's head, can hardly believe Angelo is serious:

> Is it your will Claudio shall die tomorrow?
>
> ANGELO. Did not I tell thee yea? Had'st thou not order?
> Why dost thou ask again?
>
> PROVOST.   Lest I might be too rash.
> Under your good correction, I have seen
> when, after execution, judgement hath
> repented o'er his doom.

ANGELO. Go to, let that be mine.
　　Do you your office, or give up your place,
　　and you shall well be spar'd.

It might be argued that the keeper of a prison in Shakespeare's time was unlikely to have been such a humane figure as is presented here (and proves to be later), but his misgivings highlight the radical change that Angelo is introducing. When Isabella and Lucio enter and the Provost makes to leave, Angelo instructs him to remain; not, I would suggest, to lend himself backup but, since the Provost seems so uncertain of due process, to allow him to witness the proper conduct of the law. Angelo turns to Isabella:

　　You're welcome. What's your will?
ISABELLA. I am a woeful suitor to your honour.
　　Please but your honour hear me.
ANGELO. Well, what's your suit?

Being almost as absolute as Angelo in matters of sexual morality, Isabella is at first in great difficulty. She has no intention of taking Lucio's advised course, and yet cannot muster a substantial moral argument to support her request:

　　There is a vice that most I do abhor,
　　and most desire should meet the blow of justice,
　　for which I would not plead, but that I must,
　　for which I must not plead, but that I am
　　at war 'twixt will and will not.

Angelo has little patience with this –

　　Well, the matter?

– but even less with this attempted distinction between the doer and the deed:

ISABELLA. I have a brother is condemn'd to die.
　　I do beseech you, let it be his fault
　　and not my brother.
ANGELO. Condemn the fault and not the actor of it?
　　Why, every fault's condemn'd ere it be done.
　　Mine were the very cipher of a function,
　　to fine the faults – whose fine stands in record –
　　and let go by the actor.

Isabella cannot refute Angelo's logic –

ISABELLA.   O just but severe law!
    I had a brother, then. Heaven keep your honour.

– and she turns to go. I suggest the venue for this meeting, if not a state building of some kind, might again have been Angelo's own Great Hall, the large, and to a degree public space in which lords and governors commonly received petitioners, whether on legal or commercial matters, and conducted trials – as in Act 2 Scene 1. In this case – making it all the harder for Isabella – such a petition would be witnessed, every word overheard, by various officials and servants, represented here by the Provost and the Servant who brings Isabella in (if the production can afford no more). There is an intimidating space between the judge and the petitioner, who is forced to speak up, while Lucio's *sotto voce* asides to her are credibly privately delivered, perhaps half-heard by Angelo, perhaps not (in our intimate space they were). Lucio still believes in the conventional strategy:

    [*Aside to Isabella*] Give't not o'er so. To him again,
      entreat him,
    kneel down before him, hang upon his gown.
    You are too cold. If you should need a pin
    you could not with more tame a tongue desire it.
    To him, I say!

This last line is six syllables short, suggesting Isabella's hesitation, as she tries to think of any pretext on which she can renew her appeal. All she has is this:

    Must he needs die?

She can have little hope of a rethink, and yet it does provoke an opportunity:

    ANGELO.   Maiden, no remedy.

The rapid and curt simplicity of this is too unworldly, too, too easy, and Isabella's sense of righteousness now becomes her ally rather than her obstacle. Her 'yes' is a small grenade thrown into the debate –

    Yes. I do think that you might pardon him,
    and neither heaven nor man grieve at the mercy.
    ANGELO. I will not do't.

– and she follows it up with an assault that clearly puts Angelo on the defensive –

    ISABELLA.   But can you, if you would?
    ANGELO. Look, what I will not, that I cannot do.

ISABELLA. But might you do't, and do the world no wrong,
if so your heart were touch'd with that remorse
as mine is to him?

ANGELO.   He's sentenced; 'tis too late.

LUCIO. [*Aside to Isabella*] You are too cold.

ISABELLA. Too late? Why, no.

– again the monosyllables are shocking, bravely powerful –

                                 I, that do speak a word
may call it back again. Well believe this:
no ceremony that to great ones 'longs,
not the king's crown, nor the deputed sword,
the marshal's truncheon, nor the judge's robe
become them with one half so good a grace
as mercy does.

An acute and educated intelligence, debating skills that would not disgrace a top QC, and an instinctive recognition of the vanity of her opponent have now released Isabella from her discomfort and she is momentarily in the ascendant:

If he had been as you and you as he
you would have slipp'd like him, but he, like you,
would not have been so stern.

ANGELO.   Pray you, be gone.

ISABELLA. I would to heaven I had your potency
and you were Isabel! Should it then be thus?
No. I would tell what 'twere to be a judge,
and what a prisoner.

LUCIO. [*Aside to Isabella*] Ay, touch him, there's the vein.

ANGELO. Your brother is a forfeit of the law
and you but waste your words.

ISABELLA.   Alas, alas!
Why, all the souls that were were forfeit once,
and He that might the vantage best have took
found out the remedy. How would you be,
if He, which is the top of judgement, should
but judge you as you are? O, think on that
and mercy then will breathe within your lips
like man new made.

But now Angelo begins to recover, and his next words end with the shock that adds new urgency to Isabella's petition:

ANGELO.   Be you content, fair maid,
    it is the law, not I, condemn your brother.
    Were he my kinsman, brother, or my son,
    it should be thus with him. He must die tomorrow.

ISABELLA. Tomorrow? Oh, that's sudden! Spare him, spare him!
    He's not prepar'd for death. Even for our kitchens
    we kill the fowl of season. Shall we serve Heaven
    with less respect than we do minister
    to our gross selves? Good, good my lord, bethink you.
    Who is it that hath died for this offence?
    There's many have committed it.

Now Angelo has the upper hand. The unalloyed absolutism, and the vanity of his mind is eloquently expressed in the controlled development of his response, particularly in its last, long sentence:

The law hath not been dead, though it hath slept.
Those many had not dar'd to do that evil
if the first that did th'edict infringe
had answer'd for his deed. Now 'tis awake,
takes note of what is done, and, like a prophet,
looks in a glass that shows what future evils,
either new – or by remissness new-conceiv'd
and so in progress to be hatch'd and born –
are now to have no successive degrees
but ere they live to end.

An element of barely disguised thrill in his own agency in this awakening of the law is shocking, but there is worse to come:

ISABELLA.   Yet show some pity.

ANGELO. I show it most of all when I show justice,
    for then I pity those I do not know –
    which a dismiss'd offence would after gall –
    and do him right that, answering one foul wrong,
    lives not to act another. Be satisfied.
    Your brother dies tomorrow. Be content.

The utter failure of empathy in the ludicrous, and repeated, injunction, 'Be content', refuels Isabella's indignation –

So you must be the first that gives this sentence,
and he, that suffers. Oh, it is excellent
to have a giant's strength, but it is tyrannous
to use it like a giant.

And she continues with an astonishingly bold attack, characterising Angelo as a 'pelting, petty officer' abusing his 'brief authority'. But she then moderates her tone, as Angelo is evidently captivated by her argument – or by something else, as the libidinously focused Lucio interprets:

> [*Aside*] Oh, to him, to him, wench! He will relent.
> He's coming, I perceive 't.
>
> PROVOST. [*Aside*] Pray heaven she win him!
>
> ISABELLA. We cannot weigh our brother with ourself.
> Great men may jest with saints, 'tis wit in them,
> but in the less foul profanation –

this is bitingly ironic, of course –

> LUCIO. Thou'rt i' the right, girl, more o' that.
>
> ISABELLA. That in the captain's but a choleric word,
> which in the soldier is flat blasphemy.
>
> LUCIO. [*Aside*] Art avis'd o' that? More on't.

Angelo is now at a loss:

> ANGELO. Why do you put these sayings upon me?
>
> ISABELLA. Because authority, though it err like others,
> hath yet a kind of med'cine in itself
> that skins the vice o' the top. Go to your bosom,
> knock there, and ask your heart what it doth know
> that's like my brother's fault. If it confess
> a natural guiltiness such as is his
> let it not sound a thought upon your tongue
> against my brother's life.
>
> ANGELO. [*Aside*] She speaks, and 'tis
> such sense, that my sense breeds with it. Fare you well.

Here is one of those moments when the play as we have it might have been prevented; Angelo intends to escape the feelings Isabella has aroused in him by leaving the room, but with her 'gentle' address, he is stopped, caught on what he is soon to characterise as the Devil's 'hook':

> ISABELLA. Gentle my lord, turn back.
>
> ANGELO. I will bethink me. Come again tomorrow.
>
> ISABELLA. Hark how I'll bribe you. Good my lord, turn back.
>
> ANGELO. How? Bribe me?

Bribe him? Has she almost blundered here? It is hardly likely that she could have conceived of any form of bribe other than the one she is to offer – the 'true prayers' of 'fasting maids whose minds are dedicate to nothing temporal'. The more interesting question is: is there the slightest element of *play* in her here; does she enjoy the moment of shock?

A second interview is agreed and Isabella, Lucio and the Provost leave, permitting Angelo's first soliloquy:

> ANGELO. What's this, what's this? Is this her fault or mine?
> The tempter or the tempted, who sins most, ha?
> Not she. Nor doth she tempt. But it is I
> that, lying by the violet in the sun,
> do as the carrion does, not as the flower,
> corrupt with virtuous season. Can it be
> that modesty may more betray our sense
> than woman's lightness? Having waste ground enough,
> shall we desire to raze the sanctuary
> and pitch our evils there?

'Evils' is a synonym for privies, or toilets. The literal sense is 'why pitch our privies on sanctified rather than waste ground?', the metaphorical 'why choose holy women as the objects of our lusts, given that prostitutes are plentiful?' The literal sense may well escape the modern audience, but emendation is problematic; and the attitude to female sexuality is clear enough.

> O, fie, fie, fie!
> What dost thou, or what art thou, Angelo?
> Dost thou desire her foully for those things
> that make her good? O, let her brother live!
> Thieves for their robbery have authority
> when judges steal themselves. What, do I love her,
> that I desire to hear her speak again
> and feast upon her eyes? What is't I dream on?
> O cunning enemy, that, to catch a saint
> with saints dost bait thy hook! Most dangerous
> is that temptation that doth goad us on
> to sin in loving virtue. Never could the strumpet,
> with all her double vigour – art and nature –
> once stir my temper, but this virtuous maid
> subdues me quite. Ever till now,
> when men were fond, I smil'd and wonder'd how.

John Mackay as Angelo, photo © Alan Moore 2001

With this great speech we at last see Angelo from the inside, and it should provoke some sympathy for him. Why is it 'sin', why is he 'corrupted' by his sexual attraction to Isabella, by wanting to hear her speak again and to 'feast upon her eyes'? Because we must be clear that at this point, 'fondness' is the extent of his perceived fall. If there is any element of a dirty deal in the making then it is yet to take any conscious shape. Angelo is bewildered, awakening to a new conception of himself, and it is tragic that his puritanical mind should conceive of fondness as polluting, sinful, because it will make the step into that dirty deal the easier; he already believes himself guilty, that he is already caught on the Devil's hook.

This frame of mind is not idiosyncratic; it is common to Shakespeare's Vienna. Even Claudio, who will go on to protest that he 'got possession of Julietta's bed' 'upon a true contract', has greeted his friend Lucio with this rationale for his arrest:

> As surfeit is the father of much fast,
> so every scope by the immoderate use
> turns to restraint. Our natures do pursue,
> like rats that ravin down their proper bane,
> a thirsty evil, and when we drink we die.

> Act 1 Scene 2

Even allowing for a strong vein of irony, the disgust at his own sexuality is palpable. It will be echoed later in the prison by Juliet's:

> I do repent me as it is an evil and take the shame with joy.
>
> Act 2 Scene 3

And his 'restraint' might remind us of the 'more strict restraint' that Isabella looked to find in the convent; an unacknowledged anxiety, perhaps even an element of panic, about her own sexual appetite.

The next great scene (Act 2 Scene 4) we should imagine in a smaller, more private place, perhaps Angelo's own 'great chamber' (see Girouard again). In my own production the space was now empty except for two severely upright chairs, which John Mackay took some time to place, deliberately but nervously, quite close together. A contrast with the previous scene is crucial; having endured the embarrassment of a semi-public petition, Isabella now endures the threat of a completely private encounter; now there will be no witness beyond her own eyes and ears.

From the start, Angelo is almost grimly decided on a course that will amount to rape, observing his own capitulation to a 'strong and swelling evil' with a somewhat melodramatic fascination:

> When I would pray and think, I think and pray
> to sev'ral subjects. Heav'n hath my empty words,
> whilst my invention, hearing not my tongue,
> anchors on Isabel. Heav'n in my mouth,
> as if I did but only chew His name,
> and in my heart the strong and swelling evil
> of my conception. The state, whereon I studied,
> is like a good thing, being often read,
> grown sere and tedious. Yea, my gravity,
> wherein – let no man hear me – I take pride,
> could I with boot change for an idle plume
> which the air beats for vain…

Isabella's arrival is announced, and his nervous anticipation redoubles:

> O heavens,
> why does my blood thus muster to my heart,
> making both it unable for itself
> and dispossessing all my other parts
> of necessary fitness?…

A servant ushers Isabells in.

> How now, fair maid?
>
> ISABELLA. I am come to know your pleasure.

Angelo immediately flags up the difficulty he will have in articulating his 'pleasure'. Though the Folio text is silent on the matter, this is commonly, and I believe correctly, played as an aside:

> ANGELO. That you might know it, would much better please me
> than to demand what 'tis. – Your brother cannot live.
>
> ISABELLA. Even so. Heaven keep your honour.

Isabella, who has prepared herself for a simply definitive decision, once again turns to go. Angelo, by contrast unprepared for such an acceptance – had he expected weeping and kneeling? – must hold her there somehow:

> Yet may he live awhile. And, it may be,
> as long as you or I. Yet he must die.
>
> ISABELLA. Under your sentence?
>
> ANGELO. Yea.
>
> ISABELLA. When, I beseech you? That in his reprieve,
> longer or shorter, he may be so fitted
> that his soul sicken not.

He does not answer this, but with Isabella momentarily stayed, embarks on the provocatively severe argument – very possibly preconceived – that he hopes will trap her into offering an apology for sexual sin:

> Ha? Fie, these filthy vices! It were as good
> to pardon him that hath from nature stolen
> a man already made,[16] as to remit[17]
> their saucy sweetness that do coin heaven's image
> in stamps that are forbid.

This image brings together two ideas – the sin of procreating out of wedlock (the child being the image of God), and the crime of counterfeiting the monarch's image on a coin – both ideas being repeated in the next lines:

> 'Tis all as easy
> falsely to take away a life true made
> as to put metal in restrained means
> to make a false one.

The ruse works –

ISABELLA. 'Tis set down so in heaven, but not in earth.

– and Angelo seizes on it:

> Say you so? Then I shall pose you quickly:
> which had you rather, that the most just law
> now took your brother's life, or, to redeem him,
> give up your body to such sweet uncleanness
> as she that he hath stain'd?

ISABELLA.   Sir, believe this,
> I had rather give my body than my soul.

ANGELO. I talk not of your soul. Our compell'd sins
> stand more for number than for accompt.

ISABELLA. How say you?

He has made a false move and – after a momentary hiatus, perhaps – backtracks:

> Nay, I'll not warrant that, for I can speak
> against the thing I say. Answer to this:
> I, now the voice of the recorded law,
> pronounce a sentence on your brother's life.
> Might there not be a charity in sin
> to save this brother's life?

ISABELLA.   Please you to do't,
> I'll take it as a peril to my soul,
> it is no sin at all, but charity.

ANGELO. Pleas'd you to do't at peril of your soul,
> were equal poise of sin and charity.

Here, the actor playing Isabella can choose between innocent and deliberate incomprehension, though Angelo's own tone and manner might make the innocent choice untenable:

ISABELLA. That I do beg his life, if it be sin,
> Heaven let me bear it. You, granting of my suit,
> if that be sin, I'll make it my morn prayer
> to have it added to the faults of mine,
> and nothing of your answer.

ANGELO.   Nay, but hear me.
> Your sense pursues not mine. Either you are ignorant,
> or seem so crafty, and that's not good.

Angelo is probably right that Isabella had begun to comprehend his real intent; if not, then he has just given it away. She is now on the defensive, trying to deny the implicit drift of Angelo's words:

> ISABELLA. Let me be ignorant, and in nothing good,
> but graciously to know I am no better.

But she only reinforces his intent:

> ANGELO. Thus wisdom wishes to appear most bright
> when it doth tax itself, as these black masks
> proclaim an enshield beauty ten times louder
> than beauty could, display'd. But mark me,
> to be received plain, I'll speak more gross:
> your brother is to die.
>
> ISABELLA. So.
>
> ANGELO. And his offence is so, as it appears,
> accountant to the law upon that pain.
>
> ISABELLA. True.

Now Isabella's monosyllables ring not with confidence, but with dread of what is to come:

> ANGELO. Admit no other way to save his life –
> as I subscribe not that, nor any other,
> but in the loss of question – that you, his sister,
> finding yourself desir'd of such a person,
> whose credit with the judge, or own great place,
> could fetch your brother from the manacles
> of the all-binding law, and that there were
> no earthly mean to save him, but that either
> you must lay down the treasures of your body
> to this suppos'd, or else to let him suffer,
> what would you do?

Angelo's metrically incomplete line again suggests a brief hiatus as Isabella searches for an answer. When it comes it is a powerful riposte, yet also erotically expressive, with an edge of masochism that has long disturbed Isabella's critics:

> As much for my poor brother as myself.
> That is, were I under the terms of death,
> the impression of keen whips I'd wear as rubies,
> and strip myself to death, as to a bed
> that longing have been sick for, ere I'd yield
> my body up to shame.

ANGELO. Then must your brother die.

ISABELLA. And 'twere the cheaper way.
Better it were a brother died at once,
than that a sister, by redeeming him,
should die for ever.

The absolutism is now Isabella's, and Angelo seizes on it:

Were not you then as cruel as the sentence
that you have slander'd so?

ISABELLA. Ignomy in ransom[18] and free pardon
are of two houses. Lawful mercy
is nothing kin to foul redemption.

It is a production choice as to whether Angelo is momentarily merely 'arguing the toss' here – lawyer-like identifying the contradictions in Isabella's position as a small victory in itself – or still determinedly pursuing his objective:

You seem'd of late to make the law a tyrant,
and rather prov'd the sliding of your brother
a merriment than a vice.

ISABELLA. Oh, pardon me, my lord. It oft falls out,
to have what we would have, we speak not what we mean.
I something do excuse the thing I hate
for his advantage that I dearly love.

ANGELO. We are all frail.

ISABELLA.   Else let my brother die,
if not a feodary,[19] but only he
owe and succeed thy weakness.

He is certainly back on track now:

ANGELO. Nay, women are frail too.

In her misery, Isabella fails to recognise this next trap; indeed, she digs it deeper by voicing a common prejudice against her sex:

ISABELLA. Ay, as the glasses where they view themselves,
which are as easy broke as they make forms.
Women? Help Heaven! Men their creation mar
in profiting by them. Nay, call us ten times frail,
for we are soft as our complexions are
and credulous to false prints.

Angelo has at last arrived in a place that a different mould of tyrant could have reached in a moment. A novice in sexual passion, he has sought intellectual sanction from Isabella to the sin that he is asking her to commit with him, bullying with his rhetorical skills rather than physical force – though the brutality of the proposed beheading of Claudius is an immanent violence. It has been an uneasy, even comically embarrassed progress; and though he is now explicitly unwrapping his intent, it is still expressed with a lawyer's fastidious care and – in this speech – a final euphemism:

> I think it well.
> And from this testimony of your own sex –
> since I suppose we are made to be no stronger
> than faults may shake our frames – let me be bold:
> I do arrest your words. Be that you are,
> that is, a woman. If you be more, you're none.
> If you be one, as you are well express'd
> by all external warrants, show it now,
> by putting on the destin'd livery.

For Isabella there is still a possibility that the livery of whoredom (as I read the metaphor) can be avoided, that the very suggestion can be contradicted by a reversion to Angelo's 'former language' – meaning the language that there is no alternative, that Claudio must die; perhaps even a possibility that the argument can be retrospectively reframed as a test of her own virtue, so as to extinguish the terrifying meaning that now echoes in her ears:

> I have no tongue but one. Gentle my lord,
> let me entreat you speak the former language.
>
> ANGELO. Plainly conceive, I love you.
>
> ISABELLA. My brother did love Juliet,
> and you tell me that he shall die for't.
>
> ANGELO. He shall not, Isabel, if you give me love.

She is now clutching at straws:

> ISABELLA. I know your virtue hath a licence in't,
> which seems a little fouler than it is
> to pluck on others.
>
> ANGELO.   Believe me, on mine honour,
> my words express my purpose.

But at this mention of honour, her strength of spirit reasserts itself:

ISABELLA. Ha! Little honour to be much believ'd,
and most pernicious purpose! Seeming, seeming!
I will proclaim thee, Angelo, look for't.
Sign me a present pardon for my brother
or with an outstretch'd throat I'll tell the world aloud
what man thou art.

To no avail; Angelo has now discovered a terrible confidence in the scope
of his own power; and a complete determination in his purpose. There
remains the quality of fascinated self-observation – 'and now I give my
sensual race the rein' – that is peculiar to him:

Who will believe thee, Isabel?
My unsoil'd name, th'austereness of my life,
my vouch against you, and my place i'th'state,
will so your accusation overweigh
that you shall stifle in your own report
and smell of calumny. I have begun,
and now I give my sensual race the rein.
Fit thy consent to my sharp appetite,
lay by all nicety and prolixious blushes
that banish what they sue for. Redeem thy brother
by yielding up thy body to my will,
or else he must not only die the death,
but thy unkindness shall his death draw out
to ling'ring suff'rance…

While stage action normally allows for a wide spectrum of interpretation,
John Mackay, Lucy Black and I were convinced that there must be no
grappling, barely perhaps a touch. The horror, and the eroticism, of this
scene is entirely in the words, and in the two imaginations that exchange
them. Any physical action would render those words at best unnecessary,
at worst ridiculous. Left alone, as Isabella speaks now of her hurt and
bewilderment, she does not have the feel of a bruising clutch on her wrist
or her jaw, but just the terrible sound of Angelo's words, the *action* of his
words, resounding in her head. Words have changed everything for her:

To whom should I complain? Did I tell this,
who would believe me? Oh perilous mouths,
that bear in them one and the self-same tongue,
either of condemnation or approof,
bidding the law make curtsy to their will,
hooking both right and wrong to the appetite,
to follow as it draws. I'll to my brother.

She is now dependent on her brother to be her saviour, and she must dictate to her own imagination how he will react when she tells him of Angelo's proposal:

> Though he hath fallen by prompture of the blood,
> yet hath he in him such a mind of honour
> that, had he twenty heads to tender down
> on twenty bloody blocks, he'd yield them up
> before his sister should her body stoop
> to such abhorr'd pollution.

The 'twenty bloody blocks' alerts us to a willed, rather than a settled confidence; the rhyming couplets that end the scene have an alarming simplicity that makes us distrust them; and, however deep our sympathy for Isabella's agony, her 'more than our brother is our chastity' (the last syllable perhaps offering a perfect rhyme with 'die') we must still feel as shocking:

> Then, Isabel, live chaste, and, brother, die.
> More than our brother is our chastity.
> I'll tell him yet of Angelo's request,
> and fit his mind to death, for his soul's rest.

Whetstone's *Promos and Cassandra* had Cassandra say 'Honour far dearer is than life.' Shakespeare's change from 'honour' to 'chastity' is telling.

The 'Contemptus Mundi'

Returning to the Duke, the action now moves directly to Claudio's cell in the prison (Act 3 Scene 1) where a lay impostor presumes to offer the condemned man spiritual comfort. We are evidently cutting into a scene already in train:

> DUKE. So then you hope of pardon from Lord Angelo?
>
> CLAUDIO. The mis'rable have no other med'cine
>   but only hope.
>   I have hope to live, and am prepar'd to die.

The Duke responds with his famous *contemptus mundi*, a preparation for death, which I quote here in full:

> DUKE. Be absolute for death. Either death or life
>   shall thereby be the sweeter. Reason thus with life:

if I do lose thee, I do lose a thing
that none but fools would keep. A breath thou art,
servile to all the skyey influences
that dost this habitation where thou keep'st
hourly afflict. Merely, thou art Death's fool,
for him thou labour'st by thy flight to shun
and yet runn'st toward him still. Thou art not noble,
for all th'accommodations that thou bear'st
are nurs'd by baseness. Thou'rt by no means valiant,
for thou dost fear the soft and tender fork
of a poor worm. Thy best of rest is sleep,
and that thou oft provok'st, yet grossly fear'st
thy death, which is no more. Thou art not thyself,
for thou exists on many a thousand grains
that issue out of dust. Happy thou art not,
for what thou hast not, still thou striv'st to get,
and what thou hast, forget'st. Thou art not certain,
for thy complexion shifts to strange effects
after the moon. If thou art rich, thou'rt poor,
for, like an ass whose back with ingots bows,
thou bear'st thy heavy riches but a journey
and death unloads thee. Friend hast thou none,
for thine own bowels which do call thee sire,
the mere effusion of thy proper loins,
do curse the gout, serpigo, and the rheum
for ending thee no sooner. Thou hast nor youth nor age,
but as it were an after-dinner's sleep
dreaming on both, for all thy blessed youth
becomes as aged and doth beg the alms
of palsied eld. And when thou art old and rich
thou hast neither heat, affection, limb, nor beauty
to make thy riches pleasant. What's yet in this
that bears the name of life? Yet in this life
lie hid moe thousand deaths. Yet death we fear,
that makes these odds all even.

This argument was taken by the Christian world from the classical Stoics, despite the fact that its characterisation of God's creation as 'a thing that none but fools would keep' might be considered blasphemous, and its counsel of despair a mortal sin. We should certainly feel it as a curious tactic for a Christian friar (even a bogus one). Is this merely the Duke exercising his craft as an actor, or doing his best for Claudio using the first strategy to come into his head; or does it call our attention once again to the sound and substance of the Duke's own mind? Once again I urge my belief: Shakespeare's characters say what they mean and mean what they say. The speech cannot be rattled off, as a received text; it must be thought through and, as it is, the images land with a cumulative power, devaluing human life in ways that suggest an empty chasm in the Duke's own psyche. Though he preaches resignation, he reveals his own loneliness, his own fear of ageing, of being held in impatient contempt by his children – those 'mere effusions' of his own loins – and, through it all, his own inability to enjoy, or value what is merely temporal. And, meanwhile, not a word from this supposed man of God, of the need for repentance, or of the permanence of the Christian after-life. This is a reductive and reduced spirit. But even while it allows him to act with extraordinary, sometimes even comic callousness towards those who do hold on to life as a value – Barnadine being the supreme example – perhaps we should extend him some understanding; there is evidence here that he is one among Shakespeare's many unhappy beings.

In this moment, his sermon has his desired effect:

> CLAUDIO.   I humbly thank you.
> To sue to live, I find I seek to die,
> and, seeking death, find life. Let it come on.

The neat simplicity of 'To sue to live, I find I seek to die' again suggests a fragility in the assertion.

Isabella and Claudio

And then Isabella arrives. I have long thought of her journey from Angelo's chamber to the prison as of a walk down a very long corridor, at the end of which is Claudio's condemned cell, barely glimpsed at first but growing more and more present as she proceeds; a journey from certainty to uncertainty, from confidence to nervous terror. How easy is it for her to knock on that door, and have it opened to admit her?

Believing them to be alone together, Claudio's resignation immediately falls away:

> Now, sister, what's the comfort?
> ISABELLA.   Why –

That line is two syllables short, which may well suggest a hesitation, before she attempts to assure both Claudio *and herself* that there is no alternative to the execution:

> as all comforts are – most good, most good indeed.
> Lord Angelo, having affairs to Heaven,
> intends you for his swift ambassador,
> where you shall be an everlasting leiger.
> Therefore your best appointment make with speed.
> Tomorrow you set on.
>
> CLAUDIO.   Is there no remedy?

It is to Isabella's credit that she does not offer a simple 'no'. She is too honest, but she also needs Claudio's confirmation of her decision, and so preloads the argument to that end:

> None, but such remedy as, to save a head,
> to cleave a heart in twain.
>
> CLAUDIO.   But is there any?
>
> ISABELLA. Yes, brother, you may live.
> There is a devilish mercy in the judge,
> if you'll implore it, that will free your life,
> but fetter you till death.
>
> CLAUDIO.   Perpetual durance?[20]
>
> ISABELLA. Ay, just. Perpetual durance, a restraint,
> though all the world's vastidity you had,
> to a determin'd scope.
>
> CLAUDIO.   But in what nature?
>
> ISABELLA. In such a one as, you consenting to't,
> would bark your honour from that trunk you bear
> and leave you naked.
>
> CLAUDIO.   Let me know the point!

Set out like this, we see how Claudio pressures his sister, completing her iambic line five times running in a crescendo of frustration. The immediate physical threat to Isabella is far more imminent in this moment than it ever was in the two scenes with Angelo:

> ISABELLA. O, I do fear thee, Claudio, and I quake,
> lest thou a fev'rous life shouldst entertain
> and six or seven winters more respect
> than a perpetual honour. Dar'st thou die?
> The sense of death is most in apprehension,
> and the poor beetle that we tread upon,
> in corp'ral suff'rance finds a pang as great
> as when a giant dies.

Now he cuts in on her line again, but this time with an indignation that will
– momentarily – release her from her fear:

>   Why give you me this shame?
> Think you I can a resolution fetch
> from flow'ry tenderness? If I must die,
> I will encounter darkness as a bride
> and hug it in mine arms.

We hear her intense relief:

> ISABELLA. There spake my brother. There my father's grave
>   did utter forth a voice. Yes, thou must die.
>   Thou art too noble to conserve a life
>   in base appliances.

and she continues in real confidence that Claudio will see with her eyes:

>   This outward-sainted deputy,
> whose settl'd visage and deliberate word
> nips youth i'th'head and follies doth enew
> as falcon doth the fowl, is yet a devil.
> His filth within being cast, he would appear
> a pond as deep as hell.
> CLAUDIO.   The princely[21] Angelo?
> ISABELLA. O, 'tis the cunning livery of hell,
>   the damned'st body to invest and cover
>   in princely guards! Dost thou think, Claudio,
>   if I would yield him my virginity,
>   thou mightst be freed?
> CLAUDIO.   O heavens, it cannot be!

In the following few lines there are two syllables missing somewhere. At
least one editor suggests that Claudio's 'Thou shalt not do it' completes
Isabella's previous line (even though it gives a line of twelve syllables), and
that the syllabic gap follows Isabella's 'O, were it but my life'. I prefer to lay
it out like this, suggesting there is a two-syllable hiatus before Claudio's
'Thou shalt not do it', and no break before Isabella's reply:

> ISABELLA. Yes, he would give't thee, from this rank offence,
>   so to offend him still. This night's the time
>   that I should do what I abhor to name,
>   or else thou diest tomorrow. [*Hiatus*]
> CLAUDIO. Thou shalt not do't.

ISABELLA.   O, were it but my life,
    I'd throw it down for your deliverance
    as frankly as a pin.
CLAUDIO.   Thanks, dear Isabel.
ISABELLA. Be ready, Claudio, for your death tomorrow.
CLAUDIO. Yes.

Again in this play a monosyllable carries extraordinary import.

What would happen next, if... (again)

At this point I ask that important question again: what would have happened next if Claudio had not followed up on his 'yes' of agreement to being executed? Would brother and sister have sat together in silence, waiting for the appointed time? Or reminisced through a long night? Or would Isabella have given him a final, tearful hug and kiss and left? Might the gentle Provost have strong-armed her out? – unlikely, I think. The last family visit in the condemned cell must always have been an excruciatingly painful experience for both parties, but here the sister would be walking away knowing that she could have saved her brother. However passionately she may believe that 'more than our brother is our chastity', the guilt would be inescapable, the final, parting look unbearable. There is, I suggest, no exit from that room at the end of that long corridor – until, that is, Claudio changes his tune:

    Has he affections in him,
    that thus can make him bite the law by th'nose
    when he would force it? Sure, it is no sin,
    or of the deadly seven, it is the least.

Here the missing syllables suggest the hiatus is Isabella's; she has lost her preparedness for this possibility:

[*Hiatus*]   Which is the least?
CLAUDIO. If it were damnable, he being so wise,
    why would he for the momentary trick
    be perdurably fin'd? O Isabel!
ISABELLA. What says my brother?
CLAUDIO.   Death is a fearful thing.

But now she is quick to retort:

And shamed life a hateful.

The impulse for life in Claudio's famous response is so strong that many an actor has found it hard to keep under control:

> Ay, but to die, and go we know not where,
> to lie in cold obstruction and to rot,
> this sensible warm motion to become
> a kneaded clod, and the delighted spirit
> to bathe in fiery floods, or to reside
> in thrilling region of thick-ribbed ice.
> To be imprison'd in the viewless winds
> and blown with restless violence round about
> the pendent world, or to be worse than worst
> of those that lawless and incertain thought
> imagine howling – 'tis too horrible!
> The weariest and most loathed worldly life
> that age, ache, penury and imprisonment
> can lay on nature is a paradise
> to what we fear of death.

It is an instinctive and passionate overturning of that resigned state the Duke briefly secured in him with his stoic sermon. It throws aside both honour and morality, and our Claudio, Stuart Crossman, played it with passionate conviction, without a shred of the shameful pleading that is so often seen. It is 'Nature' itself – amoral Nature – that speaks in him, and the more commandingly it does so, the more terrifying it is to Isabella:

> ISABELLA.   Alas, alas!
>
> CLAUDIO. Sweet sister, let me live!
>   What sin you do to save a brother's life,
>   Nature dispenses with the deed so far
>   that it becomes a virtue.

It is to Isabella's response –

>   O, you beast!
> O faithless coward, O dishonest wretch!
> Wilt thou be made a man out of my vice?
> Is't not a kind of incest, to take life
> from thine own sister's shame? What should I think?

– that the 'anti-Isabellists' will point, a massive over-reaction, piling up the sin-count: cowardice, dishonesty, even incest and bastardy. The distinguished American academic Harry Berger Jr, in an exhaustive analysis of the Duke's motivation and behaviour,[22] characterises Isabella here as having a 'full-throated operatic pleasure… in proclaiming her brother unfit to live', this in response to 'Claudio's cowardly reluctance to exchange his head for her maidenhead'. Such a pleasure could be played, as could Claudio's cowardice, but that is not what I hear. I hear in her overstatement panic and hysteria rather than operatic pleasure. She continues:

> Heaven shield my mother play'd my father fair.

'Shield' may easily be misheard now to mean 'protect' rather than 'forbid'. In fact, academic editors disagree as to which meaning is intended. Brian Gibbons, in the 1991 New Cambridge edition glosses 'shield' as 'ensure, grant that'; but, along with J.W. Lever in the 1965 Arden edition, and many others since, I believe 'forbid' is the intended meaning. In this moment Isabella is expressing the extraordinary wish (that surely only hysteria can explain) that her mother had committed adultery with Claudio's father rather than that Claudio should have been a true son of her own father and so her full brother. The use of 'Heaven', where Shakespeare might have originally written 'God', was required in the Folio text following the Edict of 1606: 'That if any time… any person or persons do or shall in any stage play, interlude, show, maygame, or pageant jestingly or profanely speak or use the holy name of God or of Christ Jesus, or of the Holy Ghost or of the Trinity, which are not to be spoken but with fear and reverence, shall forfeit for every offence by him or them committed, ten pounds'. If my interpretation of the line is accepted, I recommend an emendation to 'God forbid my mother…', which retains the metre, while clarifying an important thought:

> God forbid my mother play'd my father fair,
> for such a warped slip of wilderness
> ne'er issu'd from his blood. Take my defiance,
> die, perish! Might but my bending down
> reprieve thee from thy fate, it should proceed.
> I'll pray a thousand prayers for thy death,
> no word to save thee.

> CLAUDIO.   Nay, hear me, Isabel.

But she has not finished yet; her next accusation, were it expressed in a very, very different tone, could have been spoken by Angelo in Act 2 Scene 2; it has the force of the puritan fear of the fatal unruliness of sexuality:

> O, fie, fie, fie! –

four powerful syllables have assumed the space of a full line –

> Thy sin's not accidental, but a trade.
> Mercy to thee would prove itself a bawd.
> 'Tis best thou diest quickly.

Though the Duke (who has overheard all this) now enters to prevent her, I suggest that had he not done so Isabella would have exited at this point, slamming the door loudly behind her, Claudio's *betrayal* permitting her the exit his *loyalty* would have denied; a powerful, albeit unspoken, human dynamic.

This brother/sister confrontation has a clear origin in Act 3 Scene 3 of Whetstone's *Promos and Cassandra*; but the transformation Shakespeare works sets it in a different dramatic universe from Whetstone's wholly unconvincing interaction; you can read the first part of Whetstone's two-part play on my website.

Forestalling Isabella's exit, the Duke has a plot in mind:

> Might you dispense with your leisure, I would by and by
> have some speech with you. The satisfaction I would
> require is likewise your own benefit.
>
> ISABELLA. I have no superfluous leisure. My stay must be stolen
> out of other affairs. But I will attend you awhile.

The detail here – 'I have no superfluous leisure' – is quite wonderful; she speaks to the supposed friar, not as a humble novitiate, but as an impatient, highborn woman addressing a social inferior; her sense of shame has bruised her dignity.

The Duke's Plot

We notice that the scene has changed suddenly into prose. There is an element of bathos here, as the scene descends from the high passion of the Claudio/Isabella confrontation into one of plotting and lying. The Duke, now he has damning evidence of Angelo's hypocrisy, is re-energised and in scheming mood:

> Son, I have overheard what hath pass'd between you and
> your sister. Angelo had never the purpose to corrupt her.
> Only he hath made an essay of her virtue to practise his
> judgement with the disposition of natures. She, having
> the truth of honour in her, hath made him that gracious
> denial which he is most glad to receive. I am confessor to
> Angelo –

– lie upon lie upon lie –

> – and I know this to be true. Therefore prepare yourself
> to death. Do not satisfy your resolution with hopes that
> are fallible. Tomorrow you must die. Go to your knees
> and make ready.

It will soon become clear that he has every intention of saving Claudio, but he seems to have no qualms whatever about condemning him to the humiliation of believing that his appeal to Isabella was pointless, and to more hours of misery in anticipation of a beheading. Small wonder that Claudio's state is now quite abject:

> Let me ask my sister pardon. I am so out of love with life
> that I will sue to be rid of it.
> DUKE. Hold you there. Farewell.
> *Exit Claudio* [?]

Here some modern editors suggest Claudio 'retires' rather than 'exits' (a Second Folio direction only, there is no direction in F1), to allow for a dumbshow reconciliation between Claudio and Isabella as the Duke converses briefly with the Provost. I am sceptical of this, preferring the option that the Duke's 'Hold you there' refers not to Claudio's request to beg pardon of Isabella, but only to his 'I am so out of love with life that I will sue to be rid of it'. A reconciliation would seem to be a major event – and a difficult one – that Shakespeare would hardly have left to silence and to chance.

It might be argued that the Duke now has sufficient proof of Angelo's perfidy, but he is beginning to develop a plot which will deepen Angelo's guilt and make it proof against any denial. He may already envision its grand dénouement at the gates of the city. With both the Provost and Claudio gone, he has first to add in a vital piece of backstory, for Isabella and for us:

> DUKE. Have you not heard speak of Mariana, the sister of
> Frederick, the great soldier who miscarried at sea?
> ISABELLA. I have heard of the lady, and good words went with
> her name.
> DUKE. She should this Angelo have married, was affianc'd to her
> by oath

– the status, incidentally, of the Claudio/Juliet relationship –

> and the nuptial appointed. Between which time of the
> contract and limit of the solemnity, her brother Frederick
> was wreck'd at sea, having in that perish'd vessel the
> dowry of his sister. But mark how heavily this befell to the
> poor gentlewoman: there she lost a noble and renowned
> brother, in his love toward her ever most kind and
> natural; with him the portion and sinew of her fortune,
> her marriage-dowry; with both, her combinate husband,
> this well-seeming Angelo…

The revelation here that Angelo is a promise-breaker and that the Duke has known it all along might deepen our scepticism as to the Duke's motives; was he more confident than we might have imagined at the start of the play that Angelo would fall?

The sudden rush of human sympathy for a single woman with whom the Duke could have had little intimacy, unless illegitimately (not suggested), is a little awkward here and necessitated by the requirement to get Isabella's sympathy for her. The problem is compounded later (in Act 4 Scene 1) when Mariana refers to the Duke-as-Friar as her habitual comforter, a blatantly unsubtle use of a double time scheme. Shakespeare is taking great liberties to enable his greater design.

Who Believes the 'Bed-trick'?

We now come to the matter of the 'bed-trick'; the substitution of one participant in the sex-act that goes unrecognised by the other. This is the Duke's proposed strategy:

> … Go you to Angelo, answer his requiring with a
> plausible obedience, agree with his demands to the point,
> only refer yourself to this advantage: first, that your stay
> with him may not be long, that the time may have all
> shadow and silence in it, and the place answer to
> convenience. This being granted in course – and now
> follows all – we shall advise this wrong'd maid to stead up
> your appointment, go in your place…

and he rounds it off with the question, 'what think you of it?' As I was in rehearsal in 2001 a young journalist interviewing me for a preview piece told me exactly what *she* thought of it by collapsing into giggles at the very mention. How absurd! How could it possibly happen?

The bed-trick, which Shakespeare was to use again in *All's Well That Ends Well*, became very popular as a theatrical plot device – there are at least forty-four known instances of it between 1598 and the closure of the theatres in 1642 – and it has a long ancestry, going back to the story of Laban's substitution of his elder daughter, Leah, for his younger, Rachel, in Jacob's marriage bed in Genesis; to many occurrences in folklore; in classical legend to the story of Jupiter's disguise as Alcmena's husband, Amphitryon, to beget Hercules by her (a story dramatised by Thomas Heywood in *The Silver Age* (1610–12); and Chaucer used it in *The Reeve's Tale*, and Malory in *Le Morte d'Arthur*. But occurrences in scripture, in classical myth and in English poetry and drama do not of themselves answer that journalist's giggles. The question remains: is such a thing possible? In actuality, in the Jacobean context I believe it was. Almost complete darkness was vital – something our urban world can no longer provide, but on a moonless night Shakespeare's London could – and virtual silence. Add to that a convention that the virgin woman comes to the man with her modesty protected by a shift, at the least, and perhaps even a veil, and we have a very possible scenario. In both my productions of this play[23] I have staged this abhorrent coupling, largely to confirm its credibility. The text of the new scene went like this:

> *Night. Angelo's garden room with a day-bed where Angelo awaits.*
>
> *Outside, enter Duke, Isabella and Mariana (veiled).*
>
> ISABELLA. Little have you to say
> when you depart from him but, soft and low,
> 'Remember now my brother'.
>
> MARIANA.   Fear me not.
>
> DUKE. Nor, gentle daughter, fear you not at all.
> He is your husband on a pre-contract.
> To bring you thus together 'tis no sin,
> sith that the justice of your title to him
> doth flourish the deceit. [*Giving the key*] Go, get you in.
>
> *Mariana enters the garden room. She and Angelo couple.*
>
> ANGELO. Isabel!
>
> MARIANA. Remember now my brother.
>
> *Mariana rises from him and exits.*

We used almost no light; only vague shapes were visible. All the lines except for Angelo's orgasmic 'Isabel' are taken from the end of Shakespeare's Act 4 Scene 1. Our stage direction about the key is developed from Angelo's instructions to Isabella, reported by her in the same scene:

He hath a garden circummur'd with brick,
whose western side is with a vineyard back'd.
And to that vineyard is a planched gate
that makes his opening with this bigger key.
This other doth command a little door
which from the vineyard to the garden leads.

Philip Stubbes relates how a garden room – the garden kept private by high walls and a locked gate – commonly provided a form of private brothel, with keys supplied for both the owner and his lover or prostitute. In his excellent book, *The Lodger* (Penguin 2008), Charles Nicholl describes a garden on Silver Street that could have functioned in this way, and might even have been visible from Shakespeare's room in his lodging house at the time he wrote this play.

With this business with the keys, Shakespeare appoints both Isabella and the Duke as Mariana's bawds. Neither would allow themselves to think of it that way, but how else might we define it? What's more, the deed the Duke has termed 'no sin at all' is criminal in Vienna – a post troth-plight but pre-marital coupling, for which Claudio has been condemned to death. The other gain we made was to allow Mariana to whisper that 'remember now my brother' – for we remember (I hope) that it was her own brother Frederick's loss at sea, with all his wealth, that had provoked Angelo to break off his engagement to her.

Shakespeare could not have done this. To present the sex act on stage would have been impossible; and he would have had to find some alternative to actual darkness to convey its presence; neither daylight nor candlelight could have been switched off. Dominic Power and I were criticised for this example of *lèse-majesté*, but I would do it again; it made palpable – and completely credible – a profoundly ugly and joyless encounter.

How could Isabella possibly allow herself to be complicit in such a sordid charade? This is hard for the actor – and perhaps for the audience. But Isabella is in the most appalling situation; she has left her brother to face his death, with her own hysterically angry words echoing in her ears. Would we not take almost any route out of such a nightmare, particularly one advocated by a man of the cloth? I think we would.

The Dénouement

In the dénouement of this play we encounter its major difficulties. But let me first deal with the conclusion to Angelo's story, for here, at least, we are on firm ground. However strong the denials he offers in front of the 'returned' Duke, Angelo is already a broken man, as expressed in his Act 4 Scene 4 soliloquy, beginning:

> This deed unshapes me quite, makes me unpregnant
> And dull to all proceedings...

His language has changed. He speaks of himself still, but the peculiarity of his earlier self-fascination is absent. There is only a plain summation of the predicament his actions have brought him to and a profound regret:

> ... Would yet he had liv'd!
> Alack, when once our grace we have forgot
> nothing goes right. We would and we would not.

Now, with his perfidy publicly exposed, his despair is complete:

> O my dread lord,
> I should be guiltier than my guiltiness,
> to think I can be undiscernible,
> when I perceive your Grace, like power divine
> hath look'd upon my passes. Then, good Prince,
> no longer session hold upon my shame,
> but let my trial be mine own confession.
> Immediate sentence then and sequent death
> is all the grace I beg.
>
> Act 5 Scene 1

He has corrupted his public office, in intention at least committed rape, reneged on a bargain to spare a man's life, all wrapped in the deepest hypocrisy, but with all these sins now revealed before the whole city, the fate he begs is denied him. He must live on, his shame a lasting punishment – and perhaps a permanent testimony to the Duke's god-like understanding.

But how god-like is the Duke? As his behaviour becomes ever more extraordinary, the question 'what is he up to?' urgently demands an answer. Act 4 threatens to turn to black farce as the Duke hurries to secure every element in position for his grand return to the city. Surely we cannot but cheer Barnadine for his refusal to be beheaded to suit the Duke's convenience –

> I swear I will not die today for any man's persuasion.
>
> DUKE. But hear you –
>
> BARNADINE. Not a word. If you have any thing to say to me,
> come to my ward, for thence will not I today.

Act 4 Scene 3

– and we cannot but deplore the Duke's postponement of the good news of Claudio's survival, and goggle at his impatience with Isabella's tears:

> ... I will keep her ignorant of her good,
> to make her heavenly comforts of despair
> when it is least expected...
>
> ISABELLA. Hath yet the deputy sent my brother's pardon?
>
> DUKE. He hath releas'd him, Isabel, from the world.
> His head is off and sent to Angelo.
>
> ISABELLA. Nay, but it is not so.
>
> DUKE.   It is no other.
> Show your wisdom, daughter, in your close patience.
>
> ISABELLA. O, I will to him and pluck out his eyes!
>
> DUKE. You shall not be admitted to his sight.
>
> ISABELLA. Unhappy Claudio! Wretched Isabel!
> Injurious world! Most damned Angelo!
>
> DUKE. This nor hurts him nor profits you a jot.
> Forbear it therefore, give your cause to heaven...
>
> nay, dry your eyes...
>
> Command these fretting waters from your eyes
> with a light heart...

The complete failure of empathy here matches Angelo's in Act 2 Scene 2. May we regard it as a mere plot device, *Shakespeare* rather than the Duke wanting to delay the good news for the last moments of the play? If that was Shakespeare's intent, he could have accomplished the trick without putting such callous words into the Duke's mouth. We have always to judge these moments humanly; there is no get-out here for the Duke, and the repetition of his impatience makes it perfectly clear that the callousness is Shakespeare's deliberate choice.

The dénouement will restore the Duke; restore him to his authority, but in what other sense? There are many viewpoints here. At one end of the spectrum is the *deus ex machina* notion of him – that I have already suggested is insupportable – by which he fashions a circumstance that will demonstrate the inhumanity of a rigid 'measure still for measure', and successfully provoke Isabella to the virtue of forgiveness. Somewhere in the middle is the more psychological argument that he rescues himself from a state of funk, even despair, to a confidence that he can mix authority with mercy, and for that reason he can face his people again (or perhaps for the very first time). And then there is the much bleaker view, to which I incline myself: that he is restored only to the measure that Angelo is reduced; that his whole project, even if not consciously, was to bring down the man whose very being – his certainty, his rectitude – he felt diminished by; and that 'poor Mariana' is not 'advantaged' but condemned to a horrific marriage – to the same fate that for Angelo is a punishment – in what is a deliberate parody of a festive-comic conclusion; that the play is not Shakespeare's comedy but the *Duke's*.

Our problem is partly in seeking answers to my 'what would have happened next?' question, for we might ask it several times in the last scene. What if Lucio had not revealed the Duke's identity by pulling the hood off his head? What if Mariana had not pleaded for Angelo's life after her offstage shotgun wedding? What if Isabella had not joined her in asking for a reprieve for Angelo? To put it another way, since the Duke has gone to elaborate lengths to set up this dénouement, to what extent does the scene follow, or deviate from, his design? Does Lucio's action merely anticipate, perhaps only by seconds, an action the Duke would have done for himself? Do Mariana and Isabella appeal for Angelo exactly as he envisaged they would (there would be a touch of the *deus ex machina* in that) or *thwart* his own plan to send Angelo off with the Provost as if to die on the block – a 'measure for measure' mirroring of Claudio's terrifying experience – before welcoming the Provost back to the scene with Barnadine and both Claudio *and Angelo* hooded, as if for execution; two rabbits to pull out of his hat rather than one? The latter possibility is credible, but impossible to communicate to the audience. The former possibility – that the Duke is deliberately *provoking* the two women to intercede for Angelo is easier to *play*, and yet when considered in reality so much less convincing. How can the man who has so far so massively misjudged the human heart so perfectly predict how Mariana and Isabella will behave?

The *tone* of all this I fear remains uncertain, and that uncertainty is sustained through the final moments. *Measure for Measure* is no exception to the rule that comedies end with marriages or commitments to them, but the reunion between Claudio and Juliet (who, like Claudio, says not a word) is severely downplayed; and in addition to the forced marriage between Angelo and Mariana, we are promised a second punishment marriage between Lucio and his 'punk'. And what are we to make of the most eye-catching of them all, the Duke's surprising proposal – astonishing to a new audience – to Isabella, the novitiate nun? Oliver Ford Davies, in his excellent book, *Performing Shakespeare*,[24] devotes a chapter to a blow-by-blow account of the Duke's journey (he has played the part himself) and in it he questions the recent fashion for Isabella to either explicitly refuse or simply fail to respond to the Duke's proposal, remarking:

> There is no record of a sixteenth- or seventeenth-century head
> of state proposing to a non-aristocrat and being turned down.

He surmises that Isabella's famous silence indicates Shakespeare 'felt doubts about the proposal, and couldn't fashion an appropriate speech of acceptance'. While I would concur with him that in the Jacobean context refusal is not an option for Isabella, I would prefer to interpret her silence as articulating that fact as a predicament for the character rather than for the author, particularly as it is coupled with her silence towards Claudio, and his towards her; they share not a single word after he is revealed as still alive. Is that a second moment of wordless reconciliation, this time one of great smiles and a lasting hug? Shakespeare is as silent on the matter as they are, but it is easy to understand that humiliation on Claudio's part and guilt on Isabella's may have made a sibling reconciliation difficult or even impossible. But Isabella's silence to the Duke is a tougher nut. We might invoke the notion, favoured by a Protestant nation that had seen the destruction of the monasteries, that marriage and procreation were superior before God to the chaste withdrawal from the world that Isabella intended, but why could Shakespeare not address it in words? The answer I would prefer is that, from the beginning, he set out to subvert the classical form of comedy in this play, or at least to experiment with it. So the element of parody, and the incompleteness of the joy that should end a comedy is here deliberate and challenging. Our own final moment pleased the *Guardian* critic, Lyn Gardner:

> The ending is just wonderful; with her brother unexpectedly
> restored to her and the Duke rushing her into marriage,
> Isabella doesn't look suffused with joy but has the glazed,
> horrified look of a woman who has just realised that a
> juggernaut is bearing down on her at 100 miles an hour.
> (12 February 2001)

But I cannot be confident in this as Shakespeare's intention, or in my preferred answer to that question, 'What is the Duke up to?' Just how to imagine him, and how to play this last scene in particular, will continue to tease actors and directors, and only rarely will some clarity be achieved.

Production Notes

The Hungarian Wars: Among a number of other edits, I am sure that ours was not the first production to excise completely the mention of a war between the Austrian states and the King of Hungary, a plot element no sooner introduced than forgotten. Act 1 Scene 2, where it is first mentioned, we set not in the street, but in Mistress Overdone's brothel. We imagined it as early morning; two whores are sleeping off the night's work, and Froth and Lucio – in the light of the news that the brothels are to be 'plucked down' – briefly discuss Angelo's character. Overdone and Pompey enter with the news of Claudio's arrest, and in exchange Lucio gives them the news about the brothels. The oddity in the Folio that Overdone seems to hear twice of Claudio's prosecution is avoided and Froth introduced in place of two gentlemen we would never see again. We used only Shakespeare's language, except one word, to summon the sleeping Bridget back to her work.

Saskia Portway as Mariana, confessing to the Duke, photo © Alan Moore 2001

Mariana's Story: In addition to the staging of the bed-trick, for my 2001 production Dominic Power provided a new scene of fifty lines, placed between Act 2 Scene 1 and Act 2 Scene 2, in which the Duke, substituting for Friar Thomas, hears Mariana's confession. As well as eliminating the double time scheme (or at least one usage), this made more plausible the relationship between the two characters that will become so key to the plot, and filled in Mariana's unhappy backstory early in the play rather than allowing it to slow the action just as it should be gathering pace in Act 4.

The scene went completely unremarked (at least to my ears) by audience and critics; a compliment to the deftness of Dominic's work. Again, the full production text is available on my website.

3. Leontes, Hermione, Polixenes, Perdita and Florizel

Leontes' World

The Winter's Tale opens with – to our ears – another rather challenging conversation. It is between Camillo and Archidamus, respectively the chief officers of Sicilia and Bohemia. Their two Kings, Leontes and Polixenes, have been enjoying a nine-month-long reunion in the Sicilian Court, an extremely long time for Polixenes to have left his country and family. The exchange, which I quote here in full, is essentially exposition, but its elaborate courtliness sets the tone for this royal world:

> ARCHID. If you shall chance, Camillo, to visit Bohemia – on the like occasion whereon my services are now on foot – you shall see, as I have said, great diff'rence betwixt our Bohemia and your Sicilia.
>
> CAMILLO. I think this coming summer the King of Sicilia means to pay Bohemia the visitation which he justly owes him.
>
> ARCHID. Wherein our entertainment shall shame us. We will be justified in our loves, but indeed –
>
> CAMILLO. Beseech you –
>
> ARCHID. Verily, I speak it in the freedom of my knowledge. We cannot with such magnificence, in so rare – I know not what to say. We will give you sleepy drinks, that your senses – unintelligent of our insufficience – may, though they cannot praise us, as little accuse us.
>
> CAMILLO. You pay a great deal too dear for what's given freely.
>
> ARCHID. Believe me, I speak as my understanding instructs me and as mine honesty puts it to utt'rance.
>
> CAMILLO. Sicilia cannot show himself overkind to Bohemia. They were train'd together in their childhoods and there

rooted betwixt them then such an affection which cannot choose but branch now. Since their more mature dignities and royal necessities made separation of their society their encounters, though not personal, have been royally attorney'd with interchange of gifts, letters, loving embassies, that they have seem'd to be together, though absent, shook hands, as over a vast, and embrac'd as it were from the ends of opposed winds. The heavens continue their loves!

ARCHID. I think there is not in the world either malice or matter to alter it. You have an unspeakable comfort of your young Prince Mamillius. It is a gentleman of the greatest promise that ever came into my note.

CAMILLO. I very well agree with you in the hopes of him. It is a gallant child. One that indeed physics the subject, makes old hearts fresh. They that went on crutches ere he was born desire yet their life to see him a man.

ARCHID. Would they else be content to die?

CAMILLO. Yes, if there were no other excuse why they should desire to live.

ARCHID. If the king had no son they would desire to live on crutches till he had one.

Act 1 Scene 1

We have had to listen hard. But Shakespeare has given us more than just backstory and personnel. From the very first speech, the sharp-eared Jacobean would have picked up a whole series of hints about what is to come. As Kings themselves are commonly referred to by their country – here as 'Sicilia' and 'Bohemia' – the 'great difference' between the two countries that Archidamus means may also have a shadow meaning of great difference – with its sense of disagreement or dispute – between the two men. And in Camillo's central speech the hints become louder. By 'branch' Camillo intends the sense 'develop', but a shadow meaning is 'grow apart'; and while he believes this relationship has been sustained by the trumpeted exchange of gifts, letters and ambassadors, his accumulated metaphors suggest instead a growing chasm – 'absent', 'shook hands, as over a vast', 'embrac'd as it were from the ends of opposed winds'. What he describes as warmth we may hear, on the contrary, as chilly, even threatening.

Is the modern audience going to glean so much? If they are new to the play it is unlikely – they are still checking their phones are switched off and trying to get a handle on who these two men are. Does it matter? It is a loss, but not a crucial one. Is there anything to be done about it? Probably not, for it is important that these shadow notes are no more than that; that Camillo and Archidamus are as complacently confident that all is well as are Hermione, Polixenes and the whole court. So there is no nudging manipulation of tone available to the actor. But, though the audience may be deaf to the shadow notes, the production must not be.

Leontes, Polixenes, the pregnant Hermione (very close to term), and Mamillius then enter, 'Camillo following', in what the Folio marks as a new scene. Time and place are unspecified, but these are among the first questions to resolve. Andrea Montag (Designer) and I chose a late nineteenth-century setting for the first half of the play and took the opportunity to place this as an after-dinner scene, the men in formal 'white tie', and the women in long evening gowns. As the play opened we heard, from offstage, Mamillius' pure soprano voice singing a courtly setting of the Autolycus song, 'When daffodils begin to peer', and Camillo and Archidamus entered, brandy glasses in hand, for their private, informal chat. After the song finished with a round of applause, Leontes, Hermione, Mamillius and male and female courtiers entered, effectively joining Camillo and Archidamus in their more relaxed space and cutting their conversation short. With dinner and Mamillius' brief cabaret done, Polixenes took the opportunity to announce his decision that he must leave for home in the morning. There was nothing revolutionary about these choices; the nineteenth-century setting has been a popular one and, I daresay, the after-dinner timing as well; but a quickly recognisable context allows the audience to tune into the moment, to 'listen and to understand'.

Should we not ask 'Why'?

Within scarcely more than a hundred lines Leontes has been seized with jealousy. This has often been seen as a problem, even a shortcoming on Shakespeare's part. A contrary view is expressed by Stephen Greenblatt; in reference to Iago's motivation in Othello, to Lear's motivation for the love test he sets his daughters, to Hamlet's choice to put on 'an antic disposition', and to Leontes' sudden jealousy, Greenblatt coins the term 'strategic opacity', finding in the absence of rationale a deliberate and liberating choice by Shakespeare:

> Shakespeare found that he could immeasurably deepen the
> effect of his plays, that he could provoke in the audience and in
> himself a peculiarly passionate intensity of response, if he took
> out a key explanatory element, thereby occluding the rationale,

motivation, or ethical principle that accounted for the action
that was to unfold.[25]

For Greenblatt, Leontes' jealousy 'is the most extreme version in his work
of the radical excision of motive'. I cannot echo this and nor, I suspect,
would many a director or actor. We always ask the question 'why?'; and I
do find an answer (at an inchoate level) in Iago's actions, I can understand
(while deploring) Lear's demand of his daughters, and here I can find a
delicately etched-in portrait of a shared, cultural sensibility that makes
both Leontes and Polixenes vulnerable to unheralded and explosive sexual
jealousy. (I shall come to Hamlet's 'antic disposition' in Chapter 5.)

The suddenness is certainly Shakespeare's own. In his principal source
text, Robert Greene's popular prose romance, *Pandosto, the Triumph of
Time*,[26] first published in 1588, and reprinted many times, the genesis of
the jealousy is much slower, developing over the long period of Polixenes'
visit;[27] and Leontes first falls into a melancholy, which Hermione notices
but cannot diagnose.

Perhaps Shakespeare chose suddenness over Greene's slow burn
merely for dramatic effect, as an arresting beginning to his drama; but
my belief is that he departed from Greene so that Hermione should have
no inkling of a problem, allowing her, innocently and unknowingly, to
light the fuse.

From here I am going to proceed on the basis of one crucial
assumption: that Leontes and Polixenes – not blood relatives, let alone
brothers – are 'twins' in that, as characters, they are virtually
interchangeable; that Shakespeare prompts us to the suspicion that, had
Leontes spent nine months visiting Polixenes in Bohemia, and Polixenes'
wife had been eight months pregnant, that the appalling situation could
well have arisen in reverse. If I am right, then Polixenes' behaviour in Act
1 Scene 2 speaks very eloquently of his own *and* Leontes' attitudes to
childhood, to women, and to sex.

The suddenness of Leontes' jealousy *is* a problem for us now, because
our antennae are not so acutely adjusted to Shakespeare's language as this
text, and this moment in particular, require. But if the actors understand
what is going on, then much of what is *wrong* in these first hundred lines
will be communicated perfectly well. The danger that a 'fairy story' label
be attached to it must be avoided, because we must share the Jacobeans'
alarm at the idea of a king deserting his country for nine months and, like
them, wonder what on earth Polixenes is up to. Again, the design is crucial,
ensuring that the context has some recognisable reality. One of my main
reasons for choosing a relatively modern setting was to lend an

anachronistic note to Polixenes' ornate diction and metaphor – to avoid it being heard as merely early Jacobean style – and so set up the detail of his exchanges with Leontes and Hermione for sceptical listening:

> Nine changes of the watery star hath been
> the shepherd's note since we have left our throne
> without a burden. Time as long again
> would be fill'd up, my brother, with our thanks
> and yet we should for perpetuity
> go hence in debt. And therefore like a cipher,
> yet standing in rich place, I multiply
> with one 'we thank you' many thousands more
> that go before it.

With his flowery reference to the nine months that have passed, Polixenes invokes that key pastoral character, the shepherd. But the ornateness of 'and therefore like a cipher yet standing in rich place', finds no mirror in Leontes' almost curt response –

> Stay your thanks a while
> and pay them when you part.

– and the host's plainly framed, almost perfunctory, persuasion continues to contrast sharply with Polixenes' elaborate formality:

> POLIXENES.　　　　　　　Sir, that's tomorrow.
> I am question'd by my fears of what may chance
> or breed upon our absence that may blow
> no sneaping winds at home to make us say
> 'This is put forth too truly'.[28] Besides, I have stay'd
> to tire your royalty.
>
> LEONTES.　　　　　　　We are tougher, brother,
> than you can put us to't.
>
> POLIXENES.　　　　　　　No longer stay.
>
> LEONTES. One sennight longer.
>
> POLIXENES.　　　　　　　Very sooth, tomorrow.
>
> LEONTES. We'll part the time between's then, and in that
> I'll no gainsaying.
>
> POLIXENES.　　　　　　　Press me not, beseech you, so.
> There is no tongue that moves, none, none i' the world
> so soon as yours could win me. So it should now
> were there necessity in your request although
> 'twere needful I denied it. My affairs
> do even drag me homeward. Which to hinder

THE WORD AS DEED

were in your love a whip to me, my stay
to you a charge and trouble. To save both,
farewell, our brother.

When Leontes passes the baton to Hermione, she teases him for his lacklustre efforts:

LEONTES.   Tongue-tied, our queen? Speak you.

HERMIONE. I had thought, sir, to have held my peace until
you had drawn oaths from him not to stay. You, sir,
charge him too coldly. Tell him you are sure
all in Bohemia's well. This satisfaction
the by-gone day proclaim'd. Say this to him,
he's beat from his best ward.

LEONTES. Well said, Hermione.

HERMIONE. To tell he longs to see his son were strong,
but let him say so then and let him go.
But let him swear so and he shall not stay –
we'll thwack him hence with distaffs!

Language as everyday and robust as 'thwack him hence with distaffs' and later, 'I love thee not a jar of the clock behind what lady she her lord', is peculiar to Hermione on this occasion; and has prompted one American academic to complain to me that Shakespeare has negligently reduced Hermione's language to that of a 'common housewife' (his characterisation). On the contrary, her forthrightness and vigour stand in deliberate contrast to Polixenes' etiolated, courtly tones; a contrast of central importance to the play as a whole.

Hermione continues:

Yet of your royal presence I'll adventure
the borrow of a week. When at Bohemia
you take my lord I'll give him my commission
to let him there a month behind the day
prefix'd for's parting. Yet, good deed, Leontes,
I love thee not a jar o' th' clock behind
what lady she her lord. You'll stay?

POLIXENES.   No, madam.

HERMIONE. Nay, but you will.

POLIXENES.   I may not, verily.

HERMIONE.   'Verily'!
You put me off with limber vows

113

– 'limber' meaning limp, and 'verily' (a word already employed by Archidamus) a rather precious version of 'truly'. Again, Hermione would like to inject a dash of real spirit into proceedings; so now she teases Polixenes –

> but I,
> though you would seek to unsphere the stars with oaths,
> should yet say 'Sir, no going.' 'Verily',
> you shall not go. A lady's 'verily' is
> as potent as a lord's. Will you go yet –
> force me to keep you as a prisoner,
> not like a guest? So you shall pay your fees
> when you depart and save your thanks? How say you,
> my prisoner or my guest? By your dread 'verily'
> one of them you shall be.

Tone

In response Polixenes could give way in laughter, in a tone of 'OK, you win!', but he is more straight-faced than that, more solemnly courteous:

> Your guest then, madam.
> To be your prisoner should import offending,
> which is for me less easy to commit
> than you to punish.

Though Hermione is clearly convinced that both men truly wish to extend Polixenes' visit, we might have begun to wonder if that is actually so. We then come to the most revelatory passage in these hundred lines:

> HERMIONE.   Not your gaoler then,
> but your kind hostess. Come, I'll question you
> of my lord's tricks and yours when you were boys.
> You were pretty lordings then?
> POLIXENES.   We were, fair queen,
> two lads that thought there was no more behind
> but such a day tomorrow as today
> and to be boy eternal.

'No more behind' means nothing more for the future to reveal but more of the same – a continued idyll. Hermione imagines them getting up to boyish mischief:

HERMIONE. Was not my lord the verier wag o' the two?

But an ordinary, noisy boyhood is not as Polixenes chooses to remember it:

POLIXENES. We were as twinn'd lambs that did frisk i' the sun
　　　　　and bleat the one at th' other. What we chang'd[29]
　　　　　was innocence for innocence. We knew not
　　　　　the doctrine of ill-doing,[30] nor dream'd
　　　　　that any did. Had we pursu'd that life
　　　　　and our weak spirits ne'er been higher rear'd
　　　　　with stronger blood, we should have answer'd heaven
　　　　　boldly 'Not guilty', the imposition clear'd[31]
　　　　　hereditary ours.

Lisa Kay as Hermione and Peter Clifford as Polixenes, photo © Alan Moore 2002

Sometimes our choices about tone are crucial. In Blanche McIntyre's production at Shakespeare's Globe in 2018, Oliver Ryan's choice in this passage was self-mockery – 'Weren't we naive!' Perfectly possible, perfectly legitimate, yet I cannot hear that tone in these words. I hear a solemnly sentimental recollection of the two young boys 'bleating' like lambs, loaded with regret at childhood passing, and with guilt at the loss of innocence as sexuality intrudes – 'our weak spirits ne'er been higher rear'd with stronger blood'. There is a sexual pun here – on the tumescent penis – that is unlikely to be conscious on Polixenes' part, but Shakespeare's shadowing joke at the expense of a very un-self-aware man. Hermione is still eager for a taste of transgression:

> By this we gather
> you have tripp'd since.
>
> POLIXENES.   O my most sacred lady,
> temptations have since then been born to's, for
> in those unfledg'd days was my wife a girl.
> Your precious self had then not cross'd the eyes
> of my young play-fellow.

What *is* he saying? Hermione certainly follows the logic:

> HERMIONE.   Grace to boot!
> Of this make no conclusion, lest you say
> your queen and I are devils!

He has effectively said exactly that; the two women have tempted the two innocents into sin. Polixenes does not intend an accusation or a criticism; paradoxically he honours Hermione as 'precious' and 'sacred'; but the fact of Eve's betrayal of Adam powerfully informs his regret. Hermione's response is generously accommodating:

> Yet, go on.
> The offences we have made you do we'll answer –
> if you first sinn'd with us, and that with us
> you did continue fault, and that you slipp'd not
> with any but with us?

It is at this point that Leontes intervenes –

> Is he won yet?

– and Polixenes gets no chance to answer Hermione's teasing question (her question-mark is mine), though the actor playing Polixenes should know how he would have responded; it might not have been easy.

It is a production choice as to what extent Leontes has heard this exchange, for it seems implicit in his question that Hermione and Polixenes have been conversing to a degree privately. John Mackay's choice was that he heard at least some of it – how could a man in whom jealousy is about to explode not have his ears pinned back to catch his wife's teasing chatter? – and that his question is therefore disingenuous as he knows the answer:

> HERMIONE. He'll stay, my lord.

Leontes could even have misconstrued Hermione's last lines; if her 'with us' could be thought to be a use of the 'royal we', it would mean 'if you first sinned with me'. Leontes is now in urgent need of reassurance:

> At my request he would not.
> Hermione, my dearest, thou never spok'st
> to better purpose.

HERMIONE.   Never?

LEONTES.   Never but once.

He is fishing. Hermione, had she any clue of the panic within him, would not treat the matter as a game of flattery. She would home in immediately on her 'I will' to his proposal of marriage, her 'I am yours for ever'. But she is completely confident in her own loyalty, and in Leontes' confidence in it too; so the courtly game goes on:

> What, have I twice said well? When was't before?
> I prithee tell me. Cram's with praise, and make's
> as fat as tame things. One good deed dying tongueless
> slaughters a thousand waiting upon that…
> But to the goal –
> my last good deed was to entreat his stay.
> What was my first? It has an elder sister
> or I mistake you. O, would her name were Grace!
> But once before I spoke to the purpose. When?
> Nay, let me have't, I long.

LEONTES.   Why, that was when
> three crabbed months had sour'd themselves to death,
> ere I could make thee open thy white hand
> and clap thyself my love. Then didst thou utter
> 'I am yours for ever'.

HERMIONE.   It is Grace indeed.

Her next few words, and the gesture that follows them, light tragedy's fuse:

> Why, lo you now, I have spoke to the purpose twice.
> The one for ever earn'd a royal husband,
> th' other for some while a friend.
>
> *She gives her hand to Polixenes.*

The stage direction is not in the Folio, but the suggestion of the eighteenth-century editor, Capell. It is hard to fault, given that to permit Leontes' soliloquy that follows, Polixenes and Hermione must move away from Leontes, and his 'paddling palms' accusation must be given some credence.

Hermione has snatched defeat from the jaws of victory. The slightest difference in her last two lines – perhaps a reversal of the order, honouring Polixenes first and then turning to her beloved husband, the touch thereby going to him rather than her 'friend' (a term that in Shakespeare's time could mean 'lover') and the deaths and years of agony that are to follow might have been avoided.

That is not to suggest that the tragedy of the play is somehow accidental. If we now look back at the opening dialogue between Camillo and Archidamus, and at their final exchange –

> ARCHID... You have an unspeakable comfort of your young
>   Prince Mamillius. It is a gentleman of the greatest
>   promise that ever came into my note.
>
> CAMILLO. I very well agree with you in the hopes of him. It is a
>   gallant child. One that indeed physics the subject, makes
>   old hearts fresh. They that went on crutches ere he was
>   born desire yet their life to see him a man.
>
> ARCHID. Would they else be content to die?
>
> CAMILLO. Yes, if there were no other excuse why they should
>   desire to live.

– we can see that the whole Sicilian court is infected with this sentimental regret at the passing of childhood; and, as Polixenes is a severe case of it, may we not infer that the Bohemian court is as well? Polixenes is a Peter Pan exiled from a childhood paradise. In 1969, in one of the most articulate examples of Shakespeare design I have ever seen, the RSC's production of the play (directed by Trevor Nunn and designed by Christopher Morley) set this scene in Mamillius' nursery, a great white rocking-horse occupying centre stage. This was where these men were most at ease, with their children, in their children's worlds; they were unable fully to come to terms with sex, with adulthood – or with the responsibilities of power.

If Polixenes and Leontes are equally infected with this disease, is it any wonder that Leontes misreads his wife's innocent flirting –

> [*Aside*] Too hot, too hot!
> To mingle friendship far is mingling bloods.
> I have tremor cordis on me, my heart dances.
> But not for joy, not joy.

He tries to believe it innocent but cannot:

>   This entertainment
> may a free face put on, derive a liberty

from heartiness, from bounty, fertile bosom,
and well become the agent. It may, I grant.
But to be paddling palms and pinching fingers,
as now they are, and making practis'd smiles
as in a looking-glass? And then to sigh, as 'twere
the mort o' the deer? – O, that is entertainment
my bosom likes not, nor my brows! Mamillius,
art thou my boy?

MAMILLIUS.   Ay, my good lord.

John Mackay as Leontes, photo © Alan Moore 2002

A later reference to Mamillius being as yet 'unbreech'd' – i.e. still dressed in skirts – implies that he is probably no more than six years old (and Leontes no more than twenty-nine). This unguarded appeal for an affirmation of his paternity is an extraordinary burden to foist on a young child, whatever the depth of Leontes' panic and misery:

I' fecks!
Why, that's my bawcock. What, hast smutch'd thy nose?
They say it is a copy out of mine. Come, captain,
we must be neat. Not neat but cleanly, captain.
And yet the steer, the heifer, and the calf
are all call'd neat. Still virginalling

> upon his palm? How now, you wanton calf!
> Art thou my calf?
>
> MAMILLIUS.   Yes, if you will, my lord.

When I played Leontes myself as a student, I felt constrained in playing the emotional violence of the next developments right into the face of the real six-year-old child who had been cast, and it impressed on me how immature and out of control Leontes is here. No wonder the boy is unwilling to look him in the eye:

> LEONTES. Thou want'st a rough pash[32] and the shoots[33] that I have
>   to be full like me. Yet they say we are
>   almost as like as eggs. Women say so
>   that will say anything. But were they false
>   as o'er-dy'd cloth, as wind, as waters, false
>   as dice are to be wish'd by one that fixes
>   no bourn 'twixt his and mine, yet were it true
>   to say this boy were like me. Come, sir page,
>   look on me with your welkin eye. Sweet villain!
>   Most dear'st! My collop![34] Can thy dam, may't be – ?

He wants to love the boy, wants to claim him as his own, and then rejects the possibility. The boy is clasped to him and then pushed away. He seems to be a child himself. His passion draws the attention of Hermione and Polixenes, but he is able, this once, to collect himself and turn the focus back to Polixenes:

>   My brother,
>   are you so fond of your young prince as we
>   do seem to be of ours?

The question returns Polixenes to his regretful theme:

>   If at home, sir,
>   he's all my exercise, my mirth, my matter.
>   Now my sworn friend and then mine enemy.
>   My parasite, my soldier, statesman, all.
>   He makes a July's day short as December
>   and with his varying childness cures in me
>   thoughts that would thick my blood.

He seems almost to be a depressive, sustained in the prime of his life only by his own son's 'varying childness'. One begins to feel sorry for Bohemia, and for Polixenes' wife, so neglected by a head of state and a husband who prefers the playroom to both the council chamber and the marriage bed.

Leontes now invites the two to confirm his suspicions – 'I am angling now, though you perceive me not how I give line' – by continuing their tête-à-tête, while he is left alone with Mamillius and his own seething imagination:

> Gone already!
> Inch-thick, knee-deep, o'er head and ears a fork'd one!

It is a production choice as to how directly Leontes offers what follows to Mamillius, as is the tone of the repeated 'Go play, boy, play'. Does the hurt sarcasm of 'thy mother plays' begin with the 'Go play, boy, play', or is it merely provoked by it, the instruction to the boy being a kinder and more literal one? Whatever the choice, it seems the violent disgust of his imaginings possesses him completely and he loses all sense that a vulnerable young consciousness is witness to it:

> Go, play, boy, play. Thy mother plays and I
> play too, but so disgrac'd a part whose issue
> will hiss me to my grave. Contempt and clamour
> will be my knell. Go, play, boy, play. There have been,
> or I am much deceiv'd, cuckolds ere now
> and many a man there is, even at this present –
> now while I speak this – holds his wife by the arm
> that little thinks she has been sluic'd in his absence
> and his pond fish'd by his next neighbour, by
> Sir Smile, his neighbour. Nay, there's comfort in't.
> Whiles other men have gates and those gates open'd,
> as mine, against their will…

This crude and harsh reference to the wife's sex as the husband's property is no more acceptable to Shakespeare's sensibility than to our own.

Mamillius is evidently old enough to have some apprehension of what is happening, and a desire to reassure:

> I am like you, they say.
> LEONTES.   Why, that's some comfort.
> What, Camillo, there? Go play, Mamillius,
> thou'rt an honest man.

At last, with the entrance of a more appropriate confidant, Leontes can offer Mamillius an unambiguous invitation to 'go play'.

The Male Courtiers, and the Female

The tragedy of the play now unfolds, with the instruction to Camillo to poison Polixenes, Camillo and Polixenes' flight from Sicilia, and the arrest and imprisonment of Hermione. Leontes' advisers protest at this madness, chief among them Antigonus, whose language is direct and conspicuously uncourtly:

> You are abus'd and by some putter-on
> that will be damn'd for't... Be she honour-flaw'd
> I have three daughters – the eldest is eleven,
> the second and the third, nine and some five –
> if this prove true, they'll pay for't. By mine honour,
> I'll geld 'em all... They are co-heirs
> and I had rather geld myself than they
> should not produce fair issue.
>
> Act 2 Scene 1

In response, Leontes' own language has a savage bluntness –

> Cease, no more.
> You smell this business with a sense as cold
> as is a dead man's nose. But I do see't and feel't
> as you feel doing thus –

that will become crudely and insultingly derisive in the play's next movement, when Hermione gives birth in prison and Antigonus' wife, Paulina, brings the baby to the court to present to her father. Though (despite its tragic consequences) we have enjoyed the vigour Hermione has injected into courtliness, and Antigonus' passionate defence of Hermione's loyalty, they have been as nothing to the force of nature that is Paulina. The women in this play so outshine the men – only Florizel and Antigonus sharing in their clear-eyed certainty and grounded passion – and Paulina is their torchbearer. Here, while his men stand around, unmanned and helpless, she fearlessly fights Hermione's cause – 'the good Queen (for she is good)' – and armed with her confidence that the sight of the child will melt Leontes' heart, she lays the child on the floor at his feet. But she has misjudged him:

> LEONTES.   Out!
> A mankind witch! Hence with her, out o'door,
> a most intelligencing bawd!... Traitors,
> will you not push her out? Give her the bastard.
> [*To Antigonus*] Thou dotard, thou art woman-tir'd,
>   unroosted

> by thy Dame Partlet here. Take up the bastard.
> Take't up, I say. Give't to thy crone.
>
> Act 2 Scene 3

In these angry slanders – this 'crone', later 'callat' and 'gross hag', is a gentlewoman, full of grace and courage – the misogyny that Polixenes' language to Hermione so elegantly disguised is revealed in all its ugliness. Paulina does not understand that the vessel of the court's emotional world is too fragile to hold her candour, vigour and passion; nor does she realise the depth of fear of the sexually mature and autonomous woman (that she so powerfully represents) in this immature man. Leontes reacts at this moment as if a grenade has been put at his feet with the pin removed. There seems no question here of a moment of choice, of a possibility of softening on Leontes' part. He is in a boys' playground world in which all womanhood is a threat, whether wife, interfering neighbour, or new-born baby girl.

Undaunted, Paulina pursues her objective, believing to the last that her strategy will work – even to taking the near-fatal risk of leaving the court without the child:

> Look to your babe, my lord, 'tis yours. Jove send her
> a better guiding spirit! What needs these hands?

– this second of two references to being manhandled highlighting the lords' tongue-tied silence –

> You that are thus so tender o'er his follies
> will never do him good, not one of you.
> So, so, farewell. We are gone.

But her effort has failed. The baby is dispatched 'to some remote and desert place', and Hermione's trial is to go ahead.

'A language that I understand not'

It is true that this is a play of Kings and Queens, and the Delphic Oracle;[35] to some degree a fairy-tale world for Shakespeare's audience, and – if we are not very careful – so much more so for us. But what Shakespeare makes utterly clear in Hermione's first speech in her trial scene (Act 3 Scene 2) is what a deep affront it is to a Queen and to her marriage that this tragedy is played out in public:

> ... You, my lord, best know –
> who least will seem to do so – my past life
> hath been as continent, as chaste, as true,
> as I am now unhappy. Which is more
> than history can pattern though devis'd
> and play'd to take spectators. For behold me –
> a fellow of the royal bed, which owe
> a moiety of the throne, a great king's daughter,
> the mother to a hopeful prince – here standing
> to prate and talk for life and honour 'fore
> who please to come and hear.

A notorious sixteenth-century precedent, the trial of Anne Boleyn, was conducted in private before twenty-seven of her peers, *as was her right*; and the King was not present.

In production it is vital that we catch the sheer extraordinariness, as well as the cruelty of this trial, a sense of improvisation perhaps, even of the absurd. In 2002 we made clear the public nature of the scene by raising the house lights, and we had the reluctant and bewildered presiding lords (Tom Sherman and Ed Sinclair) erect their own trestle table as an improvised judges' bench. But the mockery that the trial is goes further than the physical context. There is no evidence – not even fabricated evidence – to offer to the court; no chambermaids who have spied through keyholes, no private dicks who have sat for hours behind crumpled newspapers in hotel lobbies. It is accusation and denial, a marital row that should have been played out in private, across the kitchen table, not in this most bizarre of arenas. Hermione, already cruelly punished by the loss of her baby, and still in recovery from the birth, fights hard (with some success) to retain her dignity, while Leontes loses all sense of his:

> LEONTES.   I ne'er heard yet
> that any of these bolder vices wanted
> less impudence to gainsay what they did
> than to perform it first.
>
> HERMIONE.   That's true enough.
> Though 'tis a saying, sir, not due to me.
>
> LEONTES. You will not own it.
>
> HERMIONE.   More than mistress of
> which comes to me in name of fault, I must not
> at all acknowledge. For Polixenes
> with whom I am accus'd I do confess
> I lov'd him as in honour he requir'd.
> With such a kind of love as might become

> a lady like me. With a love even such,
> so and no other, as yourself commanded.
> … Now for conspiracy
> I know not how it tastes, though it be dish'd
> for me to try how. All I know of it
> is that Camillo was an honest man
> and why he left your court the gods themselves,
> wotting no more than I, are ignorant.

LEONTES. You knew of his departure, as you know
what you have underta'en to do in's absence.

– and here Hermione encapsulates the whole appalling farce in one cryptic line:

> Sir,
> you speak a language that I understand not.

Language expresses not truth but fiction. As language supported the fiction that Leontes and Polixenes could perpetuate a childhood idyll – a fiction that even Hermione was deceived by – so here it permits the elaboration of a tragic lie that no degree of passionate denial on Hermione's part, or Paulina's, can penetrate or explode. Leontes' conviction is as extreme as his vengefulness. He has sent to the Oracle at Delphi, yet in his passion he must pre-empt it – and will later dare to contradict it. Though all-powerful in Sicilia, he is as weak as is Lear when he refuses to go back on his disowning of Cordelia. He is a prisoner of his own imaginings, born of fear of Hermione's provocative sexuality – so abundantly expressed in her pregnancy as well as her teasing – and underscored by a puritanical distrust of sexuality itself.

Language that enables and promotes, rather than obfuscates, the relationship between a man and a woman, and a world that honours rather than distrusts sexuality, will be the subject of the 'pastoral' scenes in Bohemia. Meanwhile, the Oracle declares Hermione innocent, the court receives the terrible news that Mamillius has died from grief, and Hermione collapses and is carried off. Paulina enters to announce that she has died, and to punish Leontes with another uninhibitedly passionate remonstrance. Leontes is contrite at last, but he has lost his wife, his son and his new-born daughter.

To Bohemia

Antigonus delivers the baby to the shores of Bohemia and is killed and eaten by a bear. The stage direction – '*Exit, pursued by a bear*' – has become famous, its pithiness celebrated. The moment itself has a less glorious history, and is generally risible. We chose to leave it to sounds, to the panic in Antigonus' eyes (Jonathan Nibbs again) and to the power of the audience's own imagining. At least one critic – John Peter in *The Sunday Times* – felt short-changed, but I would do it again.

The child is discovered by an old shepherd, who finds that Antigonus has left with her a considerable sum of gold, together with some jewels. There is then an interval of sixteen years, as the child grows up as the shepherd's adopted daughter.

Nature v. Art

As in *As You Like It*, the pastoral world is held in opposition to the city. This is the essential contrast, not – as has often been imagined – between Sicilia and Bohemia. As well as in the sharp difference we should see in design, it is one explored in a key passage, the Nature v. Art debate between Perdita and the disguised Polixenes. To leap ahead to that, Perdita has just made presents of rosemary and rue to welcome the disguised Polixenes and Camillo to her sheep-shearing feast:

> POLIXENES.   Shepherdess –
>   a fair one are you! – well you fit our ages
>   with flowers of winter.
>
> > Act 4 Scene 4

– note Polixenes' repeated compliments to Perdita; both these middle-aged men are rather taken with her –

> PERDITA. Sir, the year growing ancient –
>   not yet on summer's death nor on the birth
>   of trembling winter – the fairest flowers o' the season
>   are our carnations and streak'd gillyvors,
>   which some call nature's bastards. Of that kind
>   our rustic garden's barren and I care not
>   to get slips of them.
> POLIXENES.   Wherefore, gentle maiden,
>   do you neglect them? –

PERDITA.   For I have heard it said
　　　there is an art which, in their piedness, shares
　　　with great creating nature.

Polixenes' argument now is a little dense, but can be understood: the art
with which man changes Nature is itself a product of Nature:

　　　　　　　　　　　　　　Say there be.
　　　Yet nature is made better by no mean
　　　but nature makes that mean. So, o'er that art
　　　which you say adds to nature is an art
　　　that nature makes. You see, sweet maid, we marry
　　　a gentler scion to the wildest stock
　　　and make conceive a bark of baser kind
　　　by bud of nobler race. This is an art
　　　which does mend nature – change it rather – but
　　　the art itself is nature.

PERDITA.   So it is.

Perdita accepts his logic, but will not change her practice:

　　　　　　　　　　　　I'll not put
　　　the dibble in earth to set one slip of them.
　　　No more than were I painted I would wish
　　　this youth should say 'twere well and only therefore
　　　desire to breed by me.

There is a wonderful irony in this passage. Perdita, who is herself a 'gentler
scion' grafted onto the 'wildest stock' of this farming community, is deeply
suspicious of the art of cross-breeding; while Polixenes, who will shortly
oppose the grafting of his princely son, Florizel, onto what he assumes is
the 'wildest stock' of Perdita, in this purely theoretic argument about
horticulture enthusiastically supports the practice.

Perdita's last speech quoted above also strikes the keynote in her
relationship with Florizel. Her earthy characterisation of the sexual
instinct, which so befits a shepherd, whose livelihood depends on the
vigour of her ram and the robustness of her ewes, stands in rich contrast
to the rarefied world of Leontes' court. The presentation of this shepherds'
world is of crucial importance in production, yet in my experience it has
so often seemed a problem. The Trevor Nunn production I applaud above
reconceived it as a rock opera in the manner of *Hair*, with strongly middle-
class music festival associations. In a Bristol Old Vic production in which
I played Polixenes it was so sentimentalised that its vigour was lost; in that
case Florizel was the main sufferer, being played as a sweet young lad

rather than the bold twenty-one-year-old that he is, prepared to defy his father and risk everything for love.

Tom Espiner as Florizel and Lisa Kay (doubling) as Perdita, photo © Alan Moore 2002

There *is* a degree of sweetness to the scene, but Shakespeare presents it as a real world – if anything, more real than the world of the court – with a wealth of detail: Perdita's knowledge of the local flora; Autolycus' trade in picking pockets, and selling ribbons, gloves, fabrics, bracelets, necklaces, pins, perfumes and song-sheets; the young girls' competitiveness for the Clown's largesse; the sheep-shearing festival itself; and the visit of local carters, shepherds, neatherds and swineherds to offer their satyrs' dance. This last event is thought by some editors to be a late addition to the text. I am inclined to agree, and I cut it from my 2002 production. It breaks the narrative, occasioning a rather clumsy resumption in these lines of Polixenes:

> [*To Shepherd*] O Father, you'll know more of that
> hereafter.
>
> [*To Camillo*] Is it not too far gone? 'Tis time to part them.
>
> He's simple and tells much. [*To Florizel*] How now, fair
> shepherd...

Though fully appropriate to the occasion, it does seem to have been shoe-horned into an already very substantial scene. But were I to direct the play again (and given the personnel), I would revisit that choice; the satyrs add scale to the occasion and provide another, darker tone.

Shakespeare knew this world; he knew its labours, its customs and its pastimes, vividly present in his native Warwickshire. His family, on both sides, had been farmers, and his father, John Shakespeare, had indulged for a period in illegal wool-trading ('wool-brogging'). He would have known – as Corin has to point out to the urban Touchstone – that sheeps' 'fells are greasy'. He would also have known that sheep-shearing festivals featured singing contests and dancing men dressed as animals. Had Stanislavski ever directed the play, he would almost certainly have released a whole farmyard of real animals onto the stage to lend it verisimilitude; we cannot do that, but in dress and props, and in manners, we must emphasise its earthy substance. For Polixenes, it will be capable of great charm, but also of severe threat; only a real world can achieve that double.

Florizel has borrowed a shepherd's attire for himself, and brought Perdita some clothes from the court. Dressing out of one's station was frowned on in Shakespeare's time; in some circumstances it was illegal;[36] and Perdita is relieved that such folly is forgivable on a feast day:

> Your high self,
> the gracious mark o' the land, you have obscur'd
> with a swain's wearing, and me, poor lowly maid,
> most goddess-like prank'd up. But that our feasts
> in every mess have folly and the feeders
> digest it with a custom, I should blush
> to see you so attir'd, swoon, I think,
> to show myself a glass.

Florizel's joy in having met and fallen for Perdita is unqualified; but such a marriage across classes was almost unthinkable in 1610 and as a lowly subject in an autocratic state, Perdita cannot put the dangers out of her mind:

> … Even now I tremble
> to think your father, by some accident,
> should pass this way as you did. O, the fates,
> how would he look to see his work, so noble,
> vilely bound up?…

Using instances lifted directly from *Pandosto,* Florizel dismisses her anxiety:

> Apprehend
> nothing but jollity. The gods themselves,

humbling their deities to love, have taken
the shapes of beasts upon them. Jupiter
became a bull and bellow'd. The green Neptune
a ram and bleated. And the fire-rob'd god,
Golden Apollo, a poor humble swain
as I seem now. Their transformations
were never for a piece of beauty rarer,
nor in a way so chaste, since my desires
run not before mine honour nor my lusts
burn hotter than my faith.

Much of the language exchanged between them stands in direct contrast to what we heard in the court, and Florizel's sexual frankness – can we imagine Polixenes ever talking of his 'lusts' to Hermione? – is admirably refreshing. However, his references to classical mythology are fanciful and inapposite and Perdita tries again to ground him:

O but, sir,
your resolution cannot hold when 'tis
oppos'd, as it must be, by the power of the king…

But as he will prove later, Florizel is in earnest and, echoing Rosalind's 'I cannot be out of the sight of Orlando', firmly declares his resolution:

… Or I'll be thine, my fair,
or not my father's. For I cannot be
mine own, nor anything to any, if
I be not thine.

The dialogue – which becomes a confrontation – between Florizel and his father is at the heart of the scene, and threatens a tragic outcome; and in it Shakespeare returns to his exploration of Polixenes' psyche. This is how he reacts when Florizel ignores Autolycus' sales-pitch:

[*To Florizel*] How now, fair shepherd!
Your heart is full of something that does take
your mind from feasting. Sooth, when I was young
and handed love as you do, I was wont
to load my she with knacks. I would have ransack'd
the pedlar's silken treasury and have pour'd it
to her acceptance. You have let him go,
and nothing marted with him.

It is hard to imagine an uglier description of gift-giving to a young woman than 'to load my she with knacks', the love of the generic female – my 'she'

– purchased with cheap rubbish measured by weight. Florizel rightly demurs:

> Old sir, I know
> she prizes not such trifles as these are.
> The gifts she looks from me are pack'd and lock'd
> up in my heart, which I have given already
> but not deliver'd.

The 'old' of the beginning of his speech will now become 'ancient', not intended to insult Polixenes (he should be about forty-five by now, though perhaps disguised as an older man), but unlikely to better his mood:

> [*To Perdita*] O, hear me breathe my life
> before this ancient sir, who, it should seem,
> hath sometime lov'd. I take thy hand. This hand,
> as soft as dove's down and as white as it,
> or Ethiopian's tooth, or the fann'd snow that's bolted
> by the northern blasts twice o'er.
>
> POLIXENES.   What follows this?
> How prettily the young swain seems to wash
> the hand was fair before! I have put you out.
> But to your protestation – let me hear
> what you profess.

Florizel fails to pick up on the fact that this still-smiling man is inviting him to dig his way deeper into trouble:

> FLORIZEL.   Do, and be witness to't.
>
> POLIXENES. And this my neighbour, too?
>
> FLORIZEL.   And he and more
> than he, and men, the earth, the heavens and all,
> that – were I crown'd the most imperial monarch,
> thereof most worthy, were I the fairest youth
> that ever made eye swerve, had force and knowledge
> more than was ever man's – I would not prize them
> without her love…

To be just to Polixenes, this declaration – in Shakespeare's time – is radical indeed. Princes did not marry for love, though, for the fortunate, love might follow; the requirements of state, and the premium on the purity of the royal bloodline dictated differently. Where later audiences might root for Florizel purely as a handsome young man madly in love with a pretty young woman, the Jacobean audience would have been enabled in the same sentiment by knowing that Perdita is herself a princess, and that her marriage to Florizel has the potential to repair the rupture between Bohemia and Sicilia.

But Polixenes' ignorance of Perdita's true parentage throws his behaviour into sharp relief. The secular contract, about to be undertaken before witnesses, had legal force in England. (In *Measure for Measure* Claudio and Juliet's troth-plight may have been similarly witnessed.) Polixenes has to stop this one in its tracks, and his bonhomie gradually fractures as Florizel denies his father's authority in the matter:

> POLIXENES... Pray you, once more,
> is not your father grown incapable
> of reasonable affairs? Is he not stupid
> with age and altering rheums? Can he speak? Hear?
> Know man from man? Dispute his own estate?
> Lies he not bed-rid and again does nothing
> but what he did being childish?
>
> FLORIZEL.   No, good sir,
> he has his health and ampler strength indeed
> than most have of his age.
>
> POLIXENES.   By my white beard,
> you offer him, if this be so, a wrong
> something unfilial...

Florizel knows his father's approval is unthinkable and that pre-emptive action is his only recourse. Under increasing pressure, he is insistent:

> Mark our contract.

The Old Shepherd – innocent of Florizel's true identity – is about to oblige, when Polixenes rips off his own disguise:

> Mark your divorce, young sir,
> whom son I dare not call! Thou art too base
> to be acknowledg'd. Thou a sceptre's heir
> that thus affects a sheep-hook!

He then turns his fire onto the Old Shepherd:

> Thou, old traitor,
> I am sorry that by hanging thee I can but
> shorten thy life one week.

And then onto Perdita:

And thou, fresh piece
of excellent witchcraft, who of force must know
the royal fool thou cop'st with –

SHEPHERD. O, my heart!

POLIXENES. I'll have thy beauty scratch'd with briers and made
more homely than thy state. – For thee, fond boy,
if I may ever know thou dost but sigh
that thou no more shalt see this knack, as never
I mean thou shalt, we'll bar thee from succession,
not hold thee of our blood, no, not our kin,
far'r than Deucalion off, mark thou my words.
Follow us to the court. – And you, enchantment,
worthy enough a herdsman, yea him too
that makes himself, but for our honour therein,
unworthy thee, if ever henceforth thou
these rural latches to his entrance open
or hoop his body more with thy embraces
I will devise a death as cruel for thee
as thou art tender to't. *Exit*

Polixenes' paternal authority is denied and his *amour propre* deeply wounded. This is readily comprehensible. But the transformations these bring about in his attitude to Perdita are telling, and far from rational. The 'fair shepherdess', the 'gentle maiden', and 'the prettiest low-born lass that ever ran on the green-sward' is now a 'sheep-hook' (a mere rustic tool), and a 'knack' (a trifle, like Autolycus' ribbons). Her beauty is now a threat, and threatened with despoiling, and her sex – 'rural latches' has a crude sexual meaning as well as a literal reference to cottage doors – a degraded and degrading function, and the 'hoops' of her embraces illegitimate fetters. These threats and insults diminish Polixenes even as he attempts to regain authority by them, just as Leontes was diminished by his behaviour at Hermione's trial. They are further evidence of his own arrested emotional development.

Language and Being

Leontes and Polixenes are prisoners of a sickly court culture and language – that language that Hermione 'understands not'. They are not merely two irascible individuals, prone in Leontes' case to paranoid jealousy, and in Polixenes' to sentimental recollection on the one hand, and to 'heavy father' behaviour on the other. They represent their aristocratic world.

That world is not a unitary one; it includes Paulina, Antigonus and a man capable of moving from a position at its centre to challenge it, Camillo; but Leontes and Polixenes *are* their courts. As Orsino's self-indulgent passion filled his court, Leontes' volcanic jealousy fills his in the earlier part of the play; and his remorse will fill it just as completely in the later. The Nature v. Art debate between Perdita and Polixenes was habitually cut from eighteenth- and nineteenth-century productions and only restored by the American producer Winthrop Ames in New York in 1910. Yet the passage is key to the play; to the renewal that Florizel and Perdita bring to both Sicilia and Bohemia – a renewal in language and behaviour, and in relationships between men and women – born of Perdita being grafted onto the wilder stock of the rural world, and Florizel falling not only for her beauty, but for her natural grace and vigour, and her frank and untroubled acknowledgement of her own sexuality and his.

Following the storm and the death of Antigonus in Act 3 Scene 3, the Old Shepherd had greeted his son on the seashore with this:

Thou met'st with things dying, I with things new-born.

– an apt and pithy metaphor for the play.

So the 'Bohemian' section should not be viewed either sentimentally or untrustingly, as if it requires some inventive slant to breathe vitality into it. The vitality is there to be found; the sheep-shearing festival is a time-honoured one, completing for the shepherd one of the most exhausting – but most profitable – periods of the farming year. Thus the salesmen and petty crooks would home in on it, and other ranks of farmers would dignify it with their dances. The task in the modern theatre – without any help from farmyard animals – is to find and express its pulsating reality.

A final note: the renewal and rebirth extends to the discovery that Hermione is not dead after all. This always provokes a question about Paulina's own knowledge of Hermione's condition after she is carried from the trial-court, but it seems to me we must allow Shakespeare a sleight of hand here, and Zoë Aldrich and I agreed that Paulina must play her Act 3 Scene 2 attack on Leontes as if Hermione is indeed dead. The revelation at the end that she has survived would have amazed – and probably delighted – the original audience, familiar with Greene's *Pandosto*, in which no such miracle occurs. Not only that, but Pandosto, while still ignorant of his daughter's true identity, is overcome with lust for her, and even threatens to rape her. After the truth comes out and the two young lovers are married, he falls into a guilt-ridden depression and commits suicide.

Shakespeare's conclusion is sunnier than that, but still etched with loss. Sixteen years have been wasted – as the line 'Hermione was not so wrinkl'd, nothing so aged as this seems' reminds us – and Mamillius remains in his grave. (At the general exit we again heard Mamillius singing John Telfer's setting of *When daffodils begin to peer*, this time in a distant, unearthly reprise.) The comfort must be that to an extent the tragedy was inevitable, even necessary, and the renewal substantial and potentially lasting.

Production Notes

Hermione and Perdita: I asked Lisa Kay to double Hermione and Perdita, a feat I had seen Judi Dench pull off beautifully in that Stratford production in 1969, and one Lisa accomplished equally beautifully for us. There is the appearance of both women to negotiate in the last scene – no avoiding it – but Hermione pulls focus back from Perdita, who barely speaks, and a substitution is perfectly acceptable. Like the doubling of *As You Like It*'s two Dukes, it highlights the essential tonal differences between the two worlds of court and country, and here reinforces the Nature v. Art debate.

Hermione's heritage: Hermione ends her self-defence in the public court with these words:

> The Emperor of Russia was my father.
> O that he were alive and here beholding
> his daughter's trial…

That Hermione is a foreigner in the Sicilian court has not been mentioned before, and this late entry in her biography suggests that Shakespeare attached little importance to it as a mark of difference in culture or manners. Lisa and I toyed with the idea of making her Russian in accent, and so emphasise the sense that she is an interloper in Leontes' and Polixenes' fragilely reconstructed world. But this would have begged the question of how Polixenes speaks, as he is – theoretically at least – a German interloper in Leontes' Italian world; and we felt that to have followed that logic would have been to defeat the object. I wonder now if we were being too literal-minded about that and if a truly Russian Hermione might not have been rather useful?

The Setting: By placing the sixteen-year span of the action between 1890 and 1906, the production fed off the shift from the late Victorian stuffed shirt to the freer and more flowing Edwardian line. And costume can convey so much. As Andrea and I worked out our scene breakdown (the who, the where and the when) I realised how accustomed we are in the theatre to see, in Elizabethan- or Jacobean-set productions, even fabulously wealthy characters dressed in just one costume – for day and night, for home and away, for summer and winter; our image of the early modern 'look' is so uninformed, so generalised. Not so with 1890. There is evening wear, morning wear, domestic, formal and travel wear (season by season), all of which can define time, place and activity more eloquently than any number of textual references – as here, in our choice of evening wear for the opening scene, and later, when we saw Cleomenes and Dion travelling to Delphi in tweeds. As a result – in a play that already involves disguisings and the need to make vivid the sixteen-year gap – we found ourselves committed to the most enormous costume bill, the actors having to do battle for dressing-room space with their own wardrobes. But it was well worth it.

Of our frugal in-the-round design, Dominic Cavendish wrote:

> Often in the theatre, simplicity proves the best policy.
> Shakespeare at the Tobacco Factory… has a hallmark style that
> is as clear and unadorned as its name. *The Winter's Tale* is so
> no-frills that I kept wondering how designer Andrea Montag
> spends her days: her main contribution here consists of four
> high-backed wooden chairs. Andrew Hilton, who directs,
> understands completely, however, that when work is presented
> close up and in the round, the audience can enjoy other kinds
> of visual delights to do with the positioning of the actors, the
> way they look at each other, and their tiniest gestures. This
> pared-down approach is brilliantly suited to a play in which
> things get blown out of proportion. It's the manner in which
> Hermione extends her hand to her husband, Leontes, but then
> clasps instead that of his childhood friend Polixenes that tips
> the Sicilian king into his jealous rage. Here, in a court where
> everyone is attired in Victorian dress and holds themselves
> with prim rectitude, such a casually demonstrative act has the
> force of a gun blast. (*Daily Telegraph*, 16 February 2002)

Andrea Montag's 'main contribution' was, of course, the extensive costume design.

1. In quoting from this scene, I use common choices between the Second Quarto and the Folio texts, with some long-popular emendations thrown in, such as Theobald's 'pious bawds' for 'pious bonds' (1726) in a Polonius' speech late in the scene.

2. 'most modest' or 'most frugal'.

3. 'buds'.

4. 'blights', perhaps here with a military and explosive edge.

5. 'a bastard'.

6. The absence of mothers in Shakespeare – think of Cordelia, Isabella and Claudio, Hermia and Helena, Rosalind and Orlando, and many more – stems partly from the limited number of skilled boy-actors his companies could afford, but is also an artistic choice, the dramatic action so often finding the mother surplus to requirements. Though the appallingly high mortality – perhaps as much as seven per cent – of women in and after childbirth may have obviated the need for recording the particularities of death or absence, statistically mothers outlived fathers in Shakespeare's time as they do now.

7. She was speaking at the Critics' Circle Theatre Awards 2020, where she won one a Best Actress Award.

8. After a performance of *King Lear* in 2000 an audience member approached me enthusiastically: 'You've rewritten it, haven't you? It's so clear, so comprehensible.' It was hard to persuade him that – in that instance at least – we had not rewritten a word.

9. An obvious example is the word 'doubt', in Shakespeare meaning 'fear' rather than 'question'; so Hamlet's 'I doubt some foul play' means 'I fear there has been foul play' rather than 'I can't believe there has been foul play'.

10. First suggested by Edward Chalmers in 'A Supplemental Apology for the Believers in the Shakespeare-Papers', 1799. It is true that the Duke's dislike of crowds might reflect James' own, and his trumpeted arrival at the gates of Vienna at the end of the play could recall James' arrival in London early in 1604 – a ceremony Shakespeare's company could well have been employed in – but to intend the Duke as a portrait of the new King would seem to be dangerous in the extreme.

11. In *The Wheel of Fire* (1930), G.Wilson Knight writes of the Duke's 'almost divine power of fore-knowledge and wisdom. There is an enigmatic, other worldly, mystery suffusing his figure and the meaning of his acts'.

12. *Narrative and Dramatic Sources of Shakespeare*, Volume 2 (Routledge and Kegan Paul and Columbia University Press, 1987).

13. 'an equivalent centre of self, whence the lights and shadows must always fall with a certain difference' – *Middlemarch*.

14. In 1650, Cromwell's Parliament passed an Act 'for the suppression of the abominable and crying sins of incest, adultery, and fornication, wherewith this land is much defiled and Almighty God highly displeased.' The penalties were biblically prescribed, adultery being punishable by death. The Act lapsed a decade later.

15. 'to fright'.

16. i.e. murdered a man.

17. 'pardon'.

18. The shameful bargain Angelo seeks.

19. Effectively 'one among many'.

20. 'life imprisonment'.

21. The First Folio prints 'prenzie' here, and in Isabella's response. 'Prenzie' was possibly a coinage on Shakespeare's part – perhaps derived from the Italian 'prenze' meaning

'prince' – and the Second Folio itself substitutes the word 'princely'. This has not satisfied numerous editors who have sought to amend the F1 reading, most commonly to 'precise', on the grounds that 'prenzie' might have been the F1 compositor's misreading of that word. Given that 'precise' is rhymically awkward (the stress in this place in the line should come on the first syllable), I incline to believe that the F1 compositor was correct, as was the F2 editor to adjust it to a more comprehensible form.

22. *Making Trifles of Terrors* (Stanford University Press, 1997).

23. My first was for the Show of Strength Company at Bristol's Hen and Chicken in 1993.

24. Nick Hern Books, 2007.

25. *Will in the World*.

26. This text is available on my website. Greene was also the author (or co-author) of the *Groats-Worth of Wit*, the 1592 pamphlet that included the words an 'upstart crow beautified with our feathers', believed to be an attack on Shakespeare. Greene died that same year so did not survive to see Shakespeare's radical reimagining of his own, very popular story.

27. Greene's original for Leontes is 'Pandosto', for Hermione 'Bellaria' and for Polixenes 'Egistus'; Shakespeare reversed the locations, Pandosto being the King of Bohemia, and Egistus of Sicilia.

28. Polixenes' fear of what might 'breed', linked with his multiplying cipher, 'standing in rich place' – 'standing' and 'rich place' having bawdy possibilities – are detailed as unconscious triggers to Leontes' imagination by Stanley Cavell in his *Disowning Knowledge* (Cambridge University Press, 1987). I would not demur, only remarking that although these triggers may be useful to the actor playing Leontes, they are going to pass a modern audience by, as I suggest they would Polixenes himself; they are more examples of what I term 'shadow text', in this instance reflecting the auditor's mind but not the speaker's.

29. 'exchanged'.

30. The doctrine of original sin.

31. i.e. '...were the imposition clear'd that is hereditary ours.'

32. 'head'.

33. 'horns'.

34. A 'collop' is a piece of meat; a reference, therefore, to 'flesh of my flesh'.

35. Significantly, in *Pandosto*, it is Bellaria who instigates the referral to the Oracle – she begs it during her trial. That Leontes proceeds with the trial, despite having already referred the matter to the Oracle himself, but before it has pronounced, is further evidence of his unreason.

36. Elizabeth I's 1574 'Proclamation Against Excess of Apparel' (one of a number of 'sumptuary laws') was designed to curb the import of expensive fabrics from abroad and to maintain the distinctions between the classes. It defines in detail the fabrics and styles each rank was permitted to wear. Offenders could be fined.

Chapter Three

The Misery of Evil

In this chapter I extend a measure of understanding to Lady Macbeth and Goneril. They will both be driven to suicide, exhibiting depths of the misery that we commonly find – to a greater or lesser degree – in Shakespeare's portrayals of evil; in Richard of Gloucester, in Iago, in Angelo, in Claudius, perhaps even in *As You Like It*'s Duke Frederick.

History has judged the two women harshly, which may in the end be well-deserved – but we are always wrong if we take history's judgements as our starting-points. We must be careful, as director, actor or costume designer, not to allow tradition to dictate responses and choices that should be made afresh with every new performance. In rehearsal it is essential that we affect an ignorance of acquaintance with our characters. We must not know what we think of them, and not know what they will say or do – just as, in many moments, they will not know themselves. They will have stratagems, there will be premeditation, but just as often words and actions will arise out of passion, and out of confusion; they will frequently find themselves arrived, emotionally, or even physically, in a 'place' they had never imagined, or looked to find. We must not be there before them.

Just look again at the 'fiery' Duke of Cornwall's trajectory; in the first scene of the play, beyond all expectation he is given half of Britain to rule; a few weeks perhaps later, faced with a French invasion aimed at restoring his father-in-law to power, he loses his temper with the traitor, Gloucester, plucks out his eyes, and then is killed in a domestic skirmish by a previously loyal servant who cannot tolerate such cruelty. The received historic judgement that Cornwall is a practised thug – to be confident that this is how he will behave, confirmed perhaps by casting an actor who specialises in psychopathic villains – diminishes all this to a sideshow. That these extraordinary events happen in the moment, as much out of chaos as by design, is far, far more interesting – and true.

In the first of my two examples I will suggest that what happens in *Macbeth* happens not out of fixed personality traits, but in that narrow and volatile space between two people in the most intimate of relationships; a man and a woman bound together in a childless marriage.

1. Lady Macbeth

Challenging the Stereotype

Over the centuries Lady Macbeth has hardened in our imaginations into the type of the ruthlessly ambitious woman. She is able to manipulate her husband, and is prepared to humiliate him, sexually, in order to goad him into acting as she desires. She does become distressed at their deeds, even to the extent of taking her own life, but that has won her little sympathy in the public mind. She has even acquired a physical image that permits of very few variants. She is tallish, thinnish and a little sharp-featured, her hair is either raven-black or a dark red, reflecting her black or flaming red costume. She is seen as the antithesis of another theatrical type – most notably seen in the figure of Paulina – the 'earth-mother'.

She is certainly childless, though there has been at least one baby to whom she has 'given suck'. This must have gone the way of so many in the seventeenth century and, pending another pregnancy, Macbeth will fulfil the roles of both husband and child. (Tina Packer suggests the loss is recent history, that the milk Lady Macbeth would have the spirits 'take for gall' is still present in her breasts.) But as a figure of strength and ruthless determination she is herself a baby compared with that other maker of men, Caius Martius' mother, Volumnia (in *Coriolanus*), and we must examine her with as much understanding as we can muster. The actor, of course, must know her from within, must love herself, and believe that she is justified in what she does, that – at least at the beginning – she is *right*.

I directed the play in 2004, a production that was to transfer – along with Middleton and Rowley's *The Changeling* – for a five-week autumn season in the Barbican's Pit Theatre. My casting decision for Lady Macbeth – Zoë Aldrich – was a deliberate departure from the traditional type, Zoë having all the natural warmth that had served her so well as Paulina.

We meet her first on the receipt of the letter from her husband, describing his meeting with the witches:

> They met me in the day of success and I have learn'd, by the perfectest report, they have more in them than mortal knowledge. When I burn'd in desire to question them further, they made themselves air, into which they vanish'd. Whiles I stood rapt in the wonder of it came missives from the king, who all-hail'd me 'Thane of Cawdor', by which title, before, these weird sisters saluted me and referr'd me to the coming on of time with 'Hail, king that shalt be!' This have I thought good to deliver thee, my dearest partner of greatness, that thou might'st not lose the dues of rejoicing by being ignorant of what greatness is promis'd thee…
>
> Act 1 Scene 5

Here Macbeth relates the witches' golden promises without qualm or qualification, inviting his wife to rejoice in the certainty of their future greatness. In the words that follow, Lady Macbeth clearly envisages – there is no excusing her in this – the same means to wrest the future into the present that Macbeth has conceived – i.e. murder – but she also realises the obstacle that stands in the way: Macbeth's 'milk of human kindness':

> Glamis thou art, and Cawdor, and shalt be
> what thou art promis'd. Yet do I fear thy nature.
> It is too full o' the milk of human kindness[1]
> to catch the nearest way. Thou would'st be great,
> art not without ambition, but without
> the illness should attend it. What thou wouldst highly
> that wouldst thou holily; would'st not play false
> and yet would'st wrongly win. Thou'dst have, great Glamis,
> that which cries 'Thus thou must do, if thou have it,
> and that which rather thou dost fear to do
> than wishest should be undone.'

She is confident she has the remedy:

> Hie thee hither
> that I may pour my spirits in thine ear
> and chastise with the valour of my tongue
> all that impedes thee from the golden round
> which fate and metaphysical aid doth seem
> to have thee crown'd withal.

So far, however, she is unaware that an opportunity to kill the King will be offered this very night. When a servant enters with news of the King's imminent arrival her shocked excitement is evident, but quickly brought under control:

> Thou'rt mad to say it!
> Is not thy master with him? Who, were't so,
> would have inform'd for preparation.
>
> MESSENGER. So please you, it is true. Our thane is coming.
> One of my fellows had the speed of him
> who, almost dead for breath, had scarcely more
> than would make up his message.
>
> LADY.   Give him tending.
> He brings great news –

and she is pitched into what is perhaps her most famous speech:

> The raven himself is hoarse
> that croaks the fatal entrance of Duncan
> under my battlements! Come, you spirits
> that tend on mortal thoughts, unsex me here
> and fill me from the crown to the toe top-full
> of direst cruelty! Make thick my blood,
> stop up th'access and passage to remorse
> that no compunctious visitings of nature
> shake my fell purpose, nor keep peace between
> the effect and it! Come to my woman's breasts
> and take my milk for gall, you murd'ring ministers,
> wherever in your sightless substances
> you wait on nature's mischief! Come, thick night,
> and pall thee in the dunnest smoke of hell
> that my keen knife see not the wound it makes
> nor heaven peep through the blanket of the dark
> to cry 'Hold, hold!'

We know that at this moment Macbeth himself enters, and Lady Macbeth completes her pentameter line (suggesting there may be no intervening space whatever) with these words:

> Great Glamis! Worthy Cawdor!
> Greater than both, by the all-hail hereafter!

What would happen next, if... ? (again)

But what if Macbeth had not entered at this moment? What would Lady Macbeth have said next, done next? Would her soliloquy have continued? Would she have called a servant and ordered him to prepare a banquet to welcome her husband home; sharpened a dagger or two; or gone for a brisk walk?

Again, that vital question; we need to look at this soliloquy carefully with an ear to an alternative possibility: that she might have remained alone with her thoughts for a few more minutes, hours or days.

The speech is often characterised as one of a demonic strength, and indeed it begins so with that (as I read it) thrilled, even bloodthirsty cry of

> The raven himself is hoarse
> that croaks the fatal entrance of Duncan
> under my battlements![2]

The raven is traditionally hoarse to our ear – that dry croak. Perhaps here it is, as it were, hoarse within its hoarseness; even the herald of death is thrilled (or shocked) at the prospect of this particular death. 'Fatal entrance' is a common sexual pun – 'dying' being a common term for orgasm – and the implicit gate (the vulva) below the battlements provokes a sense that Duncan is entering Lady Macbeth herself, who thus impersonates Death. Her excitement is extreme.

But it provokes an urgent need and plea: that unearthly powers *do things to her* that will enable her to match up to the task; and we should note that in this instant, in the absence of her husband, the task seems to be hers alone. This is a key choice on Shakespeare's part. Both Lady Macbeth and her husband consider the deed in soliloquy; Macbeth's 'If it were done' speech I will suggest later is an urgent rehearsal of an argument as to why they will 'go no further in this business' to be offered moments later to his wife. Here Lady Macbeth considers the deed as a fatal act on her own part, and though it is very different in character from Macbeth's soliloquy, it may well be leading in the same direction. The excited eroticism of the opening, that makes her feel so acutely alive in every nerve and sinew, is immediately felt as an obstacle, or a threat; she must be 'unsexed' and such feelings replaced with 'direst cruelty'. She is also – fearfully, it seems – aware of her own 'milk of human kindness', and this too must be locked out by a thickening of the blood, and by her life-giving mother's milk being replaced with bitter gall. Finally, night must mask the deed from both heaven and her own 'keen knife', an involuntary disguising of the meaning 'my own eyes'; both must be blinded to the enormity of a deed that renders Heaven (and perhaps Lady Macbeth herself) a frightened child hiding under a blanket, hardly daring to look. Has the word 'peep' ever been used to more expressive effect?

Is this strength? And if it begins as strength, does it remain constant, or build, or diminish?

If we conclude – as I do – that Lady Macbeth is feeling her task harder and her resolution weakening with every line, that she feels herself physically shrinking from the deed, then the answer to my favourite question might be that – left on her own for a space – she would think better of the idea, and consequently there would be no murder, and no play. It is not that the timing alone can make all the difference – though in some instances it can – but that the murder will be the grotesque child of the Macbeths' relationship; like the conception of real children, it will happen only because of the sexual dynamic between them.

But there is no pause. His presence banishes her fears; and her greeting to him completes her own line:

> Great Glamis! Worthy Cawdor!
> Greater than both, by the all-hail hereafter!
> Thy letters have transported me beyond
> this ignorant present and I feel now
> the future in the instant.

MACBETH.   My dearest love,
Duncan comes here tonight.

Zoë Aldrich and Gyuri Sarossy as the Macbeths, photo © Alan Moore 2004

LADY.   And when goes hence?
MACBETH. Tomorrow, as he purposes.
LADY.   O, never
    shall sun that morrow see!

Many a Macbeth has struggled with her next sentence:

    Your face, my thane, is as a book where men
    may read strange matters.

What are these 'strange matters'? Does he wear the face of a murderer? Or is it doubt, or even horror that is now expressed in his eyes and in the line of his mouth? Macbeths I have seen have read back from this moment into his first lines in the scene:

                My dearest love,
    Duncan comes here tonight.

feeling them, not as excited and frankly murderous, but as nervous, open-ended, offered up to Lady Macbeth for her to confirm whether they will royally entertain, or brutally murder their guest. Some have read back further, into the long, unseen ride from Forres to Dunsinane, and concluded that the determination to kill the King that Macbeth expressed towards the end of Act 1 Scene 3 has faltered, bringing him home in a state of exhausted indecision.

That is a muddled strategy, and untypical of Shakespeare, whose developments are clear and precise, and with few exceptions take place within, not between scenes.

The incompleteness, metrically, of the line

    shall sun that morrow see!

is a pointer to what happens here, in this moment. Lady Macbeth's simply intended meaning is that Duncan will not wake tomorrow. But the shadow meaning that Macbeth hears, and that his face registers in those four missing beats is apocalyptic: the sun itself will not rise; the deed will be the 'promised end'. Now, and not a moment before, is where his retreat begins. But Lady Macbeth, deaf to her own metaphor, rushes him on:

            To beguile the time
    look like the time. Bear welcome in your eye,
    your hand, your tongue. Look like the innocent flower
    but be the serpent under't. He that's coming
    must be provided for and you shall put

> this night's great business into my dispatch
> which shall to all our nights and days to come
> give solely sovereign sway and masterdom.
>
> MACBETH. We will speak further.
>
> LADY.   Only look up clear.
> To alter favour ever is to fear.
> Leave all the rest to me.

And her line ends the scene; for the moment, at least, she is in charge.

Her next appearance will see her greeting the King outside the castle, her husband out of sight, hiding – one feels – from the moment. The King and Banquo have paused to admire the view:

> DUNCAN. This castle hath a pleasant seat. The air
> nimbly and sweetly recommends itself
> unto our gentle senses.
>
> BANQUO.   This guest of summer,
> the temple-haunting martlet, does approve
> by his lov'd mansionry, that the heaven's breath
> smells wooingly here. No jutty, frieze,
> buttress, nor coign of vantage, but this bird
> hath made his pendent bed and procreant cradle…
>
> Act 1 Scene 6

Lady Macbeth enters from the castle, alone, and the modest and gracious King apologises for the trouble he is putting her to:

> See, see, our honour'd hostess!
> The love that follows us sometime is our trouble
> which still we thank as love. Herein I teach you
> how you shall bid God bless us for your pains
> and thank us for your trouble.
>
> LADY.   All our service
> in every point twice done and then done double
> were poor and single business to contend
> against those honours deep and broad wherewith
> your majesty loads our house. For those of old
> and the late dignities heap'd up to them
> we rest your hermits.

The Jacobean audience would have known that the conventions of the time were being flouted. A king would expect to be met by a formal party, with the host himself at the head.[3] But Duncan's graciousness is typical of him:

> Where's the Thane of Cawdor?
> We cours'd him at the heels and had a purpose
> to be his purveyor. But he rides well
> and his great love, sharp as his spur, hath holp him
> to his home before us.

Lady Macbeth has offered no reply to Duncan's question, and he smooths the matter over with:

> Fair and noble hostess,
> we are your guest tonight.
>
> LADY.   Your servants ever
> have theirs, themselves and what is theirs in compt,
> to make their audit at your highness' pleasure,
> still to return your own.
>
> DUNCAN.   Give me your hand.
> Conduct me to mine host. We love him highly
> and shall continue our graces towards him.
> By your leave, hostess.[4]

For Lady Macbeth, the difficulty is threefold. Not only is she come face to face with the man she intends her husband will kill in a few hours' time, but she is covering for her husband's cowardice – what else can have made him commit such an outrageous *faux-pas*? – and to cap it all, this king is warm, spontaneous and generous. Small wonder her speeches in return are studiedly formal, and that in

> All our service
> in every point twice done and then done double

she seems to be trying to compensate, quite literally, for her solo appearance.

Duncan evidently recognises her on her entrance, but have they ever spoken before, let alone touched ('Give me your hand')? That is an entirely open question, but both actors must know the answer.

The Setting and the Deed

How should we set this scene? I have seen it staged against a backdrop of high, almost black, windowless walls, seeping with water, like an image of a decaying Dickensian prison. And many recent productions have taken other routes to avoid any element of architectural beauty or gracious society. The 2018 National Theatre production by Rufus Norris critics characterised as one set in a 'post-apocalyptic', 'dystopian universe'. Certainly there is an irony to the beauty of the scene as described by both Duncan and Banquo, but isn't it taking dramatic irony too far to suggest that these two men cannot recognise a death chamber when they see one? It is also pre-empting the action of the play, and making assumptions about the society of the play for which I can find no basis in the text. An actor – perhaps it was a director – once said to me that 'what we need to communicate is that *Macbeth* is set in a world where anyone might plunge a knife into anyone's back at any moment'; an attitude that for me renders the action of the play redundant. If it is not about the humane and civilised falling into catastrophic error, what is the point? In the round at the Tobacco Factory the opportunity for castle walls did not arise, but were I to film the play the setting for Dunsinane would be every bit as delightful as Duncan and Banquo testify.

We now move into the evening of the same day and the celebratory dinner held (offstage) in honour of the King himself, of victory in the war, and Macbeth's promotion to Thane of Cawdor. Again Macbeth commits a serious *faux-pas* by leaving the high table while the King is still sitting. The urgency of his need to be by himself – and in my 2004 production Gyuri Sarossy's Macbeth rushed into his private space and vomited – is often underestimated; and many actors have felt the soliloquy that opens Scene 7 to be far more meditative and open-ended than it is. It plays best as vigorously rhetorical, as if trying to persuade an unseen interlocutor that the 'deed' must not be done. The stressing of the opening lines is useful here:

> *If* it were *done*, when *'tis* done, *then* 'twere *well*
> it *were* done *quick*ly.

The first foot of the first line is reversed, opening the speech on that 'If', which immediately calls the plan into question. Of the two 'done's, the first is the stronger and fuller in meaning – 'if it were *done with, over, finished in every way*' when the killing itself is completed – and Macbeth acknowledges that speed *would* be the right strategy *if* that were the case. He repeats the equation:

> If the assassination
> could trammel up[5] the consequence and catch
> with his surcease success, that but this blow
> might be the be-all and the end-all here –
> but here, upon this bank and shoal of time –
> we'd jump the life to come.

If this were easy, and wouldn't come back to bite us in this world, then *of course* I'd say 'yes, let's do it, let's risk our eternal souls'. But it *will* come back to bite us:

> But in these cases
> we still have judgement here. That we but teach
> bloody instructions, which being taught, return
> to plague th'inventor. This even-handed justice
> commends the ingredience of our poison'd chalice
> to our own lips.

So far, so practical. He now moves into moral territory, first enlisting the medieval tradition of fealty, and then of hospitality, where the safety of the guest was the host's responsibility (even if the guest were an enemy):

> He's here in double trust.
> First, as I am his kinsman and his subject,
> strong both against the deed. Then, as his host
> who should against his murderer shut the door,
> not bear the knife myself.

And then on to more personal territory and Duncan's own inherent merit:

> Besides, this Duncan
> hath borne his faculties so meek, hath been
> so clear in his great office, that his virtues
> will plead like angels, trumpet-tongu'd, against
> the deep damnation of his taking-off.
> And pity, like a naked new-born babe
> striding the blast, or heaven's cherubim hors'd
> upon the sightless couriers of the air,
> shall blow the horrid deed in every eye
> that tears shall drown the wind.

This last is an extraordinary passage, richly rhetorical (could ever a new-born baby 'stride the blast'?) yet in its imaginative flight so utterly persuasive that Macbeth's only conclusion can be:

> I have no spur
> to prick the sides of my intent, but only
> vaulting ambition which o'erleaps itself
> and falls on the other.

But that has been a rehearsal. Now it must be played for real as Lady Macbeth finds him:

MACBETH. How now, what news?

LADY. He has almost supp'd. Why have you left the chamber?

MACBETH. Hath he ask'd for me?

LADY. Know you not he has?

What has happened between the arrival of the King, and now? We should assume that Lady Macbeth has 'conducted the King to mine host', as requested, but how competently Macbeth has dealt with that unseen meeting is for the actors to decide. But then, to Lady Macbeth's alarm, her husband has rudely left the dinner table; the King has asked for him, and Lady Macbeth has been forced to leave the King's side to follow him. She must know she is dealing with a crisis. Macbeth's 'How now, what news?' is a fearful evasion, as is the frankly stupid 'Hath he asked for me?' He is already in retreat from the drift of his soliloquy, but he plucks up courage to deliver his decision:

We will proceed no further in this business.

But the richness of his rhetorical argument is reduced to a mere shred:

He hath honour'd me of late and I have bought
golden opinions from all sorts of people
which would be worn now in their newest gloss,
not cast aside so soon.

Is this because he knows Lady Macbeth's heart and mind can only be *bought* with treats – the heavily reductive 'shallow woman' argument – or because so much of his rhetoric has been about fear; fear of the consequences in this world and the next? And fear, at this moment, is a weakness the great warrior cannot admit to? Whatever the truth, his fear is an open book to his wife:

LADY. Was the hope drunk
wherein you dress'd yourself? Hath it slept since?
And wakes it now to look so green and pale
at what it did so freely? From this time
such I account thy love. Art thou afeard
to be the same in thine own act and valour
as thou art in desire? Would'st thou have that
which thou esteem'st the ornament of life
and live a coward in thine own esteem,
letting 'I dare not' wait upon 'I would',
like the poor cat i' the adage?

The Shift of Focus

This is a crucial turning-point. The focus subtly – and unconsciously on both their parts – shifts, from the final objective, possessing the crown, to the doing itself; and it is this shift that will ensure the Macbeths' tragedy. Daring as a measure of love, and of manliness, is deeply unattractive, but it is an inherited value – from Rome, certainly, and I daresay from many other cultures – and it is required of the male of the species. Macbeth has a notion that there are actions that are not moral, not appropriate, but it is drowned out by Lady Macbeth's demand that he have the courage, the manliness, to follow through on his promises and desires:

> MACBETH.   Prithee, peace.
>   I dare do all that may become a man.
>   Who dares do more is none.
>
> LADY.   What beast was't, then,
>   that made you break this enterprise to me?
>   When you durst do it, then you were a man.
>   And, to be more than what you were, you would
>   be so much more the man. Nor time nor place
>   did then adhere and yet you would make both.
>   They have made themselves and that their fitness now
>   does unmake you. I have given suck and know
>   how tender 'tis to love the babe that milks me.
>   I would, while it was smiling in my face,
>   have pluck'd my nipple from his boneless gums
>   and dash'd the brains out, had I so sworn as you
>   have done to this.

This last claim, that she would 'dash' her baby's brains out, is extraordinary, and unless we are to assume that it is disingenuously manipulative – which I doubt – Shakespeare must surely expect us to question Lady Macbeth's self-knowledge; a question he will prompt us to again.

Macbeth is reduced to the feeblest of all responses: 'but what if it should all go wrong?' Not only does his wife have the most unanswerable response, but she woos her husband back in one of the most rapid developments in drama:

> MACBETH. If we should fail?
>
> LADY.   We fail![6]
>   But screw your courage to the sticking-place
>   and we'll not fail. When Duncan is asleep –
>   whereto the rather shall his day's hard journey

soundly invite him – his two chamberlains
will I with wine and wassail so convince
that memory, the warder of the brain,
shall be a fume and the receipt of reason
a limbeck only. When in swinish sleep
their drenched natures lie as in a death,
what cannot you and I perform upon
the unguarded Duncan? What not put upon
his spongy officers who shall bear the guilt
of our great quell?

Never mind the editorial doubts over the meaning of 'the sticking-place' (its diction alone justifies it); she is evoking – selling – an idea of an all-consuming potency. With the capacities of the King's bodyguards disabled by drink, even to being the image of death, she characterises the nature of this sordid and shameful killing as a 'great quell', as if it will be some overarching victory over a mighty enemy. And she has happened, also, on an image that answers Macbeth's 'trumpet-tongu'd' angels and his sense that the deed will never be completely 'done'. The 'quell' silences the consequences; it is complete, definitive, permanent. It is even heroic.

He is won. He flatters her in wishing that she should bear – or make – only male children; but we might hear a shadowing ambiguity, that he himself, the grown man, will be born of her womb:

> Bring forth men-children only,
> for thy undaunted mettle should compose
> nothing but males. Will it not be receiv'd,
> when we have mark'd with blood those sleepy two
> of his own chamber and us'd their very daggers
> that they have done't?

LADY.   Who dares receive it other,
as we shall make our griefs and clamour roar
upon his death?

They are both now in the extraordinarily heady mood, fatally detached from the human reality of what they intend, that will sustain them (Lady Macbeth will need to add Dutch courage) until the great scene immediately after the deed is done. Macbeth's final speech reminds us of Lady Macbeth's soliloquy, her need to abuse her body to make it capable of murder:

> I am settl'd and bend up
> each corporal agent to this terrible feat.
> Away and mock the time with fairest show.
> False face must hide what the false heart doth know.

This time it is Macbeth who completes the scene and takes charge.

With the scene set for the killing, Lady Macbeth becomes the bystander, slightly drunk, nervous of possible failure, panicked and yet excited by every sound. She drops in and out of that heady mood they were both in when we last saw them:

> That which hath made them drunk hath made me bold.
> What hath quench'd them hath given me fire. – Hark! –
>   Peace,
> it was the owl that shriek'd, the fatal bellman
> which gives the stern'st good-night. He is about it.
> The doors are open and the surfeited grooms
> do mock their charge with snores. I have drugg'd their
>   possets
> that death and nature do contend about them
> whether they live or die.
>
> MACBETH. [*Within*]   Who's there? What, ho!
> LADY. Alack, I am afraid they have awak'd
>   and 'tis not done. The attempt and not the deed
>   confounds us. – Hark! – I laid their daggers ready,
>   he could not miss 'em.
>
> Act 2 Scene 2

For the second time, I question Lady Macbeth's self-knowledge:

> Had he not resembl'd
> my father as he slept I had done't.

Does Duncan really resemble her father, or is this – much more interestingly – a trick of the unconscious? The actor, of course, must believe it to be true; it is not her job to supply a footnote. Then Macbeth enters with the bloody daggers, and she greets him as a man who has proved himself worthy of her:

> My husband!

Action then seems to be suspended, as Macbeth's consciouness overtakes the room and Lady Macbeth remains the bystander, briefly disempowered:

> MACBETH. I have done the deed. Did'st thou not hear a noise?
> LADY. I heard the owl scream and the crickets cry.
>   Did not you speak?
> MACBETH.   When?
> LADY.   Now.

MACBETH.   As I descended?

LADY. Ay.

MACBETH. Hark! –
Who lies i' the second chamber?

LADY.   Donalbain.

MACBETH. This is a sorry sight.

LADY. A foolish thought, to say a sorry sight.

MACBETH. There's one did laugh in's sleep and one cried 'Murder!'
that they did wake each other. I stood and heard them.
But they did say their prayers and address'd them
again to sleep.

LADY   There are two lodg'd together.

She is wrong-footed, well expressed in the dislocated conclusion to who
lies in the second chamber, but with her 'foolish thought, to say a sorry
sight' she attempts to regain control, but finds no point of purchase. The
scene proceeds rather as if very slowly the lights are being switched back on;
as if, almost in slow motion, the husband and wife fall back to earth. Some
actors and directors worry as to why Lady Macbeth does not see the bloody
daggers immediately; far from a problem, it is an eloquent expression of
this process. But as they both awake, Macbeth sees, hears and imagines
more and more clearly, and Lady Macbeth, beginning to live a nightmare,
knows that these thoughts, voices and imaginings must be shut out:

MACBETH. One cried 'God bless us!' and 'Amen' the other,
as they had seen me with these hangman's hands.
Listening their fear, I could not say 'Amen'
when they did say 'God bless us!'

LADY. Consider it not so deeply.

MACBETH. But wherefore could not I pronounce 'Amen'?
I had most need of blessing and 'Amen'
stuck in my throat.

LADY.   These deeds must not be thought
after these ways. So, it will make us mad.

MACBETH. Methought I heard a voice cry 'Sleep no more!
Macbeth does murder sleep'. The innocent sleep,
sleep that knits up the ravell'd sleeve of care,
the death of each day's life, sore labour's bath,
balm of hurt minds, great nature's second course,
chief nourisher in life's feast –

LADY.   What do you mean?

MACBETH. Still it cried 'Sleep no more!' to all the house,
  'Glamis hath murder'd sleep and therefore Cawdor
  shall sleep no more. Macbeth shall sleep no more.'

At last she finds the words to challenge – and if she can to suffocate – these thoughts; and, as we shall see again and again, she seeks to do so by turning to practical action:

LADY. Who was it that thus cried? Why, worthy thane,
  you do unbend your noble strength to think
  so brainsickly of things. Go get some water
  and wash this filthy witness from your hand.

And now she sees what all along have been in plain view:

  Why did you bring these daggers from the place?
  They must lie there. Go carry them and smear
  the sleepy grooms with blood.

But Macbeth is changed by the deed; their marriage is changed by the deed. He is no longer afraid to admit to fear:

           I'll go no more.
  I am afraid to think what I have done.
  Look on't again I dare not.

So Lady Macbeth must deal with the daggers herself, but first prepare her imagination for how it will cope with what her eyes will witness:

           Infirm of purpose!
  Give me the daggers. The sleeping and the dead
  are but as pictures. 'Tis the eye of childhood
  that fears a painted devil.

When she re-enters, aided by the knocking at the south entry, she is all action, persuading herself that a little wash is all the time requires. But the gulf between them is now unbridgeable, and well expressed in their relatively disorderly exit; they go together, but not together. Her 'shame' accusation is as if unheard:

  My hands are of your colour, but I shame
  to wear a heart so white.
  Knocking within.
           I hear a knocking
  at the south entry. Retire we to our chamber.
  A little water clears us of this deed.

How easy is it, then! Your constancy
hath left you unattended.
Knocking within.

                      Hark, more knocking!
Get on your nightgown, lest occasion call us
and show us to be watchers. Be not lost
so poorly in your thoughts.

MACBETH. To know my deed, 'twere best not know myself.
Knocking within.

Wake Duncan with thy knocking! I would thou could'st!

Macduff arrives to collect the King, is greeted nervously in the Great Hall by Macbeth, but then leaves for the King's chamber and discovers the body. Macbeth and Lennox rush to witness it, the alarm bell rings, and Lady Macbeth emerges in night-attire (one assumes). Her famous 'Woe, alas! What, in our house?' falls far short of what is required, and perhaps betrays a terror of the moment. She is brusquely silenced by Banquo, and Macbeth re-enters from the death-chamber:

MACBETH. Had I but died an hour before this chance
      I had lived a blessed time. For, from this instant,
      there's nothing serious in mortality.
      All is but toys. Renown and grace is dead.
      The wine of life is drawn and the mere lees
      is left this vault to brag of.

                            Act 2 Scene 3

During these lines, and those that follow – the entrance of Malcolm and Donalbain and Macbeth's revelation that in his rage he has killed the King's two guards – twenty-nine lines in all, Lady Macbeth remains silent, until her:

Help me hence, ho!

The Lady Faints

Tradition has it – I believe correctly – that she falls to the floor in a faint. But one powerful strand of that tradition has been that the faint is faked, that it is a strategy to interrupt Macbeth, on the grounds that his pretence of horror is out of control. This misses a more compelling reality. By the nature of the event – not only a moral horror, but a political crisis – she has, as a Jacobean woman, no part to play; she must stand by silently and listen. What is shocking about Macbeth's utterances is just how in control he is in this moment, how he can use his own overwhelming regret at what he has done as an instrument to disguise the truth. The lines I quote above, and then this:

> And his gash'd stabs look'd like a breach in nature
> for ruin's wasteful entrance.

are among the most eloquent in the play. And his witness also seems to come to a natural conclusion as he defends his action in killing the guards:

> Who could refrain
> that had a heart to love and in that heart
> courage to make's love known?

The faint does not interrupt him; nor is it fake. That this is far from easy to communicate to the audience is beside the point. We must know so much more about the inner lives of our characters than we can possibly express. Here we must know that the faint stems from vulnerability, not from stratagem. Lady Macbeth is ill because in this arena she has no means to shut out these terrible truths. It is as if she is being forcibly held and made to look at the body on the bed, unable to see the sight as a mere 'picture' or 'painted devil', or to displace her focus into action.

There is now a short gap of time, indicated by the brief dialogue (Act 2 Scene 4), between Ross, the Old Man and Macduff, which alerts us to the impending coronation, and we then rejoin the Macbeths, greeting Banquo, on their day of triumph:

> MACBETH. Here's our chief guest.
>
> LADY.   If he had been forgotten
> it had been as a gap in our great feast
> and all-thing unbecoming.
>
> > Act 3 Scene 1

The prelude to this moment – the murder of a king – was more than 'unbecoming', but Lady Macbeth would have everything conducted graciously from here on in – she dreams, as it were, of a new chapter – and she certainly has no complicity in Macbeth's plans for Banquo:

> Ride you this afternoon?
>
> BANQUO.   Ay, my good lord.
>
> MACBETH. We should have else desir'd your good advice,
> which still hath been both grave and prosperous,
> in this day's council. But we'll take tomorrow.
> Is't far you ride?

BANQUO. As far, my lord, as will fill up the time
    'twixt this and supper…

MACBETH.   Goes Fleance with you?

BANQUO. Ay, my good lord. Our time does call upon's.

Again, after that opening compliment, Lady Macbeth can only stand by, listen – and dread. She is dismissed together with the whole court, something that she will feel more than show, until she is on her own:

Nought's had, all's spent,
where our desire is got without content.
'Tis safer to be that which we destroy
than by destruction dwell in doubtful joy.

Act 3 Scene 2

'Safe', 'safer', 'safety' and 'safest' are words that chime through the play, a dozen uses between them, and here Lady Macbeth's use has picked up on Macbeth's double use in his intervening soliloquy:

To be thus is nothing,
but to be safely thus. Our fears in Banquo
stick deep. And in his royalty of nature
reigns that which would be fear'd. 'Tis much he dares,
and to that dauntless temper of his mind
he hath a wisdom that doth guide his valour
to act in safety.

Act 3 Scene 1

Banquo has also been tempted into error by the witches' prophecy; tempted but not succumbed; made 'safe' by his 'wisdom', by the 'dauntless temper of his mind' that will not allow his identity to be bent out of shape by ambition. Lady Macbeth is miserable at what has passed, fearful that it were better to be dead herself, yet when Macbeth enters she can disguise that thought, as if – against all probability – Macbeth, by closing the regicide chapter, can now lead her back into the light, just as she had led him into the dark:

How now, my lord? Why do you keep alone,
of sorriest fancies your companions making,
using those thoughts which should indeed have died
with them they think on? Things without all remedy
should be without regard. What's done is done.

Act 3 Scene 2

She articulates the impossible fantasy that what is done can be locked safely away, out of sight and out of mind. But Macbeth will have none of it, and in the midst of his turbulent anxiety he utters his own 'Better be with the dead':

> We have scorch'd the snake, not kill'd it.
> She'll close and be herself, whilst our poor malice
> remains in danger of her former tooth.
> But let the frame of things disjoint, both the worlds suffer,
> ere we will eat our meal in fear and sleep
> in the affliction of these terrible dreams
> that shake us nightly. Better be with the dead
> whom we, to gain our peace, have sent to peace
> than on the torture of the mind to lie
> in restless ecstasy…

Lady Macbeth can only urge him to cheer up, for this moment, for this evening:

> Come on,
> gentle my lord, sleek o'er your rugged looks,
> be bright and jovial among your guests tonight.

His agreement is momentary, quickly overwhelmed by nightmarish fears, well expressed by his forgetfulness that he has already commissioned Banquo's murder:

> So shall I, love. And so, I pray, be you.
> Let your remembrance apply to Banquo.
> Present him eminence, both with eye and tongue.
> Unsafe the while that we
> must lave our honours in these flattering streams
> and make our faces vizards to our hearts,
> disguising what they are!
>
> LADY.   You must leave this.
>
> MACBETH. O, full of scorpions is my mind, dear wife!
>   Thou know'st that Banquo, and his Fleance, lives.

This Lady Macbeth meets with:

> But in them nature's copy's not eterne.

– a platitude, perhaps, but one seized on by Macbeth as he is brought back to the present. It is impossible to exaggerate the emotional pressure Lady Macbeth is under as her husband – in some of the greatest lines ever penned – articulates his remedy:

> There's comfort yet. They are assailable.
> Then be thou jocund. Ere the bat hath flown
> his cloister'd flight, ere to black Hecate's summons
> the shard-borne beetle with his drowsy hums
> hath rung night's yawning peal, there shall be done
> a deed of dreadful note.
>
> LADY.   What's to be done?
>
> MACBETH. Be innocent of the knowledge, dearest chuck,
> till thou applaud the deed…

Is there anything more articulate of the Macbeths' changed relationship than that 'dearest chuck'? We sense that once again they go off together, perhaps even hand in hand or arm in arm. But who now is the parent, who is the child?

The banquet is prepared, the table laid and the court present:

> MACBETH. You know your own degrees, sit down. At first
> and last the hearty welcome.
>
> LORDS. Thanks to your majesty.
>
> MACBETH. Ourself will mingle with society
> and play the humble host.
> Our hostess keeps her state, but in best time
> we will require her welcome.
>
> Act 3 Scene 4

This scene, until the general exit of the court, is framed by Macbeth's 'You know your own degrees' and Lady Macbeth's 'Stand not upon the order of your going', marking first their attempt, and then their failure, to create a gracious, ordered society. Why the new Queen 'keeps her state' – in literal imagining, probably sitting on her throne on a raised dais – may be a trivial question; is Macbeth breaking the rules by 'mingling with society', or is she so shocked by Macbeth's mood that she feels she cannot speak informally? If that is the case, she digs deep to fight for their lives in what follows, first having to draw Macbeth's attention from his interrogation of the First Murderer back to their happy occasion:

> My royal lord,
> you do not give the cheer. The feast is sold
> that is not often vouch'd, while 'tis a-making,
> 'tis given with welcome.

But with the appearance of Banquo's ghost, the event careers off the rails, as Macbeth's reality takes a leap once again into a nightmare world, and it's as if we scroll back a little; his weakness begets his wife's strength, and once again she berates him for childish fear:

> O proper stuff!
> This is the very painting of your fear.
> This is the air-drawn dagger which, you said,
> led you to Duncan. O, these flaws and starts,
> impostors to true fear, would well become
> a woman's story at a winter's fire
> authoriz'd by her grandam…

This time, however – as in the matter of the bloody daggers – Macbeth's fear is invulnerable to her:

> MACBETH. Blood hath been shed ere now, i' the olden time,
> ere humane statute purg'd the gentle weal.
> Ay, and since too, murders have been perform'd
> too terrible for the ear. The times have been
> that, when the brains were out, the man would die
> and there an end. But now they rise again
> with twenty mortal murders on their crowns
> and push us from our stools. This is more strange
> than such a murder is.

She must change tactic, for a moment successfully:

> My worthy lord,
> Your noble friends do lack you.
> MACBETH.   I do forget.
> Do not muse at me, my most worthy friends.
> I have a strange infirmity, which is nothing
> to those that know me…

but Banquo reappears, Macbeth agains loses control and she knows he is beyond her reach; she must attempt to command the occasion herself:

> Think of this, good peers,
> but as a thing of custom. 'Tis no other,
> only it spoils the pleasure of the time.

Almost oblivious now, Macbeth continues to address the Ghost:

> What man dare, I dare.
> Approach thou like the rugged Russian bear,
> the arm'd rhinoceros, or the Hyrcan tiger,
> take any shape but that and my firm nerves
> shall never tremble…

> Hence, horrible shadow!
> Unreal mockery, hence! Why, so, being gone,
> I am a man again. Pray you, sit still.

But the 'great feast' they had anticipated is in ruins:

> LADY. You have displac'd the mirth, broke the good meeting
>   with most admir'd disorder.
>
> MACBETH.   Can such things be
>   and overcome us like a summer's cloud
>   without our special wonder? You make me strange
>   even to the disposition that I owe
>   when now I think you can behold such sights
>   and keep the natural ruby of your cheeks
>   when mine is blanch'd with fear.

This provokes a question that she cannot allow Macbeth to answer –

> ROSS.   What sights, my lord?

– and she must unceremoniously hustle the thanes out:

> I pray you, speak not. He grows worse and worse.
> Question enrages him. At once, good night.
> Stand not upon the order of your going
> but go at once!

The court departed, she has nothing left; we had Zoë's Lady collapsed into a seat at the far end of the long trestle table from him, head in hand, completely exhausted; no more to do, nothing to say, except a desultory answer to Macbeth's question, 'What is the night?' Even the 'sir' with which she will address him emphasises the gulf between them. Macbeth is virtually exhausted, too, but is locked into a purpose that will sustain a driven energy in him even to the end. As he puts it so succinctly, 'I am in blood stepp'd in so far that, should I wade no more, returning were as tedious as go o'er'. Lady Macbeth clutches at the straw that is sleep – 'sore labour's bath' – but we struggle, in this moment, to imagine either of them ever being able to sleep again:

> MACBETH. It will have blood, they say. Blood will have blood.
>   Stones have been known to move and trees to speak.
>   Augurs and understood relations have
>   by magot-pies and choughs and rooks brought forth
>   the secret'st man of blood. What is the night?
> LADY. Almost at odds with morning, which is which.

MACBETH. How say'st thou, that Macduff denies his person
    at our great bidding?
LADY.   Did you send to him, sir?
MACBETH. I hear it by the way. But I will send.
    There's not a one of them but in his house
    I keep a servant fee'd…
LADY. You lack the season of all natures, sleep.
MACBETH. Come, we'll to sleep. My strange and self-abuse
    is the initiate fear that wants hard use.
    We are yet but young in deed.

'Self-abuse', 'initiate fear', 'hard use' and 'deed' all have sexual meanings; Macbeth is determined to render the 'barren sceptre' in his gripe a potent one. Will there now, perhaps, be 'hard use' in bed? If so, it might well take the form of marital rape.

We shall not see a waking Lady Macbeth again; her 'sleepwalking scene' is all that remains.

The Sleepwalking

There has been a significant passage of time, enough for the Doctor to have spent two fruitless nights waiting to observe her disturbed behaviour. The Gentlewoman's account of what she has seen begins with the much debated:

> Since his majesty went into the field, I have seen her rise
> from her bed, throw her nightgown upon her, unlock her
> closet, take forth paper, fold it, write upon't, read it, after-
> wards seal it and again return to bed. Yet all this while in
> a most fast sleep.
>
> Act 5 Scene 1

What is she doing here? Writing to her husband? Or composing a confession? And why is it not the repeated action – the sleepwalking – that the Gentlewoman hopes the Doctor will see, and we are about to witness? Is it just stagecraft on Shakespeare's part, making us wait by making an ambiguous reference back to the letter from Forres, and saving up the full effect for a surprise? The question is sidelined as the Gentlewoman's hope is suddenly realised:

Lady Macbeth in her sleepwalk, observed by her Gentlewoman (Rebecca Smart) and the Doctor (Jamie Ballard), photo © Alan Moore 2004

GENTLEWOMAN. Lo you, here she comes! This is her very guise. And, upon my life, fast asleep…

DOCTOR… Look, how she rubs her hands.

GENTLEWOMAN. It is an accustom'd action with her, to seem thus washing her hands. I have known her continue in this a quarter of an hour.

LADY. Yet here's a spot… Out, damn'd spot! Out, I say! One, two. Why, then, 'tis time to do't. Hell is murky! Fie, my lord, fie! A soldier and afeard? What need we fear who knows it, when none can call our power to accompt? Yet who would have thought the old man to have had so much blood in him?

DOCTOR. Do you mark that?

LADY. The Thane of Fife had a wife. Where is she now? What, will these hands ne'er be clean? No more o' that, my lord, no more o' that. You mar all with this starting.

DOCTOR. Go to, go to, you have known what you should not.

GENTLEWOMAN. She has spoke what she should not, I am sure of that. Heaven knows what she has known.

LADY. Here's the smell of the blood still. All the perfumes of Arabia will not sweeten this little hand. O, O, O!

She rubs her hands – tries to wash off the blood ('a little water clears us of this deed') – but finds a spot that will not be washed away. She looks into Hell. She admonishes Macbeth for cowardice. She is shocked by the amount of blood that has flowed from the body. She refers to the wife of Macduff – we have not seen her receive news of that atrocity, but obviously she has, or suspected it. Again she admonishes Macbeth, it seems with reference to the banquet scene. Still the blood will not go, and she sighs heavily. So far, every moment is a reference back to words we have heard her speak, or to unseen reactions we can easily place in the sequence of her journey. Then there are some moments taken up by the Doctor and Gentlewoman, before we get her conclusion:

> Wash your hands, put on your nightgown. Look not so
> pale. I tell you yet again, Banquo's buried. He cannot
> come out on's grave.

DOCTOR. Even so?

LADY. To bed, to bed! There's knocking at the gate. Come,
come, come, come, give me your hand. What's done
cannot be undone. To bed, to bed, to bed!

> *Exit.*

DOCTOR. Will she go now to bed?

GENTLEWOMAN. Directly.

If we listen to these words carefully we are first struck by the 'I tell you yet again, Banquo's buried. He cannot come out on's grave', which we have not heard before, though one could argue that it may have been said after the exit from the banquet scene. More puzzling is the 'To bed, to bed'; it is placed precisely, as a response to the knocking at the gate, but it was not as we heard it ('Get on your nightgown, lest occasion call us and show us to be watchers'). And then there's this:

> Come, come, come, give me your hand. What's done
> cannot be undone. To bed, to bed, to bed.

– for which, as an action – the taking of the hand – there has been no scripted precedent.

What is going on here?

The framing is important. The Gentlewoman has made it clear that what we see amounts to a repeated routine of handwashing; and that it will end with a return to bed:

DOCTOR. Will she go now to bed?

GENTLEWOMAN. Directly.

We must assume, as she is already asleep, that it is indeed to *rest* in sleep. It is crucial that we obey the instructions contained in such apparently inconsequential remarks. In this case it powerfully suggests that Lady Macbeth's behaviour is more than a routine, it is a *cycle*, in which in the unconscious mind the distress is expressed and then somehow managed, permitting the return to rest. If we listen again – and try to forget the context for a moment – do we not hear a mother gently comforting an upset child? The milk is spilt, but no matter; sleep, 'the balm of hurt minds', will make all well. What is now reimagined as a more trivial hurt will, by morning, have been forgotten.

The otherwise disappointing 2015 film by Justin Kurzel, which starred Michael Fassbender and Marion Cotillard, was admirably alert to this extraordinary moment, though I would rather we had witnessed her taking an unseen hand (as did Zoë Aldrich) than the hand of the child we had seen being buried in the film's invented opening sequence. In Lady Macbeth's disturbed imagination the child is Macbeth himself.

Lady Macbeth's journey, from dizzy euphoria to fatal despair is extraordinarily swift and entirely subject to the sexual dynamic between her and her husband, itself controlled by notions of male worth and the differing roles of men and women that still pertain, though they have long been questioned and eroded. The murder is the monster-child of their relationship, and could not have happened otherwise. It is the bleakest of pictures of a marriage, but the awful glory of a text which for me has no rival in the English language.

Production Notes

A Setting Choice: In my 2004 production, designed by Andrea Montag (Bristol) and Vicki Cowan-Ostersen (the Barbican), we felt the placing of Act 1 Scene 7 (the 'If it were done...' scene) should be set in the most private and intimate space possible. A first experiment with the marital bed proved simply awkward – beds can be cumbersome things, particularly on low-tech stages – and also for Zoë's Lady, at least in that scene fully restricted by Jacobean corsetting. A happier choice proved to be a disused child's nursery with cradle and rocking-horse under dust sheets; the perfect refuge for Macbeth from the glare of the High Table (and a wash-bowl for him to vomit up his dinner); and of course we would then choose it again as the most expressive location for Lady Macbeth's obsessive wandering in Act 5 Scene 1.

Macduff: There is a tradition of casting Macduff as a good-hearted but rather rough man. Perhaps it is simply in the sound of his name. There is much more to be gained from seeing him as an almost clerical character; a peace-loving husband and father whose escape to England is informed as much by fear for his own life, as by his mission to raise an army under Malcolm. An unlikely warrior and hero, in the extremity of the hour he finally rises to the task.

2. Goneril

As I keep emphasising, we are cursed with a foreknowledge of Shakespeare's outcomes. These great plays are so famous, their stories so widely known that it is hard – impossible for many of us – to come at them completely afresh. Their characters have become the blueprints, or reference points, for vivid personality types. One consequence of this is that they can manifest themselves so easily as complete and finished from the very opening scene, often encouraged by a pressure on the actor – self-imposed or director-imposed – to 'get the character' as early as possible.

The real task, an exciting and enjoyable one, is to feel one's way. Crucial to this – and again I repeat myself – is for the actor to like their character, and to believe, for as long as it is remotely sustainable, that they are *right*; that what they are doing is justifiable, even moral.

Challenging the Stereotype (again)

The opening of *King Lear* is a classic case of ignoring this rule. Though many an actor has rightly fought against this, how often have we seen Goneril and Regan played as finished personalities, cynically offering up empty words to Lear to earn their thirds of the kingdom; to feel in both of them a cold and collected reserve born of a settled contempt for their father's old age, no blushing at their specious hyperbole required.

In this – and rather against the drift of my own argument – we are encouraged by Cordelia's words towards the end of the scene:

> The jewels of our father, with wash'd eyes
> Cordelia leaves you. I know you what you are
> and like a sister am most loath to call
> your faults as they are nam'd. Love well our father.

> To your profess'd bosoms I commit him
> but yet, alas, stood I within his grace,
> I would prefer him to a better place.
> So farewell to you both.

REGAN. Prescribe not us our duty.

GONERIL.   Let your study
> be to content your lord who hath receiv'd you
> at Fortune's alms. You have obedience scanted
> and well are worth the want that you have wanted.

CORDELIA. Time shall unfold what plighted[7] cunning hides.
> Who covers faults, at last with shame derides.
> Well may you prosper!

Neither Cordelia's judgement, nor Regan and Goneril's reactions, make it easy for us (as observers) to like the two elder sisters, and we are, perhaps, inclined to see with Cordelia's eyes. Whether she speaks as she knows for a fact, or as her instinct tells her to expect and fear, is for the Cordelia to decide. I would only caution that there are sibling dynamics here. Cordelia, previously her father's favourite, has suffered an appalling calumny and lost her inheritance. Her sisters, who have failed to leap to her defence, are the consequent winners. There is resentment and guilt, possibly on both sides. Cordelia's is not necessarily the voice of God; her judgement is yet to be proven.

We have a difficulty here, in that from our modern, western perspective, we do not understand the experience of totalitarian rule. An actor once said to me that the only way she had found to play Goneril was to create a memory that Lear had sexually abused her in her childhood. Only that way could she make sense of her cruelty to him following the division of the kingdom. I baulked at this notion, not so much because I felt Lear to be incapable of such a thing, as that I believed that to leave such a determining factor permanently unvoiced is foreign to Shakespeare's method. But the idea of abuse struck a chord, and it occurred to me that autocracy is, in itself, an abuse; that the autocrat is forever the parent, and his/her subjects forever the children, their adulthood indefinitely postponed. During the Libyan revolution against Gaddafi, a man among the protesters shouted 'I want my dignity!' He wanted to be a grown-up, with at least a degree of autonomy, not the thirty- or forty-year-old man that he was, permanently restricted and watched over like an untrustworthy adolescent.

One of the most difficult elements in the production of *King Lear*'s opening scene – and it is a very difficult scene indeed – is the silence of the assembled lords. The play's original audience in 1606 may well have had an ambivalent attitude to this, understanding only too well the nature of absolute rule and the danger of speaking out, whilst reacting with horror at the court's apparently bland acceptance of the notion of dividing the state; an acceptance which is expressed so clearly in the opening lines, where the *detail* of the division seems more interesting than the fact of it:

> KENT. I thought the king had more affected the Duke of Albany
>   than Cornwall.
>
> GLOUCESTER. It did always seem so to us. But now, in the
>   division of the kingdom, it appears not which of the
>   Dukes he values most, for qualities are so weigh'd that
>   curiosity in neither can make choice of either's moiety.

Those words, 'the division of the kingdom', placed so apparently nonchalantly as a headline for the action, in the theatre of James I, whose greatest ambition was to unite England and Scotland, must have had a sharp, political resonance. Four hundred years later – and despite the prospect of Scottish independence looming ever larger – there is a danger that they merely suggest the beginning of a fairy tale.

It is not until a deeply personal element intrudes that Lear's extraordinary and unworkable decision to divide the kingdom provokes Kent to object. This good man, who has previously remained – together with Gloucester, and we may assume the majority if not all of the court – naively unruffled, cannot remain silent while Cordelia is slandered and disinherited. His preamble to his protest lays out the nature of the relationship between King and subject:

> Royal Lear,
> whom I have ever honour'd as my king,
> lov'd as my father, as my master follow'd,
> as my great patron thought on in my prayers...

This is how even Lear's most senior advisers relate to him; the absolute ruler as king, father, master and patron. Lear's own imagining might add to that the Lord of Nature:

> Of all these bounds, even from this line to this,
> with shadowy forests and with champains rich'd,
> with plenteous rivers and wide-skirted meads
> we make thee lady. To thine and Albany's issues
> be this perpetual...
> To thee and thine hereditary ever
> remain this ample third of our fair kingdom,
> no less in space, validity and pleasure
> than that conferr'd on Goneril.

In his inflated sense of self he presumes to dictate the future as completely as he has the past.

It is crucial that we recognise this debilitating failure to question as deeply ingrained, as a product of perhaps six decades of the rule of one man. That Shakespeare articulates this only by the absence of words, that there is no one to draw attention to it (how might the Fool have behaved, had he been present?), does make this difficult to stage, and my 2012 production certainly failed to satisfy Michael Billington in this respect:

> When Lear savagely rejects his youngest daughter and banishes his most loyal follower in the opening scene, it causes scarcely a ripple of consternation among his courtiers. (*Guardian*, 17 February 2012)

The personal dimension to this is that, in the case of Goneril, Regan and their respective husbands, four married people have been living an extended childhood, inevitably with inchoate resentments bubbling underneath. In the coda to the scene, there is a measure of sounding each other out, of talking around the issue, that suggests this might be the first time that long-breeding hurts (including, of course, Lear's openly professed preference for his youngest daughter) have been voiced:

> GONERIL. Sister, it is not little I have to say of what most nearly
>   appertains to us both. I think our father will hence tonight.
>
> REGAN. That's most certain, and with you. Next month with us.
>
> GONERIL. You see how full of changes his age is. The
>   observation we have made of it hath not been little. He
>   always lov'd our sister most and with what poor
>   judgement he hath now cast her off appears too grossly.
>
> REGAN. 'Tis the infirmity of his age. Yet he hath ever but
>   slenderly known himself.
>
> GONERIL. The best and soundest of his time hath been but rash.
>   Then must we look from his age to receive not alone the
>   imperfections of long-engraff'd condition, but
>   therewithal the unruly waywardness that infirm and
>   choleric years bring with them.

This is very different from Kent's loving and respectful, yet outraged protest. But for all his 'lov'd as my father' Kent is not an actual child of Lear's. His habits of loyalty and obedience have not been muddied or tested by familial ties and jealousies. This difference is a familiar pattern in the experiencing of famous and powerful men; and so often a further burden on those bound to them by blood or marriage.

So let us tread as carefully as we can with Goneril and try to resist a rush to judgement.

In her scenes in her own home (Act 1 Scenes 3 and 4), she has to cope with the impossible reality into which her father has thrust her. He has given her the key to her new domain in one moment, but taken it back in the next. Rehearsal of these scenes often stalls around the question of the behaviour of Lear's retinue of a hundred knights. Are they truly awful? Or when Goneril complains that they're 'debosh'd and bold' and turning her 'grac'd palace' into 'a riotous inn' is she just fabricating charges to provide a pretext for handing half of them their cards? Shakespeare doesn't show us the answer. He doesn't give us drunken knights rollicking around in the middle of the night like so many Belches and Aguecheeks, nor does he demonstrate that this large, private bodyguard is a model of sobriety and discretion. He knows it's not the point, which is that authority is divided within the household and Goneril's rightful supremacy is usurped. In much more ordinary circumstances, grown-up children and their parents have warred over authority forever, so often focusing on the relatively trivial – the state of the bathroom or the table manners of the third generation. Goneril may be exaggerating, but it is not guile; whatever the actual truth of the matter, she *feels* Lear's knights are like this because they render her impotent in her own house.

My contention is that Goneril is governed not by contempt for her father – though she is so often played that way – but by fear of him; within which fear she may indeed also love him. If we play Goneril and Regan merely as the Ugly Sisters, from the very start cold and ruthless in pursuit of the main chance, then we lose the excitement of a yet-to-be determined development, and we destroy one of the many uncomfortable glories of this play. And a settled nastiness, like the settled sadism so often foisted on Cornwall, can be of interest only briefly. Goneril's journey is a voyage of self-discovery and self-empowerment. It's with extreme difficulty, not contemptuous ease, that she weans herself from her father's authority, that she moves from obedient child to autonomous adult. This difficulty is superbly well rendered.

Her short twenty-five-line scene with Oswald, her Steward (Act 1 Scene 3), that begins:

> GONERIL. Did my father strike my gentleman for chiding of his
> fool?
>
> OSWALD. Ay, madam.

is a little masterpiece of development. Goneril's speeches have a staccato, improvisatory feel, with a number of very short sentences, instruction added upon instruction, as her mood rapidly swings.

She begins in misery. The punishment of her gentleman (who may or may not be Oswald himself) provokes a crisis that cannot be ignored, encapsulating for all to see the challenge to her authority.

> By day and night he wrongs me. Every hour
> he flashes into one gross[8] crime or other,
> that sets us all at odds. I'll not endure it.
> His knights grow riotous, and himself upbraids us
> on every trifle.

Evidently she dare not simply confront her father – 'Father, we need to talk.' So, as so many of us do when we shrink from *initiating* a confrontation, she takes, instead, an easier step that will initiate it remotely – here by *not* talking to him:

> When he returns from hunting
> I will not speak with him. Say I am sick.
> If you come slack of former services
> you shall do well. The fault of it I'll answer.

That irrevocable step taken, though Lear's return is imminent, she begins to grow in confidence:

> OSWALD. He's coming, madam, I hear him.
>
> GONERIL. Put on what weary negligence you please,
> you and your fellows. I'd have it come to question.
> If he distaste it, let him to our sister,
> whose mind and mine, I know, in that are one.

In her mind she is gathering backup, from her household, from her sister. Then come lines that are so often spoken only to express a casual contempt for Lear, but can express something very different. They are – unfortunately in my view – omitted from the Folio and I quote them here from the 1608 Quarto (which renders the speech in prose):

> ... whose mind and mine, I know, in that are one, not to
> be over-rul'd. Idle old man, that still would manage those
> authorities that he hath given away! Now, by my life, old
> fools are babes again and must be us'd with checks as
> flatteries when they are seen abus'd.

Is she not *reassuring herself* that her father is no longer to be feared; that he is indeed merely an idle old man, with no power to command, no power to hurt; and that the task of reprimanding him is both just and necessary? The weight lifts and she becomes bolder still:

> And let his knights have colder looks among you. What
> grows of it, no matter. Advise your fellows so. I would
> breed from hence occasions, and I shall, that I may speak.
> I'll write straight to my sister to hold my very course.

Finally she is cheerful, she even has an appetite:

> Go, prepare for dinner.

And there the scene ends.

But this new-found ease doesn't last. When in Act 1 Scene 4 she finally obeys Lear's command to come into his presence, she has prepared herself to be commandingly definitive – there is now no going back – and she has sufficient self-control to seize on the Fool's audacity as her springboard:

> Not only, sir, this your all-licens'd fool,
> but other of your insolent retinue
> do hourly carp and quarrel, breaking forth
> in rank and not to be endur'd riots. Sir,
> I had thought, by making this well known unto you,
> to have found a safe redress, but now grow fearful,
> by what yourself too late have spoke and done,
> that you protect this course, and put it on
> by your allowance.

But though this is strong meat, it lacks the freedom she would have liked to have had to chastise the erring child. There is a sense of a speech half-rehearsed, her passion mediated through convoluted grammar; and when she arrives at the threat of sanction she becomes hard to understand at all:

> Which, if you should, the fault
> would not 'scape censure, nor the redresses sleep,
> which in the tender of a wholesome weal
> might in their working do you that offence,
> which else were shame, that then necessity
> will call discreet proceeding.

I have known these five and a half lines to be cut from performance, their obscurity judged to be accidental – an example of our occasional difficulty with early seventeenth-century expression – rather than as deliberate, and telling.

This is a speech, not coldly efficient, but inhibited by the dread of the reaction it might provoke. The narrative itself is distorted. She has not 'made this well known unto you'; this is her first voiced protest. Challenged by her father, she becomes freer in her expression:

> This admiration, sir, is much o' the savour
> of other your new pranks.

– 'pranks' following through her 'old fools are babes again' –

> I do beseech you
> to understand my purposes aright.
> As you are old and reverend, should be wise.
> Here do you keep a hundred knights and squires,
> men so disorder'd, so debosh'd and bold
> that this our court, infected with their manners,
> shows like a riotous inn. Epicurism and lust
> make it more like a tavern or a brothel
> than a grac'd palace. The shame itself doth speak
> for instant remedy.

Now we can smell the Mansion polish, and know that there will be no dust to be found along the tops of the picture frames. But she is being less than frank:

> Be then desir'd
> by her, that else will take the thing she begs,
> a little to disquantity your train.
> And the remainders that shall still depend,
> to be such men as may besort your age
> which know themselves and you.

She has *already issued* the order to dismiss half Lear's retinue. Though this has puzzled some editors and directors, who have complained of an error in Shakespeare's plotting, the psychology should be plain enough. She is asking her father to volunteer a choice that she has herself pre-empted. She dreads Lear's reaction to this order – issued a little too easily perhaps, from the safety of her own quarters – and hopes now to disguise it as a mutual agreement. But the request alone provokes Lear's fury:

> Darkness and devils!
> Saddle my horses, call my train together.
> Degenerate bastard, I'll not trouble thee.
> Yet have I left a daughter.

This in turn provokes Goneril's most uncomplicated protest:

> You strike my people and your disorder'd rabble
> make servants of their betters!

174

One can imagine her in tears of both frustration and guilt at this moment, but in vain, as Lear's rage negotiates Albany's bewildered intervention, to find its most extreme expression:

> Hear, Nature, hear, dear goddess, hear!
> Suspend thy purpose, if thou didst intend
> to make this creature fruitful.
> Into her womb convey sterility,
> dry up in her the organs of increase
> and from her derogate body never spring
> a babe to honour her! If she must teem
> create her child of spleen, that it may live
> and be a thwart disnatur'd torment to her… !

It is hard to imagine a more appalling message from a father to a daughter. It is equally hard to imagine that this isn't at an instinctive level what Goneril has foreseen, and dreaded. Her father's power to call down such revenges from the heavens is a living terror to her.

Challenged now by her husband – 'Now, gods that we adore, whereof comes this?' – she is curt and unbending; also, I would suggest, raw, guilty, deeply hurt and shocked. And Lear has still to react to the dismissal of the knights:

> Blasts and fogs upon thee!
> Th' untented woundings of a father's curse
> pierce every sense about thee…
> I have another daughter
> who I am sure is kind and comfortable.
> When she shall hear this of thee, with her nails
> she'll flay thy wolvish visage…

Lear exits in his rage, and we now get the first of three dialogues between husband and wife, which will take Albany from passive bewilderment, through horrified disbelief to a passionate certainty of judgement in the play's closing scene; another of this play's extraordinary roll-call of wonderful character-journeys:

> GONERIL.   … A hundred knights?
> 'Tis politic and safe to let him keep
> at point a hundred knights? Yes, that on every dream,
> each buzz, each fancy, each complaint, dislike,
> he may enguard his dotage with their powers
> and hold our lives in mercy. Oswald, I say!
> ALBANY. Well, you may fear too far.

GONERIL.   Safer than trust too far.
> Let me still take away the harms I fear,
> not fear still to be taken. I know his heart.
>   … No, no, my lord,
> This milky gentleness and course of yours,
> though I condemn not, yet, under pardon,
> you are much more at task for want of wisdom
> than prais'd for harmful mildness.

ALBANY. How far your eyes may pierce I can not tell.
> Striving to better, oft we mar what's well.

GONERIL. Nay, then –

ALBANY. Well, well, th'event.

This first spat can be played to the formula of a cold, mannish woman putting down her weak husband. And, of course, she does exaggerate – there has never been a suggestion that Lear's knights offer a threat to Goneril and Albany's lives – but, however badly judged her tactics in reducing the private army by half, it is hardly a criminal desire, and her own intransigence is made inevitable by Lear's astonishingly cruel curses. I feel I have seen this scene played as if the curses were *deserved*; how could that possibly be? As Lear finally exits, Goneril is not rubbing her hands and saying to herself 'job done'; she is shaking from the experience. No wonder she gives Albany's hesitant criticism short shrift.

Her last scene with her father, Act 2 Scene 4, at Gloucester's castle is capable of differing interpretations; the slightest variations in tone have radical consequences in how we react to the scene's humiliation of Lear, and how we judge Goneril's role in it. Why does she travel to Gloucester? It is a change of intent; she had sent Oswald off with the letter to Regan, instructing him to hurry back with her response. Is it a fear that Regan will not hold the line when faced with their father's rage, or rather a half-formed plan to combine conclusively with her against the old man? Her opening exchange with Lear is capable of either choice:

LEAR. O Regan, wilt thou take her by the hand?

GONERIL. Why not by the hand, sir? How have I offended?
> All's not offence that indiscretion finds
> and dotage terms so.

Step by Step (again)

But for me the latter choice is too premeditated, and renders the scene flatly sadistic. Again, that crucial sense of ignorance of the next beat in the story is lost. The scene's power is in Goneril and Regan's step-by-step loosening – their weaning – from Lear's control and dominance, a long-delayed release into autonomy, into adulthood. It is ugly, as revolts against tyranny so often are, but the ugliness is born of abuse. Lear will always evoke sympathy in this scene – his 'O reason not the need' has resonated through the centuries. Yet his own part in it, his:

> But yet thou art my flesh, my blood, my daughter,
> or rather a disease that's in my flesh,
> which I must needs call mine. Thou art a boil,
> a plague-sore, or embossed carbuncle
> in my corrupted blood…

is again beyond forgiveness; if ever we questioned the quality of his parenting, its shocking failings are transparent here.

It is too easy to see Goneril and Regan pushing this scene through to a premeditated conclusion. But Lear's choices are equally decisive. What would have happened next (that question yet again) if his answer to this proposal from Regan –

> I pray you, father, being weak, seem so.
> If till the expiration of your month
> you will return and sojourn with my sister,
> dismissing half your train, come then to me.

– had been to back down? If Regan has the end of the scene – the reduction from a hundred knights to none – in mind from the beginning, then she is going about it very strangely. No, here, as almost always in Shakespeare, emotionally charged scenes have their own momentum, with the participants only fitfully in control as their passions take them into undreamt-of territory.

When the black farce of numbers-trading is done, and the anguished Lear, declaring to his Fool that he 'will go mad', rushes out into the night, Shakespeare highlights the shock felt by both Regan and Goneril at what they have done by setting it off against Cornwall's relative indifference:

CORNWALL. Let us withdraw. 'Twill be a storm.

REGAN. This house is little. The old man and's people
cannot be well bestow'd.

> GONERIL. 'Tis his own blame. Hath put himself from rest
>   and must needs taste his folly.
>
> REGAN. For his particular, I'll receive him gladly,
>   but not one follower.
>
> GONERIL.   So am I purpos'd.

It is the returning Gloucester's protest that gives the sisters a choice, to be persuaded by him to send after Lear to seek a reconciliation, or to deny their guilt and take their cue from Cornwall:

> CORNWALL. 'Tis best to give him way. He leads himself.
>
> GONERIL. My lord, entreat him by no means to stay.
>
> GLOUCESTER. Alack, the night comes on, and the high winds
>   do sorely ruffle. For many miles about
>   there's scarce a bush.

Regan now casts any doubt aside:

> REGAN.   O, sir, to wilful men,
>   the injuries that they themselves procure
>   must be their schoolmasters. Shut up your doors.
>   He is attended with a desperate train,
>   and what they may incense him to, being apt
>   to have his ear abus'd, wisdom bids fear.
>
> CORNWALL. Shut up your doors, my lord. 'Tis a wild night.
>   My Regan counsels well. Come out o' the storm.

There is now no turning back, for either sister, in their relationship with their father, and their focus moves on to one that, far from a coming-together, will split them apart. For they are both to fall in love with Edmond. For Goneril it is a downhill progression; even when experiencing that new-found passion she will refer – I think to our shock and surprise – to her 'hateful life'. And it will end in the murder of her sister and her own suicide. It is a tragic story.

Her next appearance – after her one-line contribution to the 'eyes' scene – sees her accompanying Edmond north to Albany and having a loud and angry row with her husband. That scene, Act 4 Scene 2, though heavily cut in the Folio, should be played in its full Quarto version, not least because it contains a crucial turning-point in the Duke of Albany's personal journey.

Julia Hills as Goneril and Jack Whitam as
Edmond, photo © Graham Burke 2012

Arrived outside her gracious home, Goneril offers Edmond the welcome
that, in formal terms, should have been offered by her husband – a parallel
with Duncan's arrival at Inverness:

> GONERIL. Welcome, my lord. I marvel our mild husband
>   not met us on the way.

Oswald enters from the house with news of a transformation in his master:

> OSWALD. I told him of the army that was landed.
>   He smiled at it. I told him you were coming.
>   His answer was 'The worse.' Of Gloucester's treachery
>   and of the loyal service of his son,
>   when I inform'd him, then he call'd me sot
>   and told me I had turn'd the wrong side out…

and Goneril sends Edmond back southwards:

> GONERIL.   … Back, Edmond, to my brother.
>   Hasten his musters and conduct his powers.
>   I must change arms at home and give the distaff
>   into my husband's hands. This trusty servant
>   shall pass between us. Ere long you are like to hear,
>   if you dare venture in your own behalf,

a mistress's command. Wear this. Spare speech.
Decline your head. This kiss, if it durst speak,
would stretch thy spirits up into the air.
Conceive, and fare thee well.

EDMOND. Yours in the ranks of death.

GONERIL.   My most dear Gloucester!

Exit Edmond.

O, the difference of man and man!
To thee a woman's services are due.
My fool usurps my body.

Here is something more than just a new plot line, the infatuation of a married woman for a man newly entered into her life. It is part of the experience of release from her father's dominion, almost as if she is discovering her sexuality, or at least her own agency in her sexuality, for the first time. There is an intense pleasure in the frank innuendo in 'stretch thy spirits up into the air' and in Edmond's even franker response, 'Yours in the ranks of death'. This excitement of Goneril's will find an interesting counterpoint in Regan's jealously nervous question to Edmond in Act 5 Scene 1:

> But have you never found my brother's way to the
> forfended place?

which, in Regan's very different mood, makes her sound like a nervous teenager who has never before talked sex. There is something about them both that smacks of belated sexual awakening.

Edmond's intentions, and how he might have responded to Goneril's implied suggestion of a murder followed by a marriage had she not stopped him with 'Spare speech', remain unreadable, despite his declaration that he is 'hers'; but we can be sure that he is enjoying her excited arousal.

Albany confronts her. He has awoken to the journey both women are travelling; 'the event' has revealed itself in all its ugliness and he has decided, with no misgivings whatever, where he stands. It could be argued that as he – unlike we the audience – is as yet ignorant of the blinding of Gloucester, his 'Tigers, what have you perform'd' and 'these vile offences' are overstated, and that Shakespeare is allowing a transference (an old dramatic trick) from our knowledge to his. The Quarto-only lines I put here in italics:

GONERIL. I have been worth the whistle.

ALBANY.   O Goneril,
you are not worth the dust which the rude wind

blows in your face. *I fear your disposition...*
She that herself will sliver and disbranch
from her material sap perforce must wither
and come to deadly use.

GONERIL. *No more. The text is foolish.*

ALBANY. *Wisdom and goodness to the vile seem vile,*
filths savour but themselves. What have you done?
Tigers, not daughters, what have you perform'd?
A father and a gracious aged man
whose reverence even the head-lugg'd bear would lick,
most barbarous, most degenerate, have you madded.
Could my good brother suffer you to do it?
A man, a prince, by him so benefited!
If that the heavens do not their visible spirits
send quickly down to tame these vile offences,
it will come,
humanity must perforce prey on itself,
like monsters of the deep.

Goneril is not careless of these judgements, so she turns the issue, Lady Macbeth-like, to a matter of courage and manliness; and to Albany's impotence, as she sees it, in the face of the French invasion under way many miles to the south:

Milk-liver'd man,
that bear'st a cheek for blows, a head for wrongs,
who hast not in thy brows an eye discerning
thine honour from thy suffering, *that not know'st*
fools do those villains pity who are punish'd
ere they have done their mischief. Where's thy drum?
France spreads his banners in our noiseless land,
with plumed helm thy state begins to threat,
whil'st thou, a moral fool, sit'st still, and criest
'Alack, why does he so?'...

Her 'Hateful Life'

But when a messenger enters with news of the death of Cornwall at the hand of his servant, the political dynamic is radically changed:

GONERIL.   [*Aside*] One way I like this well.
But being widow, and my Gloucester with her,
may all the building in my fancy pluck

upon my hateful life. Another way,
the news is not so tart.

No sooner has she conceived an intention to do away with Albany and marry Edmond – with an even greater ambition to become sole Queen with him – than Cornwall's death, although it clears the way to that in one regard, puts Regan in pole position to take Edmond for herself. Some editors gloss Goneril's 'my hateful life' as a conditional notion – conditional upon Regan gaining the prize; others that it is a simple reference to her present life with Albany. I hear in it neither of those; rather an element of self-loathing that adds enormous depth to Goneril's experience, and will eventually inform her desperation and her suicide.

And then the scene ends with Albany's arrival at certainty of judgement and firm resolution:

Gloucester, I live
to thank thee for the love thou show'dst the king
and to revenge thine eyes.

The scene has begged the question of this marriage: has it ever been worthy of the name in terms we would understand now? The priority would have been political rather than personal; it was almost certainly arranged. 'Albany' was a synonym for Scotland in Shakespeare's time, so – ironically, perhaps – a cementing of unity only shortly preceded the disastrous division. That they have had a sex life is clear: 'My fool usurps my body'. But it is hard to imagine there was ever much physical delight or warmth, let alone a meeting of minds. There have as yet been no children.

Goneril's journey now quickly degenerates. Her sparring with Regan in the scene following the end of the battle (Act 5 Scene 3) is almost comic; they compete gracelessly for Edmond, as he shapes up to challenge Albany for dominance in the uneasy league:

ALBANY.   Sir, by your patience,
I hold you but a subject of this war,
not as a brother.

REGAN.   That's as we list to grace him.
Methinks our pleasure might have been demanded,
ere you had spoke so far. He led our powers,
bore the commission of my place and person,
the which immediacy may well stand up
and call itself your brother.

GONERIL. Not so hot.
    In his own grace he doth exalt himself,
    more than in your addition.

REGAN. In my rights,
    by me invested, he compeers the best.

GONERIL. That were the most, if he should husband you.

REGAN. Jesters do oft prove prophets.

GONERIL. Holla, holla!
    That eye that told you so look'd but a-squint.

However, this is no comedy; Goneril has already given her sister poison:

REGAN. Lady, I am not well, else I should answer
    from a full-flowing stomach. General,
    take thou my soldiers, prisoners, patrimony.
    Dispose of them, of me, the walls is thine.
    Witness the world that I create thee here
    my lord and master.

GONERIL. Mean you to enjoy him?

ALBANY. The let-alone lies not in your good will.

EDMOND. Nor in thine, lord.

ALBANY. Half-blooded fellow, yes.

REGAN. [*To Edmond*] Let the drum strike, and prove my title
    thine.

Albany, now in possession of the letter Goneril wrote to Edmond advocating he murder her husband, intervenes with his own vein of black humour:

Stay yet. Hear reason. Edmond, I arrest thee
on capital treason, and in thine arrest,
this gilded serpent. [*To Regan*] For your claim, fair sister,
I bar it in the interest of my wife.
'Tis she is subcontracted to this lord
and I, her husband, contradict your banns.
If you will marry, make your love to me,
my lady is bespoke.

With Regan carried off to die, Goneril's rapidly shrinking world now hangs entirely on Edmond's defeat of Albany's mysterious champion – Edgar still in disguise. When Edmond is defeated, she protests that the duel was not fought according to the rules:

> This is practice, Gloucester.
> By the law of war thou wast not bound to answer
> an unknown opposite. Thou art not vanquish'd,
> but cozen'd and beguil'd.

But this has scant currency with Albany:

> Shut your mouth, dame,
> or with this paper shall I stop it. Hold, sir,
> thou worse than any name, read thine own evil.
> No tearing, lady – I perceive you know it?
> GONERIL. Say, if I do, the laws are mine, not thine.
> Who can arraign me for't?
> ALBANY. Most monstrous! O,
> know'st thou this paper?
> GONERIL. Ask me not what I know.
> *Exit.*

Though in the Folio Goneril's exit is marked two lines earlier and Albany's question, 'O know'st thou this paper?' is address'd to Edmond, and answer'd by him, the Quarto's choice, as given here, seems the better one. In one sense Goneril has become the type of the Jacobean villain and most audiences will thrill at Albany's 'Shut your mouth, dame, or with this paper shall I stop it' (or 'stople it', as in the Quarto), but her suicide will be her only escape from what she 'knows' and the last act of an unhappy life; if a 'monstrous' one, then it was largely of her father's making.

It has been a journey of the unexpected, of barely controlled, at times chaotic passions, more than the cold calculation of tradition.

Production Notes

These follow at the end of the next chapter.

1. There has been a longstanding academic debate about 'human kindness', several editors urging that it should be felt as a single word, 'humankindness', the 'kind' meaning 'nature' rather than gentleness. This demands that it be stressed only on the first syllable, rather than on the first and the third. Any actor would confirm that the rhythm of the line demands the latter.

2. This exclamation mark is mine.

3. I have seen it asserted, though in a reference I can no longer trace, that the higher the status of the visitor, the further from the host's gates he would expect to be met. If that is true, then Macbeth's failure here is all the more glaring, and Duncan's indulgence all the more generous.

4. In his *Prefaces to Shakespeare*, Harley Granville-Barker claims that Duncan's 'by your leave' implies he kisses her on the cheek. I don't know what authority he had for that, though I would like it to be true!

5. 'catch in a net'.

6. Again, the exclamation mark is mine, following Rowe and others. The Folios have a question mark.

7. 'folded', therefore 'dissembling'.

8. 'blatant' rather than 'large'.

Chapter Four

The Self, Lost and Found

As we saw initiated in *The Comedy of Errors*, the fragility of individual identity is a career-long theme in Shakespeare. Twenty years ago, the American scholar, Harold Bloom, in his massive book *Shakespeare: The Invention of the Human*,[1] went so far as to argue that Shakespeare invented the notion of human personality, of human inwardness; and so, in effect, invented us. This is a mighty but questionable thesis, far beyond the competence of this book, but I would like to pursue it in one respect. At the moment that the Elizabethan or Jacobean actor climbed into a costume, he took on a role. And we may imagine that – rather more than for us now – this had its parallel in real life. Subject (unlike the actor) to one's birth, to a great degree life-roles were defined by status and function – and costumed accordingly – rather than by what we might define as personality. The social hierarchy was well defined, social mobility severely limited; at the top was the strict hierarchy of royalty and the court, wielding autocratic power; at the bottom, or close to it, were the functionaries: 'Bottom, the weaver', 'Snug, the joiner', and 'Flute, the bellows-mender'.

In our more egalitarian age we are defined less by what we do, as by what and how we are considered to *be* – as people, as personalities. And we pay enormous attention to detail – in looks, tastes in dress, quirks of behaviour, fitness and health, possessions, place and mode of living, choice of partner; all these, and more – choices we are largely free to make – contribute to the way we perceive ourselves and each other. In some instances these factors can hugely outweigh the role we fulfil during our working hours, which may be seen to be merely a means of financing *being ourselves*.

In constructing performances in modern drama, the actor may pay great attention to these details, may argue with the designer that 'my character would just not wear a frock that colour', or decide that a stammer, or a habit of repeatedly polishing the top of the piano, is a key to the reality within.

And in Shakespeare, too, we find elements of this characterfulness, in comic roles such as Falstaff, Launce, Dogberry, Touchstone, Audrey and Phebe – vivid personalities that actors might well flesh out with tics or idiosyncrasies. They are largely unchanging creations that we recognise as types who have their counterparts on the modern stage. They may affect us profoundly, like Falstaff, or merely make us laugh.

But there is another category of character, generally taking central roles in both tragedy and comedy, for whom tricks of speech, eccentricities of dress, or other everyday details seem unnecessary or inappropriate. It is the extreme nature of their experiences, and the changes those experiences prompt in them, that make them so vivid, not character detail. In his book, *The Genius of Shakespeare*,[2] Jonathan Bate puts it this way:

> Shakespeare's characters are not the fixed entities they tend to be in his sources. Rather they are embodiments of the fluidity, the play, of emotion.

The fluidity, the wide range of possibility to be accessed, voluntarily or involuntarily by Shakespeare's central characters is, perhaps, the central concern of this book. It permits them to carry a huge metaphorical resonance, one that cannot be borne by the modern, fully realised and detailed stage personality. It is such characters that I am concerned with here, and I would like to look at one of them in detail…

Edgar

'Please introduce yourself in a sentence or two.'

'My name is John Smith. I am twenty-three. I am training to be an actor at the Bristol Old Vic Theatre School.'

'Thank you. Now could you introduce yourself as your character in *King Lear*?'

'I am Edgar. I am the eldest son of the Duke of Gloucester, and his heir. I have a younger half-brother, Edmond, a bastard.'

This is a typical exchange in an oft-repeated experiment. I have yet to hear a reference to family in answer to the first question, or to activity, work, or ambition in answer to the second.

If we were to ask the student to expand on his answers, we know that he could continue almost indefinitely about himself; his *choice* to become an actor, his likes and dislikes, hobbies, favourite colour, his desert island discs; he might *eventually* go into his background and parentage.

But in the person of Edgar he might be pushed to expand his answer at all. He could pluck details out of the air – a passion for falconry perhaps, or if he thinks of him as a more artistic soul, for the Elizabethan miniature, or Italian garden design – but the central fact of his identity would not be informed by any such choice or ambition. Because what Edgar *is* – as the student rightly pointed out – is his father's heir. He may become a great Duke of Gloucester, or make a complete hash of it, but doing it, *being it*, is non-negotiable. This is the reality, the identity, that is snatched from him by Edmond's plot; and once cast into the wilderness, his journey, from heath to battlefield, from victim to victor, will become one of Shakespeare's greatest journeys in the human mind.

When we first see him he is colourless, credulous, almost a *tabula rasa*; as if he merely waits to have the personality of power drop upon him on his father's death. This is in sharp contrast to Edmond, who is vividly and uncomfortably defined by his bastardy. Edmond's position on the periphery of society, in addition to giving cause for a burning resentment, demands that he self-invent; and it lends him the advantage of a degree of perspective and clear sight, something he shares with other outsiders in Shakespeare – Aaron, Iago, Apemantus and Richard of Gloucester. Though he is the younger brother, to us Edmond feels older, more complete and finished. His language crackles with energy and wit; he engages us, even makes us like him briefly as he scorns his father's astrological nonsense, plays with that fiddly-silly word 'legitimate', and claims Nature as his goddess.

Edmond forges a letter, supposedly from Edgar, that proposes the murder of their father. Gloucester is completely taken in by it; Edgar, who seems to lack any tools to confront the calumny, is persuaded to flee; and that rough and ready instrument of Elizabethan law, the 'hue and cry', is set up to capture him. By pure good fortune he evades his pursuers:

> I heard myself proclaim'd
> and by the happy hollow of a tree
> escap'd the hunt. No port is free, no place
> that guard and most unusual vigilance
> does not attend my taking. Whiles I may 'scape
> I will preserve myself...

> Act 2 Scene 3

And here he chooses a new identity. This is often played as a strategic choice only, a disguise that will hide him in plain view. The speech is far more interesting – and only justifies its length – if it has a more profound purpose. He first locates an identity that expresses his misery and sense of rejection:

> …I will preserve myself and am bethought
> to take the basest and most poorest shape
> that ever penury, in contempt of man,
> brought near to beast. My face I'll grime with filth,
> blanket my loins, elf all my hairs in knots
> and with presented nakedness outface
> the winds and persecutions of the sky.

But then, in a second pass, he reaches further still, finding in the Bedlam beggar who abuses his own flesh – we would say 'self-harms' – an even more acute expression of his profound distress:

> The country gives me proof and precedent
> of Bedlam beggars, who with roaring voices
> strike in their numb'd and mortified arms
> pins, wooden pricks, nails, sprigs of rosemary,
> and with this horrible object, from low farms,
> poor pelting villages, sheep-cotes and mills,
> sometime with lunatic bans, sometime with prayers,
> enforce their charity.

Like an abused child this unformed young man does not protest or ask why, but takes the sin upon himself. He tests it out:

> 'Poor Turlygod!' 'Poor Tom!'
> That's something yet. Edgar I nothing am.

It is a reach-me-down identity that is yet a profound fit; and 'Edgar', the young Duke-in-Waiting, is left behind in the pile of rich clothes that he discards on the forest floor.

As so often in Shakespeare, in this great speech we find that the thought travels, that a journey of some degree is made to a new destination. It is so much more than a mere narrative set-up – a task that could have been achieved in half the time, or less. It is the dismantling of a paper-thin identity, the reconstruction of which will form, I repeat, one of the boldest, and in its outcome most significant, character journeys in Shakespeare.

Christopher Staines as Edgar, photo © Graham Burke 2012

Journey of the Mind or Masquerade?

The jury is divided on what follows. My belief is that Edgar's immersion in Poor Tom is profound. Though he has one or two moments of self-recognition, and the span of his immersion is relatively short, it seems to me that the life of Poor Tom, far from being pieced together from fancy and hearsay, actually wells up from within him, from the chaos and bewilderment that has come from rejection and denial by his father ('I never got him', says Gloucester) and by the abandonment of his name. Poor Tom is but the first of a series of personalities that Edgar will inhabit as he searches for the very nature of himself. Reduced to the 'poor, bare, forked animal' that is man's inheritance from Nature, Edgar is reborn in crisis and pain. So it was that in our 2012 production, with the help of some clever artificial skin, we witnessed Christopher Staines' Edgar abuse his own flesh with thorns and twigs. In contrast to this approach, the New Cambridge Edition refers to Edgar's role as Mad Tom as a 'masquerade'.[3] Shakespeare did, of course piece together much of his madness from various sources, including from these lines in Samuel Harsnett's *Declaration of Egregious Popish Impostures:*[4]

> Frateretto, Fliberdigibbet, Hoberdidance, Tocobatto were four
> devils of the round, or Morrice, whom Sara in her fits, tuned

together, in measure and sweet cadence. And least you should conceive, that the devils had no music in hell, especially that they would go a maying without their music, the Fidler comes in with his Taber, and Pipe, and a whole Morice after him, with motley visards for their better grace.

But the idea that Edgar is speaking deliberately from informed memory, like an actor, rather than spontaneously from a fevered imagination, in speeches such as these –

> Take heed o' the foul Fiend. Obey thy parents. Keep thy words justice, swear not, commit not with man's sworn spouse, set not thy sweet-heart on proud array. Tom's a-cold.
>
> LEAR. What hast thou been?
>
> EDGAR. A servingman, proud in heart and mind, that curl'd my hair, wore gloves in my cap, serv'd the lust of my mistress' heart, and did the act of darkness with her. Swore as many oaths as I spake words, and broke them in the sweet face of Heaven. One that slept in the contriving of lust, and wak'd to do it. Wine lov'd I dearly, dice dearly, and in woman out-paramour'd the Turk. False of heart, light of ear, bloody of hand. Hog in sloth, fox in stealth, wolf in greediness, dog in madness, lion in prey. Let not the creaking of shoes nor the rustling of silks betray thy poor heart to woman. Keep thy foot out of brothels, thy hand out of plackets, thy pen from lenders' books, and defy the foul Fiend. Still through the hawthorn blows the cold wind, says suum, mun, nonny, Dolphin my boy, boy, sessey! Let him trot by.
>
> Act 3 Scene 4

– is very hard, even impossible, to sustain. This version of himself is full of the guilt that he has too readily assumed; that is the spring of its vividness. There *is* a doubleness, an awareness of self that permits this aside in Act 3 Scene 6 –

> My tears begin to take his part so much,
> they mar my counterfeiting.

– and ones that will follow as he meets his blinded father and leads him to the cliff at Dover; but his madness is far deeper than a 'masquerade'. When Lear responds to him this way:

> Thou wert better in a grave than to answer with thy uncover'd body this extremity of the skies. Is man no

192

more than this? Consider him well. Thou ow'st the worm
no silk, the beast no hide, the sheep no wool, the cat no
perfume. Ha? Here's three on's are sophisticated. Thou art
the thing itself. Unaccommodated man is no more but
such a poor, bare, forked animal as thou art.

Act 3 Scene 4

it is not to a vaudeville act, but to a reality.

The Folio rightly omits the six rhyming couplets the Quarto gives to
Edgar at the end of Act 3 Scene 6, which begin:

When we our betters see bearing our woes
we scarcely think our miseries our foes…

It is a speech that requires Edgar to perform an authorial task in drawing
the two plots together, lending him a sureness of perspective that actually
diminishes his own pain and difficulty. It is wholly unnecessary and well
deserves its place on the cutting-room floor. Edgar's emergence from Mad
Tom is much more convincingly portrayed in his brief soliloquy at the
beginning of Act 4 Scene 1:

Yet better thus, and known to be contemn'd,
than still contemn'd and flatter'd. To be worst,
the low'st and most dejected thing of Fortune,
stands still in esperance, lives not in fear.
The lamentable change is from the best,
the worst returns to laughter. Welcome, then,
thou unsubstantial air that I embrace.
The wretch that thou hast blown unto the worst
owes nothing to thy blasts.

With another huge shock sustained – the appearance of his blinded father,
led by the Old Man –

O Gods! Who is't can say 'I am at the worst'?
I am worse than e'er I was.

– he will maintain his guise as Mad Tom for a while longer, but only with
great difficulty:

Poor Tom's a cold. I cannot daub it further.

Some commentators struggle with his choice not to reveal his true identity,
as if he is as well informed of Edmond's treachery as we are and so should
seize a golden opportunity to be reconciled to his penitent father –
a reconciliation that would, to some degree, repair them both. Again, this

193

is to underestimate the depths of despair and bewilderment – the sense of *not being Edgar* – to which he has been reduced. At the end of the scene he says to his father –

> Give me thy arm.
> Poor Tom shall lead thee.

– the simplest of speeches, yet redolent of both compassion and questioning: who are we, what is our relationship, where are we going?

Arriving at, or near to, the south coast, it dawns on Gloucester that his companion no longer speaks like Mad Tom:

> Methinks thy voice is alter'd, and thou speak'st
> in better phrase and matter than thou didst.
> EDGAR. You're much deceiv'd. In nothing am I chang'd
> but in my garments.
> GLOUCESTER. Methinks you're better spoken.
>
> Act 4 Scene 5

But it seems that Edgar still needs to postpone recognition by choosing this spot to serve as the cliff from which his father has determined to fall. It is likely he has planned the deception but has shrunk from enacting it, for fear of its consequences. But now the alternative consequence – the revelation of his true identity – is the greater fear. He throws himself into an extraordinarily well-conjured description of an abyss of both beauty and terror:

> Come on, sir, here's the place. Stand still. How fearful
> and dizzy 'tis to cast one's eyes so low.
> The crows and choughs that wing the midway air
> show scarce so gross as beetles. Half way down
> hangs one that gathers samphire, dreadful trade.
> Methinks he seems no bigger than his head.
> The fishermen, that walk upon the beach,
> appear like mice, and yond tall anchoring bark,
> diminish'd to her cock, her cock a buoy
> almost too small for sight. The murmuring surge,
> that on th' unnumber'd idle pebble chafes
> cannot be heard so high…

And then he places his father at the edge of a precipice that is no precipice at all, and once again Shakespeare is lured into making Edgar his own commentator:

> EDGAR. [*Aside*] Why I do trifle with his despair
> is done to cure it.

His purpose will become apparent soon enough. The scene is the more powerful without the line, for by making Edgar's intention rationally explicit, it merely invites the criticism that this is all entirely unnecessary. Played at a more instinctive level, provoked by his desire to both oblige his father and preserve him, and with a deep-seated fear of revelation – perhaps even of a second rejection – the action proves more comprehensible, more humanly muddled in intent.

Gloucester falls to the ground, and Edgar reaches for a second clearly inhabited character, one of the fishermen he had imagined walking on the beach:

> What are you, sir?
>
> GLOUCESTER.   Away, and let me die.
>
> EDGAR. Hadst thou been aught but gossamer, feathers, air,
>   so many fathom down precipitating,
>   thou'dst shiver'd like an egg. But thou dost breathe,
>   hast heavy substance, bleed'st not, speak'st, art sound.

He is now more comfortably an actor, picking a simple seaman's metaphor to describe the extent of Gloucester's fall:

> Ten masts at each make not the altitude
> which thou hast perpendicularly fell.
> Thy life's a miracle.

And now Edgar finally bids farewell to Mad Tom, as he describes the figure he saw standing with Gloucester on the top of the cliff as a fiend tempting the old man to the sin of suicide:

> … methought his eyes
> were two full moons. He had a thousand noses,
> horns whelk'd and wav'd like the enraged sea.
> It was some fiend. Therefore, thou happy father,
> think that the clearest gods, who make them honours
> of men's impossibilities, have preserv'd thee.

His purpose – at least temporarily – is achieved:

> GLOUCESTER. I do remember now. Henceforth I'll bear
>   affliction till it do cry out itself
>   'Enough, enough,' and die. That thing you speak of,
>   I took it for a man. Often 'twould say
>   'The Fiend, the Fiend!' He led me to that place.
>
> EDGAR. Bear free and patient thoughts.

At this point the deranged Lear appears and he and Gloucester have their painful reunion, Shakespeare again employing Edgar, somewhat unnecessarily, as a spokesman for our own feelings (we again cut some of them out). Then when Lear runs from the search party Cordelia has sent to find him, Gloucester asks of Edgar – perhaps believing him to be a fisherman, perhaps suspecting all is not as it seems:

> Now, good sir, what are you?

In the repeated offer of his hand, Edgar moves closer to revelation, but still holds back from it:

> A most poor man, made tame to Fortune's blows,
> who by the art of known and feeling sorrows
> am pregnant to good pity. Give me your hand,
> I'll lead you to some biding.

But Oswald's entrance forestalls their exit. The Oswald sequence will be key to the design of the dénouement, but will also allow Edgar to adopt yet another persona, one in which he will flex his muscles as a champion and grow in confidence and authority. Armed only with a cudgel, but with a liberating zest for language, he defends his father, whom Oswald views as a 'proclaimed prize':

> OSWALD. Wherefore, bold peasant,
>   dar'st thou support a publish'd traitor? Hence,
>   lest that th' infection of his fortune take
>   like hold on thee. Let go his arm.
>
> EDGAR. Ch'ill not let go, zir, without vurther 'casion.
>
> OSWALD. Let go, slave, or thou diest.
>
> EDGAR. Good gentleman, go your gait, and let poor volk pass. An
>   chud ha' bin zwagger'd out of my life, 'twould not ha' bin zo
>   long as 'tis by a vortnight. Nay, come not near th' old man.
>   Keep out, che vor ye, or ise try whether your costard or my
>   ballow be the harder. Ch'ill be plain with you.
>
> OSWALD. Out, dunghill!
>
> EDGAR. Ch'ill pick your teeth, zir. Come, no matter vor your foins.

They fight, and Edgar kills Oswald. He then finds Goneril's incriminating letter to Edmond. He determines to take it to Albany, and for a third time offers his hand to his father:

Give me your hand.
Far off methinks I hear the beaten drum.
Come, father, I'll bestow you with a friend.

The repetition in the words and the gesture – 'give me your hand' – highlights Edgar's progress. He knows now who he is, and what he must do. His 'father' is not his first use – the term is a polite form of address by a young man to an old one – but may now suggest an easy negligence towards his disguise.

His Metaphorical Resonance

Out of his Dover odyssey Edgar recreates himself as a man competent to challenge Edmond to combat; and the articulation of that challenge is deeply impressive:

> Draw thy sword,
> that if my speech offend a noble heart
> thy arm may do thee justice. Here is mine.
> Behold, it is my privilege,
> the privilege of mine honours,
> my oath, and my profession. I protest –
> maugre thy strength, place, youth and eminence,
> despite thy victor-sword and fire-new fortune,
> thy valour and thy heart – thou art a traitor,
> false to thy gods, thy brother and thy father,
> conspirant 'gainst this high illustrious prince,
> and from the extremest upward of thy head
> to the descent and dust below thy foot
> a most toad-spotted traitor. Say thou 'no',
> this sword, this arm, and my best spirits are bent
> to prove upon thy heart, whereto I speak,
> thou liest.

Act 5 Scene 3

The balanced phrasing, the powerful rhythms and the confidently rooted judgements declare that not only has Edgar arrived at an active and capable maturity but that this whole landscape of chaos and brutality has carried within it the seeds of hope and renewal. Edmond, who once, in contrast to Edgar, seemed so extraordinarily vivid – and powerful – now seems shrill and boastful in his own defence:

In wisdom I should ask thy name,
but since thy outside looks so fair and warlike
and that thy tongue some say of breeding breathes,
what safe and nicely I might well delay
by rule of knighthood, I disdain and spurn.
Back do I toss these treasons to thy head,
with the hell-hated lie o'erwhelm thy heart,
which, for they yet glance by and scarcely bruise,
this sword of mine shall give them instant way,
where they shall rest for ever. Trumpets, speak!

In his book, *Shakespeare's Fathers and Daughters*,[5] Oliver Ford Davies notes, correctly, that this exchange is frequently heavily cut. This is a fundamental mistake, losing the metaphorical resonance in the two men's contrasting sounds and the trial of strength that follows. The clash of speech should be felt as of equal moment to the clash of steel; and our own fight directors – Kate Waters in 2000 and John Sandeman in 2012 – both choreographed the duel to reflect the two men's contrasting rhythms and diction in action.

I claimed at the beginning of this account that Edgar's journey is one of the most significant in Shakespeare. That is because it is more than one of individual psychology; he embodies the necessary renewal of the state; the state that has become, like Lear himself, sclerotic, its language a false currency, an impediment rather than an aid to human relationships. For this monumental play – that in its final moments repudiates the comic model in which the old are successfully confronted by youth (think Egeus and Hermia in *A Midsummer Night's Dream*), in which tyrants who appropriate law are converted to humility (think 'bad Duke' Frederick in *As You Like It*), and the vigour and promise of new life and the cohesion of community is celebrated in marriage (think any number of comedies) – offers instead a tragic vision of the world in which the aged survive to lock down the energies of those that would challenge them, and silence those that would criticise them; who as they age grow ever more brittle, fearful and paranoid and at the last split apart, sometimes only to release into the world in their place those they have abused and damaged. In such a scenario a cyclical conception of the state is born, in which the new beginning becomes not optional, but inevitable; and in which the job of recreation is both necessary and awesomely difficult: the burden that Malcolm shrinks from in *Macbeth*, the task that Edgar sets about at the end of this play knowing only that the start must be in plainspeaking, in saying 'what we feel, not what we ought to say', a line that takes us right back to the beginning of the play, to Lear's demand for declarations of love and Goneril and Regan's meaningless compliance.

It is a huge journey from an insubstantial and bewildered beginning. 'One of Shakespeare's most unfathomable characters' Michael Billington once bizarrely remarked of Edgar;[6] on the contrary, one of the boldest of Shakespeare's creations, and one of the greatest of all opportunities for an actor.

Production Notes

Setting: I believe this play is moved forward over the centuries only at considerable thematic cost, while it is utterly counter-productive to take it back to its supposed historical and pre-Christian moment around the time of the creation of Rome. So in both our productions (in 2000, with Roland Oliver as Lear, and 2012 with John Shrapnel), I and my designers (James Helps and Harriet de Winton) chose early Jacobean settings. In 2012, however, Harriet and I decided that the Jacobean image should break down as society fragmented, and we introduced more modern elements to the battlefield, losing the hierarchies always retained in Jacobean warfare; and when we finally found Lear in the care of Cordelia's doctor, he was sitting in a modern wheelchair.

Eleanor Yates as Cordelia and John Shrapnel as Lear, photo © Graham Burke 2012

But when Simon Armstrong's Kent re-entered, as himself, in the last scene, he had reassumed his original court costume, striking an anachronistic figure and emphasising, by contrast, the more basic nature of the human interactions on which Edgar's new society would be built. In Kent's 'I have a journey, sir, shortly to go. My master calls me, I must not say no' we finally bade farewell to Lear's world.

Edmond: Edmond's 'Thou, Nature, art my goddess' soliloquy arrives unheralded and seemingly coincidentally with the opening action of the play. In 2012 we had him present during the first scene (acting as the court's stenographer), and the speech – and his stratagem against Edgar – arose as if prompted in that moment by Cordelia's disobedience, and the fracturing of the family and the state. Forging the letter from Edgar at the same time as delivering one of Shakespeare's most famous speeches was far from easy, but Jack Whitam carried it off with aplomb. The ink was still wet, of course, as he affected to hide the letter from his father.

1. Fourth Estate, 1999.

2, Picador, 1997.

3. Cambridge University Press, 2005, ed. Jay L. Halio.

4. A book commissioned by the Anglican Church and published in 1603. It was the fruit of an inquiry into public exorcisms performed by Catholic priests in Denham, Buckinghamshire in the 1580s.

5. Bloomsbury, 2017.

6. *Guardian*, 26 August 2016. On an earlier occasion he had termed it 'near-unplayable'.

Chapter Five

The Unstable Text

I then observed Shakspeare [*sic*] standing between Betterton
and Booth, and deciding a difference between those two great
actors concerning the placing an accent in one of his lines: this
was disputed on both sides with a warmth which surprised me
in Elysium, till I discovered by intuition that every soul
retained its principal characteristic, being, indeed, its very
essence. The line was that celebrated one in *Othello* –

Put out the light, and then put out the light,

according to Betterton. Mr Booth contended to have it thus:

Put out the light, and then put out THE light.

I could not help offering my conjecture on this occasion, and
suggested it might perhaps be –

Put out the light, and then put out THY light.

Another hinted a reading very sophisticated in my opinion –

Put out the light, and then put out THEE, light,

making light to be the vocative case. Another would have
altered the last word, and read –

Put out thy light, and then put out thy sight.

But Betterton said, if the text was to be disturbed, he saw no
reason why a word might not be changed as well as a letter,
and, instead of 'put out thy light,' you may read 'put out thy
eyes.' At last it was agreed on all sides to refer the matter to the
decision of Shakspeare himself, who delivered his sentiments
as follows: 'Faith, gentlemen, it is so long since I wrote the line,

I have forgot my meaning. This I know, could I have dreamt so much nonsense would have been talked and writ about it, I would have blotted it out of my works; for I am sure, if any of these be my meaning, it doth me very little honour.

Henry Fielding, *A Journey from this World to the Next* (1749)

Hamlet

I have written already about some textual choices my company has made in plays that enjoy only a single Folio text. Those choices were entirely voluntary, but where more than one text has been handed down to us, choosing between versions is unavoidable. I begin this last chapter by looking at the disputed provenance of the three main Hamlet texts that we have, and then move on to look at how their differences affect key issues of interpretation and casting; and, finally, I question the failure of moral judgement that we so often see in responses to this play.

His Three Texts

The absence of secure texts of Shakespeare's plays has sustained an editorial industry over four centuries, much of it concerned with detail – should we read 'precise' in preference to 'prenzie', 'solid' in place of 'sullied' (or 'sallied'), or 'Innogen in place of 'Imogen'?[1] – but there have been much larger arguments, including about collaborative authorship and the nature of genius itself.

Hamlet has accumulated by far the greatest wealth of editorial material, not only because it is the best known and most commonly admired play in world theatre, but because its structure and provenance have been relentlessly questioned and debated. It may even be that its popularity stems in part from its portfolio of ambiguities and puzzles; it sets directors and actors the delicious task of bringing it into focus, of finding new insights and emphases, of making it their own. These thoughts of mine will be threaded with questions – and doubts – about the choices I made myself in 2016, and with speculation as to why this great play is in some narrative respects such a mess. 'Mess' is perhaps bold of me; for a contra view I recommend a book now over ninety years old, but still in print and still widely read in schools and universities: John Dover Wilson's *What Happens in Hamlet.*[2] Dover Wilson makes a case for Shakespeare's 'master-craftsmanship' in the Second Quarto text of the play and refutes almost every imaginable criticism of the play's construction. I will refer to his judgements repeatedly, as the most complete expression of a major strand in *Hamlet* interpretation, and one that, although it may have been superseded in academic circles, still reflects dominant attitudes to the play in the theatre.

The puzzles in the play are many, and will never be conclusively resolved; but, as I say, practitioners must make choices. In addressing those choices myself, I have found the trail so often leading back to provenance; how did the *Hamlet* we know come about, and to what degree can it be said that any of the extant texts are the play as Shakespeare would have recorded it for posterity, had he troubled to manage his literary legacy? Any company should look into this at least briefly, so I will begin with a short summary of the play's principal versions.

In the main they are these: the 'First Quarto' (Q1), commonly known as the 'Bad Quarto',[3] published in 1603; the 'Second Quarto' (Q2) – believed to have been printed from Shakespeare's working papers – published in 1604/5; and the 'First Folio' (F1), probably taken from a revised theatre copy by the two members of Shakespeare's company, John Heminges and Henry Condell, who edited the first collected edition of the plays, published in 1623. Further quarto editions are based on Q2, and further folios are revisions of F1.

There are two further, fairly early texts of relatively minor significance. The 'Players' Quarto' is a cut version of Q2 and has a claim to Shakespearean authenticity as it was prepared for Sir William Davenant's productions at the Duke of York's Theatre following the 1660 Restoration. It was believed that Davenant was Shakespeare's godson, even – by some – his natural son; but he was only ten years old when Shakespeare died, so any notion that he was well apprised of Shakespeare's textual intentions in *Hamlet* is a little far-fetched on that basis. A stronger argument may be that Davenant's Hamlet was Thomas Betterton, and Betterton knew Joseph Taylor who had succeeded Richard Burbage as the King's Men's Hamlet; so there was a possible line of inheritance there in approaches to the play and the part.

The other early text is a German version of the story, *Der Bestrafter Brudermord* (*Fratricide Punished*), published in 1781 from a manuscript (now lost) dated 1710. The play is in prose, contains knockabout comedy and is introduced by a Senecan Prologue in which Night orders the three Furies to revenge the murder of Old Hamlet. Its provenance and relationship to Shakespeare's play is yet another area for voluminous speculation, but it seems almost certain that its author had some cognisance of the original Shakespeare texts.

To put those last two versions aside, the version generally regarded as the full, genuine article is Q2, and – except where indicated otherwise – that is the version I shall quote from in this chapter. That the widely derided Q1 was *published* earlier than Q2 we have known for four centuries, but only because of the implication of this sentence on Q2's title page:

> Newly imprinted and enlarged to almost as much
> againe as it was, according to the true and perfect
> Coppie.

Q1's actual text was lost, and only came to light in 1823 when Sir Henry Bunbury discovered a copy in the Manor House of Great Barton in Suffolk. That may sound like the discovery of a crucial clue in an Agatha Christie novel, but it happens to be true. A second copy then turned up over thirty years later in a Dublin bookshop. They remain the only two copies known.

How long Q1 had been lost we cannot know; but it seems almost certain that the first post-Restoration editors – Rowe, Pope, Theobald, Johnson, Capell, Malone and others – were ignorant of it. And so in 1823 its peculiar readings, not least its version of the 'To be or not to be' speech, came as a rude shock –

> To be, or not to be, ay, there's the point.
> To die, to sleep, is that all? Ay, all.
> No, to sleep, to dream – ay, marry, there it goes,
> for in that dream of death, when we awake,
> and borne before an everlasting judge,
> from whence no passenger ever returned,
> the undiscovered country, at whose sight
> the happy smile, and the accursèd damned –
> but for this, the joyful hope of this,
> who'd bear the scorns and flattery of the world,
> scorned by the right rich, the rich cursed of the poor,
> the widow being oppressed, the orphan wronged,
> the taste of hunger, or a tyrant's reign,
> and thousand more calamities besides,
> to grunt and sweat under this weary life,
> when that he may his full quietus make
> with a bare bodkin? Who would this endure,
> but for a hope of something after death,
> which puzzles the brain, and doth confound the sense,
> which makes us rather bear those evils we have
> than fly to others that we know not of?

> Ay, that. Oh, this conscience makes cowards of us all. –
> Lady, in thy orisons be all my sins remembered.

– and it led to the text as a whole being derided by many of its new readers. To its fiercest critics ('garbled rubbish' was one verdict) it belongs with those lambasted in the preface to the First Folio as 'stol'n and surreptitious copies, maimed and deformed by frauds and stealths of injurious impostors'.

Q1 certainly has many lines that sound unworthy of, or simply unlike, the Shakespeare we know. Little more than half the length of Q2 – about 17,000 words against Q2's almost 32,000 – it frequently feels truncated, like the crudest of cuts, and yet it also differs, sometimes consistently, from Q2 in ways that suggest that passages of it may relate to other – my guess is earlier – manuscripts or versions of the Hamlet story. Only in this sense is Q1 really of more than academic interest. Can it shed light on some of the knottier mysteries of Q2? In one or two instances I think it can, and so I am going to pause again to summarise the most vigorously championed theories about Q1's status:

'**Bad Quarto**' theory: first fully developed over eighty years ago by G.I. Duthie in *The Bad Quarto of Hamlet*,[4] this argues that Q1, though published earlier, in composition *postdates* Q2, and is a pirated version of the play which Shakespeare's company may have first performed in 1600; that it is a poor 'memorial reconstruction' of the as yet unpublished 'official' text, probably by the actor who had performed Marcellus and doubled as Lucianus, since these characters' scenes seem to be accurately remembered, while the others are not. This actor, the argument runs, might have worked freelance for Shakespeare's company, and then on finishing his contract sold his inaccurate recollection to the eager publisher.

'**Evolution**' theory: this involves reference to an even earlier play, the text of which has never been found. This is the so-called '*Ur-Hamlet*', some suggest by Thomas Kyd, others that it was Shakespeare's own first attempt. We know that it existed, and had been performed by the Chamberlain's Men (possibly in a co-production with Henslowe's Admiral's Men), at Newington Butts in 1594, and there are references to it as early as 1589. Shakespeare may well have played in it himself in 1594, alongside Richard Burbage and Will Kemp. This would have been six or seven years before the time when the play as we know it was written and first produced.

This theory has it that Shakespeare evolved his famous play from this earlier one (be it his own, or Kyd's, or some other writer's work) rather than starting afresh in perhaps 1599 and working directly from the source in Belleforest's *The Hystorie of Hamblet*.[5] This would make Q1 just a stage in a relatively long evolution. It was hurried into print, perhaps even at the company's own instigation, but before the evolution was complete. Q2 quickly followed in 1604 in an attempt to erase the memory of that unsatisfactory, transitional version. F1 followed nearly twenty years later and represents the text, substantially cut for performance, though it also offers lines unknown to Q1 and Q2 and many different word and line-readings.

'Alternative Version' theory: this argues that Q1 may be a poorly printed but otherwise fairly accurate record of a version of the play that was edited and modified from the form of the 1600 Globe production of Q2 in order to be toured with a reduced company; one of its peculiarities is that, while it refers to attendant lords and others, it gives no speeches at all to lords, servants, messengers, sailors or soldiers.

The attention the academic world has paid to this question has been colossal, involving minute examination of all the texts, their variations and interrelations, and I won't pretend to have studied more than a tiny fraction of the analyses and commentaries that it has spawned in the UK and America. But it must be true to say that 'Bad Quarto' theory holds sway now, as it has done ever since Duthie's book. The programme note for the 2010 National Theatre production stated: 'The First Quarto... was a pirate edition, heavily truncated and possibly transcribed (badly) by the actor who played Marcellus at the Globe.' And James Shapiro has gone even further:

> one or more of those involved in the touring production,
> including the hired actor who played Marcellus (we know it
> was this actor because in putting the text together he
> remembered his own lines a lot better than he did anyone
> else's) cobbled together from memory a 2,200 line version of
> the road production and sold it to publishers in London.[6]

Here Shapiro not only supports 'poor memorial reconstruction' but implies that the recording actor was remembering not the Globe production of Q2 but the significantly adapted or shortened touring version of Q2 imagined by 'alternative version' theory. A leading academic's presentation of a double hypothesis as fact I find a little surprising.

For the 'Piracy' hypothesis – attractive though it is in many respects – provokes a number of questions. Why are Q1's Polonius and Reynaldo called 'Corambis' and 'Montano'? Why do some of the supposedly garbled passages make sense on their own terms? Why is Gertrude's behaviour sometimes closer to *The Hystorie of Hamblet* than to Q2? (In Belleforest, at the end of the 'closet' scene, Hamlet and Gertrude agree to combine to revenge the death of Old Hamlet. This is replicated in Q1 and leads to a scene between Horatio and Gertrude of some thirty-five lines in which Horatio acts as a go-between between Hamlet and his mother. None of this is in Shakespeare's play as we perform it.) Why did the reputable publishers, Nicholas Ling and John Trundell, agree to print a version of a celebrated play that they must have known was 'pirated' from the work of the leading theatre company of the day – and poorly pirated into the bargain? These are among many questions provoked by the 'Bad Quarto' theory. Speculation is heaped upon speculation. Proponents explain away 'Corambis' and 'Montano' by noting that Q1's title page refers to performances 'in the two universities of Cambridge and Oxford'. One of Oxford University's honoured founders was Robert Pullen, whose Latin name was 'Polenius'. In Shakespeare's time the President of Corpus Christi College was John Rainolds (or Reynolds), well-known for his enmity to the theatre. Thus the changes of name from 'Polonius' and 'Reynaldo' were conceived specifically for that performance in order to avoid offence. Well, *maybe…*

But the 'Alternative Version' theory is even more suspect, particularly when it is advocated as a touring version designed to be played by members of Shakespeare's company to unsophisticated provincials – presumably including those ignorant Oxbridge students. It is not just the patronising assumption behind this; the idea that a single company of actors could carry about in their heads two versions of the same play that diverged in a thousand or more details, while agreeing in countless others, is sheer fantasy. A heavily cut version could be managed, yes, but a widely altered one, no.

The mysteries connected to the development of the *Hamlet* we know as Q2 are also internal to that text. Why is it almost impossibly long – one question, incidentally, that Dover Wilson, in his master craftsman argument, signally fails to address? We know that Shakespeare's company was allowed a three-hour window in which to perform and then clear the house at the Globe (by 5 p.m.), so perhaps twenty per cent of the Q2 text, or even more, would have had to be cut. Even the full First Folio version, which may well represent something more like the performed version of the play, is only about 1,500 words shorter than Q2, still considerably longer than any other play in the Folio and a huge text to cram into less than three hours.

There are also narrative issues. Why create an image in the opening scene of an Elsinore in panic at an impending invasion – all that expenditure on brazen cannon, the impress of shipwrights 'whose sore task does not divide the Sunday from the week' – only, as the new day dawns, to present Claudius as completely in control of public events and able to resolve the crisis, if that is what it is, with one stiff letter to Fortinbras' uncle? Why create a similar situation later in the play (Q1 is innocent of this one), when briefly it seems the Danish state is threatened by a revolutionary mob, only to forget that mob in a matter of minutes, the King not even bothering to dispatch a flunkey to cool their fury? This is not great dramaturgy. And there other examples of dubious plotting that I will detail later.

And, above all, there are key character issues – about Hamlet's age, the nature of his 'madness', and the cast of his mind and supposed 'delay'. I will introduce these briefly in turn, before looking at key moments in his journey.

Hamlet's Age

The clearest clue to Hamlet's age – in the sense of putting an actual number on it – comes late in the play in Q2, in the graveyard scene, Act 5 Scene 1. The Sexton says he has been Sexton 'man and boy thirty years' and that he came to the job 'that very day that young Hamlet was born'. He also claims that Yorick's skull 'hath lyen you i'th'earth twenty-three years'. As Hamlet remembers being carried on Yorick's back as a small child, this corroborates the idea of a thirty-year-old Hamlet. This has long been taken as textual authority for casting Hamlet as a mature man. Leading actors can usually lose a few years on stage, so Albert Finney in the 1976 NT production, David Tennant in the RSC's 2008 production, and Benedict Cumberbatch when he played it at the Barbican in 2015 were all in their very late thirties. But there are contrary indications. Laertes' 'violet in the youth of primy nature' suggests a much younger Hamlet, perhaps even an adolescent; as does the naivety of his love letter to Ophelia, and a current university career, seventeen or eighteen being a more common age for entry to university in Shakespeare's day[7] than thirty or thirty-five.

In contrast to the castings above, in 1965 at Stratford Peter Hall cast the twenty-four-year-old David Warner as Hamlet; in 2004 at London's Old Vic Trevor Nunn cast the twenty-three-year-old Ben Whishaw, pretty much fresh from RADA; I followed suit in 2016 by casting the twenty-three-year-old Alan Mahon; and in that year, too, Greg Doran cast the twenty-five-year-old Paapa Essiedu for the RSC (shortly after he had given a blazing Romeo for stf in a production by Polina Kalinina). The only authority for *that* choice lies in Q1, which does not include the 'man and boy thirty years' line and has an alternative version of the line about Yorick's skull:

> Look you, here's a skull hath been here this dozen year.

Of course Yorick could still have carried the young Hamlet on his back nearly thirty years earlier (he may have spent years in retirement); but there is nothing in the Q1 scene to prompt the definition of Hamlet as a thirty-year-old man.

Does Hamlet's age matter? Dover Wilson thinks not –

> Hamlet's age... possesses no theatrical importance, since
> Hamlet is the age his impersonator makes him...

– and the theatre, over centuries, has concurred. It has gone further, making the actor's status almost the only arbiter in casting. Providing the actor has a command over us, the presence and charisma to embrace us, versions of him, such as Ophelia's

> The courtier's, soldier's, scholar's, eye, tongue, sword;
> th' expectation and rose of the fair state,
> the glass of fashion and the mould of form...
>
> Act 3 Scene 1

are diminished, barely heard. Casting practice supposes he need not conform to any element of this description – except, perhaps, the scholar – nor to Laertes' 'violet in the youth of primy nature', nor to Claudius' 'his youth and haviour' (Act 2 Scene 2).

In the theatre, name, reputation and charisma have almost always dictated the casting of Hamlet; and many leading actors have continued to play the role, as of right, for decades. Edwin Booth, for example, played it for over three decades, Betterton and Garrick both for four.

But I believe Hamlet's age matters crucially – as does some degree of accordance with Ophelia's description – and later in this account I will attempt to explain why. To add a speculation of my own, could it be relevant that Richard Burbage, who we know was Shakespeare's Q2 Hamlet in 1601, was thirty-four at the time? By then he had been the company's leading actor for some years; could he have first laid claim to the role in the lost 'Ur' text at Newington Butts in 1594 at the age of twenty-seven, or perhaps even in 1589 when he was only twenty-two?

His 'Madness'

Turning now to his 'madness', did Shakespeare intend this to be real or feigned? Or sometimes one, sometimes the other? The Belleforest source is unequivocal: it is public knowledge that Claudius ('Fengon' in Belleforest, but to avoid confusion I use Shakespeare's character names) has murdered Hamlet's father so Hamlet *feigns* madness – simple-mindedness, actually – to protect himself from the likelihood that Claudius will consider him a potential avenger and murder him as well. By behaving like an idiot Hamlet demonstrates that he is incapable of posing a threat to anyone. Meanwhile, coolly and rationally, and over a long period, he plots a revenge against the whole, complicit court that he will eventually carry out with devastating success. Could the notion of Shakespeare's Hamlet feigning madness ('as I perchance hereafter shall think meet to put an antic disposition on') be simply a hangover from that source text, or from its successor, the '*Ur-Hamlet*'? If not, then what is its purpose?

In my 2016 production, we cut the 'antic disposition' line, not to banish the *possibility* of feigned madness, only its *necessity*; if you like, to remove the headline. We would take Hamlet's behaviour on its merits, line by line, moment by moment. And as we advanced through the play Alan Mahon and I found we talked less and less of a premeditated feigning, more and more of distinct and immediate emotional responses to Polonius, to Ophelia, to Rosencrantz and Guildenstern, to Gertrude, and to Claudius. In this we were completely at one with T.S. Eliot's view that 'the levity of Hamlet, his repetition of phrase, his puns, are not part of a deliberate plan of dissimulation, but a form of emotional relief'.[8]

Dover Wilson's view – and I have no doubt that he would have been outraged at our cut – was that Shakespeare's Hamlet adopted the 'antic disposition', not to divert suspicion of a threat to Claudius, but to provoke it, to alert his uncle that he had him in his sights. This is intimately bound up with Dover Wilson's certainty that both 'Old' and 'Young' Hamlets have been usurped by Claudius, a view that discounts the difference between royal succession in Denmark and in England. Denmark's was, until 1660, an elective monarchy, in which the crown passed almost always to a relative of the deceased king (and always a male), but not necessarily to his eldest son; it could well be to a brother (like Claudius), or even to a younger son. The electorate was the immediate court circle; their choice was then put to representatives of the people for ratification. Some commentators relate Hamlet's 'popped in between the election and my hopes' to this historical fact, which makes Claudius' accession perfectly acceptable to the court – assuming it is ignorant of the regicide he has committed – and moreover perfectly understandable if Hamlet is a late adolescent rather than a mature man. Dover Wilson gives that argument very short shrift, claiming that Claudius' actions must be judged by Elizabethan norms and that the whole court must be considered complicit in an illegal usurpation. The virtual silence on the matter, apart from Hamlet's reference above to his hopes, and his later one to lacking advancement, Dover Wilson attributes to the very obviousness of the fact; the usurpation is the unmentionable 'elephant in the room'. Julia Reinhard Lupton[9] is only one current academic commentator to reject that argument, citing the further reference in the play – Hamlet's own 'I do prophesy the election lights on Fortinbras: he has my dying voice' – as a third allusion to the Danish sytem of succession. What's more, if Dover Wilson were right, then the lack of clarity about that political reality would, in my view, be one more argument against his 'master craftsmanship' argument.

His Melancholy

The matter of Hamlet's cast of mind – often defined as 'melancholic' – and the delay in revenging his father's murder commonly attributed to it, are not only at the heart of the interpretation of this play, but raise a very general question about how Shakespeare views his characters and their worlds.

Hamlet's melancholy has often been presumed to be a baseline factor in his personality, and to predate the death of his father, the first spring of the play's action. Historically, this has been supported by the generally accepted idea that in Shakespeare's time melancholy was believed to be a pathological condition resulting from too much 'black bile' in the blood. Modern scholarship has modified that perception, crediting sixteenth- and seventeenth-century diagnosis with a more complex and dynamic model, in which contextual and environmental factors also played their part. But the theatre has remained attached to its image of the 'melancholy Dane', rather as it has persisted in its image of Chekhov's characters being umbilically attached to a languorous *ennui*.

Both images should be challenged. In the case of my own experience of Shakespeare, it is that he habitually writes about *us*. Not in the sense that we are all Scottish Thanes, Danish Princes or Egyptian Queens, but that he places human beings, with capacities, like us, for both vice and virtue, with manifold ambitions, emotions and needs, into contexts – frequently extreme or unusual contexts – to which they respond, often in extreme, though rarely ever in inexplicable ways. I do not need to diagnose Hamlet as idiosyncratically and pathologically melancholic to understand his behaviour – his hesitation, his introspection – in the extreme circumstances of this play. But I do need to see him as a very young man, for the very reason that if he is thirty or more then I would indeed have to reach to pathology to explain his behaviour towards Ophelia and his mother. Of course, that may be perfectly legitimate; but then it demands of us perhaps the greatest choice we have to make: is the play *Hamlet* an exploration of a very particular personality, or of a very particular world as experienced by a highly intelligent and sensitive but otherwise representative psyche? The 'case' study is for me far less interesting, and significant, than the interaction between the individual and his or her circumstance – the prison that is Elsinore for Hamlet, the freedom that is the forest for Rosalind and Orlando, the inhuman law that entraps both Isabella and Claudio. Yes, some of these elements well up from within – the panic within Laertes and Polonius, and the remorse at the loss of innocence in Leontes and Polixenes, are prime examples – but they are elements held in common and culturally conditioned; they are not examples of purely idiosyncratic temperament.

Apart from his questionable interpretation of the political realities, Dover Wilson makes almost no mention of Hamlet's 'world', and shows little interest in Act 1 Scene 3 – the Laertes/Polonius/Ophelia trio – which I have already suggested is, in part, a searing diagnosis of the mind of Elsinore. For Dover Wilson, the world is a given, Hamlet's personality the beginning and the end of his interest. Such has been a powerful strand in *Hamlet* interpretation and production across the centuries.

Hamlet's Journey

These are among the issues I will attempt to pursue in looking at just a few key moments in Hamlet's journey. We first encounter him in the second scene of the play:

> CLAUDIUS.... Take thy fair hour, Laertes, time be thine,
> and thy best graces spend it at thy will.
> But now, my cousin Hamlet, and my son.

Shakespeare introduces him with extraordinary economy, with a quick, mordant wit (we may choose between a quick aside and a direct rebuke):

> HAMLET. A little more than kin, and less than kind.
>
> CLAUDIUS. How is it that the clouds still hang on you?
>
> HAMLET. Not so much, my lord; I am too much in the sun.

Claudius' question may well be more heavily freighted than a mere 'why are you still sad?', but it is deftly parried by Hamlet, and Gertrude steps in with a thought that is either simply sincere, or – given the guilt she must feel about her remarriage (see below) – the only version of reality that she can contemplate, which is that Hamlet suffers only from an inappropriately excessive grief:

> Good Hamlet, cast thy nighted colour off,
> and let thine eye look like a friend on Denmark.
> Do not for ever with thy vailed lids
> seek for thy noble father in the dust.
> Thou know'st 'tis common, all that lives must die,
> passing through nature to eternity.

HAMLET. Ay, madam, it is common.

GERTRUDE.   If it be,
> why seems it so particular with thee?

HAMLET. Seems, madam? Nay it is. I know not 'seems'.
> 'Tis not alone my inky cloak, good mother,
> nor customary suits of solemn black,
> nor windy suspiration of forc'd breath,
> no, nor the fruitful river in the eye,
> nor the dejected 'haviour of the visage,
> together with all forms, moods, shapes of grief,
> that can denote me truly. These indeed seem,
> for they are actions that a man might play,
> but I have that within which passes show,
> these but the trappings and the suits of woe.

Here he has given the heaviest of hints that far more is amiss than the loss of his father, but Claudius is either deaf to it, or chooses to be so:

CLAUDIUS. 'Tis sweet and commendable in your nature, Hamlet,
> to give these mourning duties to your father:
> but, you must know, your father lost a father;
> that father lost, lost his, and the survivor bound
> in filial obligation for some term
> to do obsequious sorrow. But to persever
> in obstinate condolement is a course
> of impious stubbornness; 'tis unmanly grief;
> it shows a will most incorrect to heaven,
> a heart unfortified, or mind impatient;
> an understanding simple and unschool'd;
> for what we know must be and is as common
> as any the most vulgar thing to sense,

> why should we in our peevish opposition
> take it to heart?…

In however gently avuncular a tone Claudius attempts to preface these thoughts, he cannot long hide the iron fist they mask. His 'man up' message goes beyond the British stiff upper lip; characterising Hamlet's grief as 'peevish' might be thought, in this relatively public arena,[10] to be deliberately humiliating, and the question that enfolds the word would be callous in any context, but Claudius is talking of his own brother and of Denmark's last monarch. He does not name him, of course. Old Hamlet is old news. This is a new regime, and the old must not even be named, let alone held vividly in the memory. Claudius then turns his attention to Hamlet's immediate plans:

> For your intent
> in going back to school in Wittenberg,
> it is most retrograde to our desire,
> and we beseech you, bend you to remain
> here, in the cheer and comfort of our eye,
> our chiefest courtier, cousin, and our son.
>
> GERTRUDE. Let not thy mother lose her prayers, Hamlet:
> I pray thee, stay with us, go not to Wittenberg.

We might ask why – apart from allowing the play to happen – Hamlet is forbidden to return to his studies in Wittenburg. The Wittenberg connection is not in Belleforest. Perhaps inherited from the *Ur-Hamlet*, is it chosen as Luther's city and the cradle of the reformation? 'In the comfort of our eye' enjoys an ambiguity as to whose comfort Claudius means; should we feel Hamlet longs to return to a city associated with a challenge to the status quo, even with revolution? Actors often take the opportunity here to openly insult Claudius by pointedly stressing the 'you' in the next line, though the subtler choice is to accept the inevitable – that Claudius' request is a barely veiled order – and to dress his acquiescence as a courteous concession to maternal desire:

> I shall in all my best obey you, madam.

Having got his way, the insensitive usurper's attention turns, without more ado, to feasting and celebration:

> Why, 'tis a loving and a fair reply.
> Be as ourself in Denmark. Madam, come,
> this gentle and unforc'd accord of Hamlet
> sits smiling to my heart; in grace whereof,

no jocund health that Denmark drinks today,
but the great cannon to the clouds shall tell,
and the King's rouse the heavens shall bruit again,
respeaking earthly thunder. Come, away.

The court party exits and Hamlet reveals to us the full burden of his spirit. There is one certain elephant in the room, which undoubtedly outweighs Dover Wilson's unspoken one and is now forcefully articulated: Gertrude's over-hasty and incestuous remarriage:

O, that this too too sallied flesh would melt,
thaw and resolve itself into a dew!
Or that the Everlasting had not fix'd
His canon 'gainst self-slaughter. O God, God,
how weary, stale, flat and unprofitable
seem to me all the uses of this world!
Fie on't, ah fie, 'tis an unweeded garden
that grows to seed; things rank and gross in nature
possess it merely. That it should come to this,
but two months dead – nay, not so much, not two –
so excellent a king, that was to this
Hyperion to a satyr; so loving to my mother
that he might not beteem the winds of heaven
visit her face too roughly. Heaven and earth,
must I remember? Why, she would hang on him,
as if increase of appetite had grown
by what it fed on, and yet, within a month –
let me not think on't, frailty, thy name is woman –
a little month, or ere those shoes were old
with which she follow'd my poor father's body,
like Niobe, all tears, why she –
O God, a beast that wants discourse of reason
would have mourn'd longer – married with my uncle,
my father's brother, but no more like my father
than I to Hercules. Within a month,
ere yet the salt of most unrighteous tears
had left the flushing in her galled eyes,
she married. O most wicked speed, to post
with such dexterity to incestuous sheets!
It is not nor it cannot come to good.
But break, my heart, for I must hold my tongue.
Enter Horatio, Marcellus, and Barnardo.

The first thing that should strike us about this magnificent soliloquy is its energy, its anger and frustration. The 'weary, stale, flat and unprofitable' world is eloquently suggestive of depression, but not one characterised – as it so often is in performance – by a reflective sadness. Hamlet rails against the world, the 'unweeded garden that grows to seed', and against his mother's almost incomprehensible behaviour. Her 'frailty' – her inconstancy, or her too-easy surrender to her sexual needs – has led her into what Hamlet rightly, according to the canon law of the times, defines as incest, a crime that 'cannot come to good'. There is an acutely painful wonder in the speech, of discovering with shocked dismay, and for the first time, the underbelly of things, an experience we associate with youth. It is the flipside to Ophelia's 'the expectancy and rose of the fair state, the glass of fashion and the mould of form' which offers us a glimpse of Hamlet before his father's death, secure and feted as a young man enjoying every blessing. Hamlet, when we first encounter him, in the aftermath of the death and the 'o'er hasty marriage', is reeling from the loss of innocence. We need not reach for pathology, for 'black bile', to comprehend that.

The final line is often wasted as having the sense of 'Someone's coming, I'd better shut up', whereas its real force is 'I am alone in this and outranked; however heartbroken I am, I am forbidden to speak of it.' In that sense at least, the Danish court is, as he will define it later to Rosencrantz and Guildenstern, Hamlet's 'prison'. The news brought to him of the Ghost of his father walking the night on the battlements provokes more questions[11] about the context of this development that I will not explore here. But the placing is crucial; Hamlet's profound distress concerns principally the behaviour of his mother and is vividly characterised *before* he is apprised by the Ghost of his uncle's crime. It will remain at the front of his mind, only to be displaced briefly, at intervals, by a commitment to revenge.

A Double Time Scheme?

The Ghost's terrible news received, we are pitched into the longstanding debate about Hamlet's 'antic disposition'. As I have already remarked, Belleforest's Hamlet plots his uncle's assassination with great care over a period of time, all the while acting the harmless idiot. Does Shakespeare's Hamlet now take time out to develop an 'antic' persona before we get Ophelia's report of his distraction in Act 2 Scene 1?

The prompt that this is the case is in the opening lines of that scene, the exchange between Polonius and Reynaldo:

POLONIUS. Give him this money and these notes, Reynaldo.
REYNALDO. I will, my lord.

> POLONIUS. You shall do marvels wisely, good Reynaldo,
>   before you visit him to make inquire
>   of his behaviour...

This suggests an intervening passage of time, since Polonius would hardly be sending Laertes money and letters only the day after he had left for Paris. Later, in the 'play scene', Ophelia suggests that it is then four months since Hamlet's father died, rather than the two months Hamlet has referred to in his first soliloquy. There seems to be no other likely placing[12] for that additional two months than here, in the gap between Act 1 Scene 5 and Act 2 Scene 1. But should we take these clues literally, or might Shakespeare be playing with a double time scheme? Could Hamlet – despite Polonius' lines to Reynaldo – have gone from his meeting with the Ghost almost directly to confront Ophelia?

The possibility of such a double time scheme has been raised many, many times, and just as often rejected. Back in 1877 the Variorum editor of the play, Horace Howard Furness, introduced Act 2 Scene 1 with these words:

> The supposition that Hamlet went to Ophelia directly after the interview with the Ghost is incorrect, and for the following reasons: first, the interview between Polonius and Reynaldo implies that some little time has elapsed since the departure of Laertes for Paris; secondly during this time Ophelia has returned Hamlet's letters, and denied him access; her father asks her, 'Have you given him any hard words of late?' The letter which Polonius reads to the King must, therefore, have belonged to a period before the opening of the drama. Ophelia had strictly obeyed her father's commands, and returned all Hamlet's letters. Thirdly, Polonius goes at once to the King, and yet, when he speaks to him of Hamlet, the King already knew of Hamlet's (feigned) insanity, and therefore must himself have seen the Prince before Ophelia saw him. Fourthly, between the close of the first act and the present scene, Rosencrantz and Guildenstern must have been summoned on account of Hamlet's changed demeanour, and of the King's suspicions which that demeanour had aroused.

Just over a hundred years later the Penguin editor, T.J.B Spencer, concurred:

> Some time has elapsed: Laertes has arrived in Paris and is settling down there; Ophelia has repelled Hamlet's letters and 'denied | His access'... the King already knows of 'Hamlet's transformation' [Act 2 Scene 2] and has summoned Rosencrantz and Guildenstern.

Neither critic answers the charge that a gap of time, particularly so early in the play, is peculiar – perhaps even pointless – dramaturgy.[13] There are longer gaps within Shakespeare plays, not least in *Pericles* and *The Winter's Tale*, but there they are explicitly heralded (in *The Winter's Tale* by Time himself) and absolutely key to the development of those two stories; the babies Marina and Perdita are grown to adulthood. No matter of similar use or importance is evident here. One does not have to be a devotee of the classical unities to complain that a weakly heralded and vaguely defined gap of time of unexplained purpose is a poor thing in a play.

This is one moment when the Q1 text may help us. Here I put Q1's version of the Ophelia/Polonius dialogue in Act 2 Scene 1 immediately before Q2's. It concerns the news that 'Ofelia' brings to her father, 'Corambis', with elements that are substantially absent from Q2 in italics:

> CORAMBIS. How now Ofelia, what's the news with you?
>
> OFELIA. *O my dear father, such a change in nature,*
> *so great an alteration in a Prince,*
> *so pitiful to him, fearful to me,*
> *a maiden's eye ne'er looked on.*
>
> CORAMBIS. Why what's the matter, my Ofelia?
>
> OFELIA. *O young Prince Hamlet, the only flower of Denmark,*
> *he is bereft of all the wealth he had,*
> *the jewel that adorn'd his feature most*
> *is filch'd and stol'n away, his wit's bereft him.*
> He found me walking in the gallery all alone,
> there comes he to me, with a distracted look,
> his garters lagging down, his shoes untied,
> and fix'd his eyes so steadfast on my face,
> as if they had vow'd, this is their latest object.
> Small while he stood, but grips me by the wrist,
> and there he holds my pulse till with a sigh
> he doth unclasp his hold, and parts away
> silent, as is the mid time of the night:
> and as he went, his eye was still on me,
> for thus his head over his shoulder look'd,
> he seem'd to find the way without his eyes:
> for out of doors he went without their help,
> and so did leave me.
>
> CORAMBIS.   Mad for thy love.
>   What, have you given him any cross words of late?
>
> OFELIA. I did repel his letters, deny his gifts,
>   as you did charge me.

CORAMBIS.   Why, that hath made him mad.
    By heav'n 'tis as proper for our age to cast
    beyond our selves, as 'tis for the younger sort
    to leave their wantonness. Well, I am sorry
    that I was so rash: but what remedy?
    Let's to the King, this madness may prove,
    though wild awhile, yet more true to thy love.

And here is Q2's version, this time with its own unique elements in italic:

POLONIUS. How now Ophelia, what's the matter?

OPHELIA. O my lord, *my lord, I have been so affrighted.*

POLONIUS. With what i' the name of God?

OPHELIA. My lord, as I was sewing in my closet,
    Lord Hamlet, with his doublet all unbrac'd,
    no hat upon his head, his stockings foul'd,
    ungarter'd and down-gyved to his ankle,
    pale as his shirt, his knees knocking each other,
    and with a look so piteous in purport
    as if he had been loosed out of Hell
    to speak of horrors, he comes before me.

POLONIUS. Mad for thy love?

OPHELIA. My Lord, I do not know, but truly I do fear it.

POLONIUS. What said he?

OPHELIA. He took me by the wrist and held me hard.
    Then goes he to the length of all his arm
    and with his other hand thus o'er his brow,
    he falls to such perusal of my face
    as 'a would draw it. Long stay'd he so.
    At last, a little shaking of mine arm
    and thrice his head thus waving up and down,
    he rais'd a sigh *so piteous and profound*
    as it did seem to shatter all his bulk
    and end his being. That done, he lets me go,
    and with his head over his shoulder turn'd,
    he seem'd to find his way without his eyes,
    for out o' doors he went without their helps,
    and to the last bended their light on me.

POLONIUS. Come, go with me. I will go seek the King.
    This is the very ecstasy of love
    whose violent property fordoes itself
    and leads the will to desperate undertakings
    as oft as any passions under heaven

that does afflict our natures. I am sorry.
What, have you given him any hard words of late?
OPHELIA. No, my good lord, but, as you did command
I did repel his letters and denied
his access to me.
POLONIUS.   That hath made him mad.
I am sorry that with better heed and judgement
I had not quoted him. I fear'd he did but trifle
and meant to wreck thee. But beshrew my jealousy!
By heaven, it is as proper to our age
to cast beyond ourselves in our opinions
as it is common for the younger sort
to lack discretion. Come, go we to the King.
This must be known, which being kept close might move
more grief to hide than hate to utter love.
Come.

I find it very difficult to read the Q1 version as a poorly recollected version of the Q2 – how could any actor forget the line 'loosed out of hell to speak of horrors'? But I could very easily read deliberate development and change – from Q1 to Q2. In contrast to Q2, Q1's Ofelia immediately confirms the notion of the 'antic disposition'; she tells us in so many words that Hamlet is mad – 'his wit's bereft him'. She is the first witness (in our hearing) to this change in Hamlet, but though obviously concerned, she is not 'affrighted'; 'fearful to me' is weaker, less immediate. Much more collected than in Q2, her account reads perfectly as witness to a performance of feigned madness.

Elements of this do survive into Q2; Hamlet still seems to have adopted both the dress –

his doublet all unbrac'd,
no hat upon his head, his stockings foul'd,
ungarter'd and down-gyved to his ankle

– and the melodramatic deportment of the man feigning madness –

and with his head over his shoulder turn'd,
he seem'd to find his way without his eyes,
for out o' doors he went without their help,
and to the last, bended their light on me.

But the added lines –

and with a look so piteous in purport
as if he had been loosed out of Hell
to speak of horrors,

– and –

> he rais'd a sigh so piteous and profound
> as it did seem to shatter all his bulk
> and end his being.

– powerfully suggest, not a man acting distraction, but one undergoing an existential crisis. The Ghost's revelation has incriminated Gertrude as well as Claudius. We must not undervalue the moral horror expressed in Hamlet's line in Act 1 Scene 5, 'O most pernicious woman' – a line, incidentally that is not to be found in Q1. We could well understand if he goes immediately to Ophelia, whom he has undoubtedly loved, to interrogate her face, the mirror of the heart, to test its veracity as a witness to the truth within; for 'woman' is now revealed as guilty of much more than 'frailty'. Hamlet's profoundest, even his defining, relationship has been with his mother,[14] and her betrayal is his chaos.

My suggestion is that in Q1 the Polonius/Reynaldo dialogue is indeed placed to indicate a passage of time, during which Hamlet prepares a show of madness, but that for Q2 Shakespeare couldn't resist developing that dialogue into a very funny and – of Polonius – revealing scene, while employing a double time scheme to bring Hamlet almost straight to Ophelia from his traumatic encounter with the Ghost. Whether I am right or wrong, this unseen episode is one that must be explored in rehearsal, and its timing decided; it is Hamlet's experience as well as Ophelia's.

From this I would throw into the Q1 debate the possibility that if that text is a 'memorial reconstruction', then the recording actor is filling in the gaps in his backstage memory of Q2 with tracts of text from his perhaps more acute memory of the earlier, *Ur-Hamlet*. Q1 does seem to look backwards to Belleforest in ways that suggest that defective memory of Q2 cannot be the only begetter of Q1.

Narrative Confusion

While Q1 will feel more and more truncated as it progresses, in Acts One and Two it has some logic and integrity. Its first scene between Corambis and Ofelia (Q2's Act 1 Scene 3) concludes with these lines, not seen in Q2:

> CORAMBIS. Ofelia, receive none of his letters,
> for lovers' lines are snares to entrap the heart.
> Refuse his tokens, both of them are keys
> to unlock chastity unto desire.

> Come in, Ofelia, such men often prove
> great in their words, but little in their love.
>
> OFELIA. I will, my lord.

Corambis' instruction to Ofelia, to refuse Hamlet's letters and tokens, is specific, and she acts upon it during the unambiguous gap of time ('I did repel his letters, deny his gifts, as you did charge me'). So when Claudius' first meeting with 'Rossencraft' and 'Gilderstone' begins with this:

> Right noble friends, that our dear cousin Hamlet
> hath lost the very heart of all his sense
> it is most right, and we most sorry for him...

we have an echo of Ofelia's 'his wit's bereft him' and a witness to the whole Court's observation, over a period, of an apparently deranged mind. Here we are surely to recognise that the madness is feigned and that Corambis' account of its development, very close to that of Q2, is a comically unwitting tribute to Hamlet's histrionic skill:

> Now since which time, seeing his love thus cross'd,
> which I took to be idle, and but sport,
> he straightway grew into a melancholy,
> from that unto a fast, then unto distraction,
> then into a sadness, from that unto a madness,
> and so by continuance, and weakness of the brain,
> into this frenzy, which now possesseth him.

The development in Q2 is, narratively, less clear. First, though in Act 2 Scene 1 Ophelia says to her father that 'as you did command, I did repel his letters and denied his access to me', the command that we had heard in Act 1 Scene 3 was only not 'to slander any moment leisure as to give words or talk with the Lord Hamlet', with no mention of letters. And then, in the light of the marked differences in Act 2 Scene 1 that for me cast serious doubt on the notion of a passage of time, we have from Claudius and Gertrude a less outspoken description of madness:

> CLAUDIUS. Welcome, dear Rosencrantz and Guildenstern!
> Moreover that we much did long to see you,
> the need we have to use you did provoke
> our hasty sending. Something have you heard
> of Hamlet's transformation; so call it,
> sith nor th' exterior nor the inward man
> resembles that it was. What it should be,
> more than his father's death, that thus hath put him

> so much from the understanding of himself,
> I cannot dream of…
>
> GERTRUDE. Thanks, Guildenstern and gentle Rosencrantz:
> and I beseech you instantly to visit
> my too much changed son.

Claudius' 'transformation', his 'sith nor the exterior nor the inward man resembles that it was', his 'so much from the understanding of himself', and his later reference to 'your son's distemper', can certainly be witnesses to real or feigned madness, but they are markedly less explicit than the Q1 version. Indeed, they could refer to no more than the behaviour that Claudius and Gertrude had tried to address in the opening Court scene. I do sense, at the least, a rolling back, to some degree, from the Belleforest Hamlet's deliberate performance of madness.

Q1 and Q2 also diverge, narratively, following the exit of Rosencrantz and Guildenstern in Act 2 Scene 2. The stage direction for Corambis' entry in Q1 is *Enter Corambis and Ofelia*; in Q2 it is merely *Enter Polonius*. The latter is odd, since Polonius has just instructed Ophelia (three times) to go with him to the King; but the omission of Ophelia is evidently intentional, since the opportunity to 'loose' his daughter on Hamlet, which would have been immediately available had she been with him, is not taken up, Q2 preferring that – in Ophelia's absence – Polonius should 'board' Hamlet himself for the famous 'You are a fishmonger' dialogue (in Q1 placed *after* the 'nunnery' scene). In contrast Q1 follows the logic of Corambis' intention –

> Let's to the king, this madness may prove,
> though wild a while, yet more true to thy love.

– and has the unfortunate Ofelia witnessing the reading aloud of Hamlet's love letter and her father's proposal that she be used as bait to reveal Hamlet's true condition. Hamlet then enters 'poring upon a book' and we are straight into the 'To be or not to be' soliloquy and the 'nunnery' scene, which in Q2 do not happen until after Hamlet's first meeting with Rosencrantz and Guildenstern and the arrival of the Players. Here Q1 has a developmental rhythm I find extremely attractive – and I adopted the arrangement in 2016 (so allowing the scene pictured overleaf). I was by no means the first director to do so; Michael Benthall did it in 1957 with John Neville as Hamlet at the Old Vic, Tony Richardson in 1969 with Nicol Williamson at the Roundhouse, and Ron Daniels in 1989 with Mark Rylance at the RSC, and no doubt there have been more. I assume, like me, they questioned Hamlet's Q2 relapse into introspection – his 'To be or not to be' – after the scene with the Players that ends with the extremely upbeat 'The play's the thing wherein I'll catch the conscience of the King'. But for those who see Hamlet's melancholy as a factor under diagnosis, such an extreme fluctuation in mood is a key symptom of that malaise.

Isabella Marshall as Ophelia and Ian Barritt as Polonius, photo © Mark Douet 2016

But if the Q2 sequence is Shakespeare's profounder choice, the practicalities are not entirely thought through; not only because Polonius seems inexplicably to mislay Ophelia on his way to speak to Claudius but because it sets up the Hamlet/Ophelia confrontation twice; first in Act 2 Scene 2:

CLAUDIUS.   · How may we try it further?

POLONIUS. You know, sometimes he walks four hours together
      here in the lobby.

GERTRUDE.   So he does indeed.

POLONIUS. At such a time I'll loose my daughter to him.
      Be you and I behind an arras then,
      mark the encounter…

and then again in Act 3 Scene 1, after the King and Queen's second meeting with Rosencrantz and Guildenstern:

CLAUDIUS. Sweet Gertrude, leave us two,
      for we have closely sent for Hamlet hither,

> that he, as 'twere by accident, may here
> affront Ophelia.

The explanation to Gertrude in this second sequence is largely superfluous since she was present when the plan was first proposed in Act 2 Scene 2. The 'closely sent for Hamlet hither' also sounds a little oddly, as the request (or command) is not followed through; Hamlet arrives on cue, but it seems coincidentally, not by appointment; he carries no sense of having been summoned, but to be following his common practice of walking in the lobby as described above. Here it seems that Q2 encompasses alternative narrative possibilities.

Hamlet and Ophelia

In the 'nunnery' scene – wherever it is placed – we at last see Hamlet and Ophelia together. It begins with another reference to a gap of time – again, it seems to me, an extremely curious one, a possible, rather than a fully realised narrative element – now between the meeting reported in Act 2 Scene 1 and this moment in Act 3 Scene 1:

> HAMLET.   Soft you now,
>   the fair Ophelia. Nymph, in thy orisons
>   be all my sins remember'd.
> OPHELIA.   Good my lord,
>   how does your honour for this many a day?
> HAMLET. I humbly thank you: well.
> OPHELIA. My lord, I have remembrances of yours,
>   that I have longed long to re-deliver.
>   I pray you, now receive them.
> HAMLET.   No, not I,
>   I never gave you aught.

But we are not drawn to the time-lapse implied in 'many a day' and 'longed long' but to the ambiguity of Hamlet's response – the denial of the remembrances, or the denial of the self – 'that was not me'? Or even, following the distant formality of 'I humbly thank you: well, well, well', a pretended denial of recognition. 'Nymph' suggests to me an address for his own ears only; Q1's 'Lady', perhaps a formal greeting. But these are all choices; so many in so short a space.

Now we arrive at two much-debated and related issues: Ophelia's own agency in this scene, and the question of when, if at all, Hamlet realises that they are being overheard. For the first, it has often been assumed from this speech –

> OPHELIA. My honour'd lord, you know right well you did;
>   and, with them, words of so sweet breath compos'd
>   as made these things more rich. Their perfume lost,
>   take these again, for to the noble mind
>   rich gifts wax poor when givers prove unkind.
>   There, my lord.

– that Ophelia has been instructed to return Hamlet's 'remembrances' at this point; but, in our hearing, Polonius has only said:

> Read on this book
> that show of such an exercise may colour
> your lowliness.[15]

And, if we listen carefully to Ophelia's speech, we may feel it to be very much her own, not one learned by rote, or even half-prepared. She begins by forcefully contradicting Hamlet's lie and ends, perhaps, by pressing the gifts firmly on him, an action not in her father's scenario. She is no mere dupe in Polonius' strategy but a very hurt young woman, perhaps inclined to believe that her brother and father were right in their Act 1 Scene 3 warnings after all. Hamlet, feeling on the contrary that it is Ophelia who is in the wrong, responds angrily to her passionate criticism – and perhaps specifically to her 'unkind', if he has heard its sense of 'unnatural':

> Ha, ha! are you honest?
> OPHELIA. My lord?
> HAMLET. Are you fair?
> OPHELIA. What means your lordship?
> HAMLET. That if you be honest and fair, you should admit no
>   discourse to your beauty.

Here we feel, very powerfully, the presence of Gertrude in Hamlet's bruised imagination. This is far more telling than the choice to seize this first possible opportunity for Hamlet to suspect they are overheard – a choice that would feed off the mistaken assumption that, in returning the gifts, Ophelia is transparently obeying orders rather than following her passion.

Still Ophelia is no dupe. She fights her corner:

> Could beauty, my lord, have better commerce than with
> honesty?

> HAMLET. Ay, truly, for the power of beauty will sooner
> transform honesty from what it is to a bawd than the
> force of honesty can translate beauty into his likeness.
> This was sometime a paradox, but now the time gives it
> proof. I did love you once.
>
> OPHELIA. Indeed, my lord, you made me believe so.
>
> HAMLET. You should not have believ'd me, for virtue cannot so
> inoculate our old stock but we shall relish of it. I lov'd you
> not.

Hamlet's confusion and self-disgust are dismaying, to us and to Ophelia, whose tone is perhaps sharply indignant, rather than pathetic:

> I was the more deceiv'd.

Again Hamlet rises to an accusation – how dare she talk of 'deceit'?

> Get thee to a nunnery. Why wouldst thou be a breeder of
> sinners? I am myself indifferent honest, but yet I could
> accuse me of such things that it were better my mother
> had not borne me. I am very proud, revengeful,
> ambitious, with more offences at my beck than I have
> thoughts to put them in, imagination to give them shape,
> or time to act them in. What should such fellows as I do
> crawling between earth and heaven? We are arrant
> knaves, believe none of us. Go thy ways to a nunnery.

Here we arrive at a more popular – and more useful – choice for a moment in which Hamlet realises they are overheard; perhaps an involuntary reference to where Claudius and Polonius are hidden on Ophelia's part, as the conversation has gone beyond her own understanding of the rift between them, or because she hears an intended pun by Hamlet on the meaning of nunnery as 'brothel':

> HAMLET. Where's your father?
>
> OPHELIA. At home, my lord.

That here she lies is uncontrovertible, and perhaps she makes a poor liar. Hamlet's realisation that Polonius is within earshot is not obligatory, but seems highly likely –

> HAMLET. Let the doors be shut upon him, that he may play
> the fool nowhere but in's own house. Farewell.

– and his bitterness is redoubled. He now sees Ophelia as a willing dupe indeed, and is provoked into a fervid development of the theme 'frailty, thy name is woman':

> If thou dost marry, I'll give thee this plague for thy
> dowry: be thou as chaste as ice, as pure as snow, thou
> shalt not escape calumny. Get thee to a nunnery, go,
> farewell. Or, if thou wilt needs marry, marry a fool, for
> wise men know well enough what monsters you make of
> them. To a nunnery, go, and quickly too. Farewell.
>
> OPHELIA. Heavenly powers, restore him!

The puritanism of what follows I read as yet one more symptom of youth:

> HAMLET. I have heard of your paintings too, well enough. God
> has given you one face, and you make yourselves another.
> You jig and amble, and you – list you – nick-name God's
> creatures, and make your wantonness ignorance. Go to,
> I'll no more on't, it hath made me mad. I say, we will have
> no more marriage. Those that are married already, all but
> one, shall live. The rest shall keep as they are. To a
> nunnery, go. [*Exit.*]

I must confess to some slight disappointment in the conclusion to Ophelia's part in the scene:

> O, what a noble mind is here o'erthrown!
> The courtier's, soldier's, scholar's, eye, tongue, sword,
> th' expectation and rose of the fair state,
> the glass of fashion and the mould of form,
> th' observ'd of all observers, quite, quite down!
> And I, of ladies most deject and wretched,
> that suck'd the honey of his music'd vows,
> now see what noble and most sovereign reason,
> like sweet bells jangled, out of time and harsh;
> that unmatch'd form and stature of blown youth
> blasted with ecstasy. O, woe is me,
> t'ave seen what I have seen, see what I see! [*Exit.*]

She seems suddenly to opt out of what is to some degree a lovers' tiff, reaching for the safety – albeit a distressing one – of the idea that Hamlet is mad, an idea barely justified by the content of Hamlet's anger. Certainly that was extreme and probably bewildering, but it was hardly 'blasted with ecstasy'; and one would expect Ophelia to have some sense that she has allowed herself to be used by her father, and some recognition that Hamlet has found her out. And there is the very formality of the soliloquy, its collectedly summarising and descriptive qualities that seem at odds with the chaotic passions that have provoked it; and an awkwardness in the necessary delay, to permit the speech, before the entry of Claudius and Polonius with their immediate responses to what they have overheard. Again, I wonder if we don't have here a further instance of incomplete transformation (or revision), Ophelia's response being derived from an older notion of the function of Hamlet's display of 'madness'.

Hamlet and Gertrude

The 'closet' scene, Act 3 Scene 4, is one of the great glories of the play and contains only one real mystery, the second appearance of the Ghost of Hamlet's father, initially 'to whet thy almost blunted purpose' and, secondarily, to urge Hamlet to comfort his mother. This episode has been endlessly debated on two scores: the stage direction in the Q1 text – 'Enter the Ghost in his night gown', in place of Q2's mere 'Enter the Ghost', which has been used to support Freudian interpretations of the scene; and the question of why the Ghost is invisible to Gertrude, while it had been seen by Marcellus, Barnardo and Horatio.

Francesca Ryan as Gertrude and Jamie Ballard as Hamlet in Jonathan Miller's 2008 stf production, photo © Graham Burke 2008

The Freudian issue is linked to the question, what is a 'closet' in this context? Historians insist that it is *not* a bedroom, and so protest at productions – such as Jonathan Miller's – that set this scene around a bed, possibly even the royal bed that Gertrude has so polluted. But the presence of a bed in the scene predates both Freudian theory and the rediscovery of the Q1 text, as illustrations of eighteenth-century productions confirm. Interestingly, the Q1 text never uses the term 'closet', while it is used repeatedly in Q2 – one example of *consistent* differences between the two texts that 'Bad Quarto' theory struggles to explain.

While issues of setting and the Ghost's apparel present us with intriguing choices, the play offers us no guidance as to Gertrude's blindness to the Ghost. The text is clear that *we* both see and hear him, so while, to Gertrude, Hamlet's address to the air is a symptom of his madness –

> Alas, how is't with you,
> that you do bend your eye on vacancy
> and with the incorporal air do hold discourse?
> Forth at your eyes your spirits wildly peep,
> and, as the sleeping soldiers in the alarm,
> your bedded hair, like life in excrements,
> start up, and stands on end. O gentle son,
> upon the heat and flame of thy distemper
> sprinkle cool patience...
> This is the very coinage of your brain.
> This bodiless creation ecstasy
> is very cunning in.

– to us it perhaps reflects more on Gertrude, on the element of wilful blindness in her own imagination that we have seen before and will see again. The middle sentence of the first speech above is commonly and rightly cut, as a descriptive passage that should be rendered unnecessary by the Hamlet-actor's performance, and may not accord with that performance in every, or even any detail. It seems like a voiced stage direction, the clause 'and, as the sleeping soldiers in the alarm' sounding particularly literary and considered for such a moment (to me it sounds, like Ophelia's soliloquy, like earlier period Shakespeare). Again 'madness' has raised its head, though it will be only the madness of the sword-thrust through the curtain that Gertrude will report to Claudius. Ghosts make for good melodrama, but many modern productions, directed and played by sceptical minds, have struggled to define the purpose of this second incarnation, except to provide a radical change in tempo and mood. The 'call to arms' – to get on with the task of revenge – will be repeated by the

Fortinbras sequence and provoke the great 'How all occasions do inform against me' soliloquy; the Ghost's entrance here appears to achieve nothing in terms of the revenge impulse. But is that perhaps the point – Hamlet's focus on Gertrude, and the killing of Polonius, renders the Ghost impotent?

The Murder of Polonius

Hamlet's intensely, even feverishly passionate attack on Gertrude, his determination to 'wring [her] heart' is, for me, not only symptomatic of youth – the difficulty with sex itself, the incomprehension at the fact of a mature woman's, and one's own mother's, sexuality –

> You cannot call it love, for at your age
> the hey-day in the blood is tame, it's humble,
> and waits upon the judgement...
> O shame, where is thy blush? Rebellious hell,
> if thou canst mutine in a matron's bones,
> to flaming youth let virtue be as wax,
> and melt in her own fire...

– but is also informed, quite crucially, by his own guilt at the murder of Polonius. I have rarely seen that event given its true value on stage. And some commentators – without any misgivings about their hero – define Hamlet's reaction to it as coolly careless, taking his speech at the end of the scene –

> I'll lug the guts into the neighbour room.
> Mother, good night. Indeed this counsellor
> is now most still, most secret and most grave,
> who was in life a most foolish, prating knave.

– entirely at face value, dismissing Gertrude's 'he weeps for what is done' (another line absent from Q1) as her deluded imagination (or just a plain lie), and ignoring Hamlet's own remorse:

> For this same lord,
> I do repent: but heaven hath pleas'd it so,
> to punish me with this and this with me,
> that I must be their scourge and minister.
> I will bestow him, and will answer well
> the death I gave him. So, again, good night.
> I must be cruel, only to be kind.
> Thus bad begins and worse remains behind.

This use of 'behind' to mean 'to come' we have seen before (see Polixenes on page 114); its sense of the hidden, the unrevealed, adds to Hamlet's foreboding. That all these elements of remorse are absent from Q1 for me only highlight their crucial importance in Q2; but for the Oxford World's Classics editor, G.R.Hibbard, our hero

> has all the hauteur of the Renaissance monarch or aristocrat…
> True to his breeding, he feels no compassion for Polonius
> whom he has killed, or for Rosencrantz and Guildenstern
> whom he sends to their deaths. All three have deliberately and
> knowingly intervened in matters that are no proper concern of
> theirs.

Hibbard thus ignores the distinction between a deed for which Hamlet weeps, and refers to as his punishment, and one that he will assert is 'not near my conscience'.

Earlier I have warned against the rush to judgement, the desire to cast a character as simply good or evil. But here are we not in danger of suspending our own notions of morality? Hamlet's action is a rash error, and we understand the enormous pressure that led him into it, but are we to applaud Polonius' death as 'his just deserts', as so many commentators seem in danger of doing? That would be the morality of the theatre – more specifically of revenge drama – not of real life. For truly humanly, the Polonius murder is the most significant event in Elsinore since Claudius' murder of Old Hamlet. Polonius may be dislikeable, he may even have been implicated in Old Hamlet's death – though we have not a shred of evidence to support that – and his choices may have been unintentionally malign, but he has hardly deserved to die for them; and his death will have consequences, not least the wholly innocent Ophelia's fatal breakdown. The dialogue with Claudius that follows can certainly be played according to the coolly careless interpretation:

> CLAUDIUS. Now, Hamlet, where's Polonius?
>
> HAMLET. At supper.
>
> CLAUDIUS. At supper? Where?
>
> HAMLET. Not where he eats, but where a is eaten. A certain
> convocation of politic worms are e'en at him. Your worm
> is your only emperor for diet. We fat all creatures else to
> fat us and we fat ourselves for maggots. Your fat king and
> your lean beggar is but variable service – two dishes, but
> to one table. That's the end.
>
> CLAUDIUS. Alas, alas!

HAMLET. A man may fish with the worm that hath eat of a king
  and eat of the fish that hath fed of that worm.

CLAUDIUS. What dost you mean by this?

HAMLET. Nothing but to show you how a king may go a
  progress through the guts of a beggar.

CLAUDIUS. Where is Polonius?

HAMLET. In heaven. Send hither to see. If your messenger find
  him not there seek him i' the other place yourself. But if
  indeed you find him not within this month, you shall
  nose him as you go up the stairs into the lobby.

Act 4 Scene 3

But a subtext is equally possible – that here we have a flight from reality and responsibility, a protective wall of gallows humour erected against a deep and unacknowledgeable pain; as close as Hamlet ever comes to real madness.

Hamlet's flippancies can only be forgiven and understood – in life, rather than by the crude values of revenge fiction, which is stony-hearted towards fools and meddlers – if we find them emanating from pain. I suggest that Shakespeare subtly transformed the sword-thrust through the curtain that he found in the revenge fiction of Belleforest – and possibly in the *Ur-Hamlet* – into a massive turning-point in Hamlet's journey and the fount of everything that is to follow within him. The tragic irony is that this intelligent, sensitive, troubled young man, overwhelmed by his mother's sexual betrayal of his father and the Ghost's demand that he kill his uncle, on a momentary impulse commits an irrelevant and squalid murder. A grisly sideshow invades his life and ruins him.

Hamlet and Laertes

The tragic results of this are to be seen most immediately in the graveyard scene, Act 5 Scene 1. Are we so under Hamlet's spell that we cannot see his intervention in Ophelia's funeral as little short of obscene? A young man, his father recently murdered, in huge distress, is burying his only sibling. Then there suddenly appears his father's killer – and the indirect cause of the young girl's suicide – to compete with the young man for the ownership of grief:

HAMLET.   What is he whose grief
  bears such an emphasis, whose phrase of sorrow
  conjures the wand'ring stars, and makes them stand
  like wonder-wounded hearers?

Then comes comes a declaration which better befits the Revenger of stage tradition (and perhaps recalls the personality of his warrior father) than the scrupulous self-questioner in whose company we had spent Acts One to Three:

> This is I,
> Hamlet the Dane!

Unsurprisingly, Laertes attacks him

> The devil take thy soul!

and an ugly scrap invades the solemn occasion:

> HAMLET.   Thou pray'st not well.
> I prithee, take thy fingers from my throat;
> for, though I am not spleenative rash,
> yet have I in me something dangerous,
> which let thy wisdom fear. Hold off thy hand.

On Claudius' orders attendants part them, but Hamlet is not to be silenced:

> HAMLET.... I will fight with him upon this theme
> until my eyelids will no longer wag.
>
> GERTRUDE. O my son, what theme?
>
> HAMLET. I loved Ophelia. Forty thousand brothers
> could not, with all their quantity of love,
> make up my sum. What wilt thou do for her?
>
> CLAUDIUS. O, he is mad, Laertes.
>
> GERTRUDE. For love of God, forbear him.
>
> HAMLET. 'Swounds, show me what thou'lt do:
> Woo't weep. woo't fight, woo't fast, woo't tear thyself?
> Woo't drink up eisel, eat a crocodile?
> I'll do't. Dost thou come here to whine,
> to outface me with leaping in her grave?
> Be buried quick with her, and so will I.
> And if thou prate of mountains, let them throw
> millions of acres on us, till our ground,
> singeing his pate against the burning zone,
> make Ossa like a wart!

Love cannot be reckoned in multiples, or in competitions in daring. However we assess Hamlet's love for Ophelia, these lines offer no reliable witness. If we are determined to like and support Hamlet through this sequence then we must assume we have another use of a subtext; beneath this brutally insensitive barrage of words must be an inexpressible protest or cry of pain and guilt at the terrible consequence of the Polonius killing. If we are not moved to interpret them that way (as I am not) then we can only be shocked to find Hamlet trying to push Laertes out of focus, like a leading actor fearing he is being upstaged by a junior, with the only redeeming feature being that he does show some measure of self-awareness:

> Nay, an thou'lt mouth,
> I'll rant as well as thou.

But his final lines –

> Hear you, sir:
> what is the reason that you use me thus?
> I lov'd you ever. But it is no matter –
> let Hercules himself do what he may,
> the cat will mew and dog will have his day.

– make the task of sympathy very hard indeed; his 'what is the reason that you use me thus?' is breathtaking.[16] His 'rant' admission seems a confession to the overblown nature of his language, and perhaps to a discovered emptiness in his heart, where only the shadow of his love for Ophelia has survived his trauma.

Hamlet and Rosencrantz and Guildenstern

Some talk of an admirable serenity that Hamlet achieves following this outburst. I couldn't agree less. During the sea journey a part of him seems to have been cauterised – as Lady Macbeth would have had it, the 'access and passage to remorse stopp'd up'. There is nothing admirable in the absence of any sense of responsibility for Ophelia's fate, nor in his triumphalism about the trick he has played upon Rosencrantz and Guildenstern, who we are to understand will be immediately beheaded on their arrival in England, 'not shriving time allow'd'. However unsympathetically that pair have been portrayed on stage, unlike their predecessors in Belleforest – who were fully aware of the fate awaiting Hamlet in England – in this play they are innocents, caught up in matters beyond their understanding, trying, as they see it, to assist the King to *help* Hamlet, not to betray him. It is too easy to decry them, as Dover Wilson and many others do, as Claudius' 'spies', with all that that pejorative term implies (Greenblatt throws in 'oily', and Bate remarks that they 'have betrayed not only him but the precious virtue of friendship'[17]). This is an autocratic state, in which the royal autocrat requests a service of two young subjects. What are Rosencrantz and Guildenstern to do – say 'Sorry, guv, not interested', or conspire with an emotionally volatile old friend against the King? Either is a huge ask in any circumstance; if one takes Dover Wilson's line that Hamlet has been usurped by his uncle, meaning the political situation is volatile, then the stakes are even higher. Once again, in so much of the commentary on this play the action seems to be held at one remove from reality, only *theatrical* judgements and *theatrical* morality applied.

Again in contrast to his behaviour in Q1, where Horatio is completely untroubled by Rosencrantz and Guildenstern's fate, Q2's Horatio makes his dismay perfectly clear:

> So Guildenstern and Rosencrantz go to't.

Here F1 adds a line to amplify the point:

> HAMLET. Why, man, they did make love to this employment.

– a claim without foundation, as far as we know. Then Q2 continues:

> They are not near my conscience. Their defeat
> does by their own insinuation grow.
>
> Act 5 Scene 2

Is Horatio wide of the mark here, lacking in understanding, or moral sense, or is it Hamlet that is so lacking? Is Shakespeare asking us to cheer what awaits Rosencrantz and Guildenstern in England? If he is, why does he allow Horatio to demur?

The Dénouement

Moving rapidly towards the dénouement, we enjoy the relative relief of the passage with Osric, before we are pitched back into the moral maze, and another longstanding controversy that begins with Claudius' insistence that Hamlet and Laertes shake hands:

> Come, Hamlet, come, and take this hand from me.
> HAMLET. [*To Laertes*] Give me your pardon, sir, I've done you
>   wrong.
> But pardon't, as you are a gentleman.

This presence knows,
and you must needs have heard, how I am punish'd
with a sore distraction. What I have done
that might your nature, honour and exception
roughly awake, I here proclaim was madness.
Was't Hamlet wrong'd Laertes? Never Hamlet.
If Hamlet from himself be ta'en away,
and when he's not himself does wrong Laertes,
then Hamlet does it not, Hamlet denies it.
Who does it, then? His madness. If't be so,
Hamlet is of the faction that is wrong'd,
his madness is poor Hamlet's enemy.
Let my disclaiming from a purpos'd evil
free me so far in your most generous thoughts,
that I have shot mine arrow o'er the house
and hurt my brother.

Many critics, at least as far back as Dr Johnson, have found this 'madness' justification for the murder of Polonius distasteful. Johnson regarded it as taking 'shelter in falsehood'. However, the impulse to back Hamlet to the last is strong and many actors, directors and academic commentators (including Dover Wilson) have yielded to it; but it should be resisted. This is the last use in the play of the 'madness' excuse, and it is the most transparently bogus. The very elegance of Hamlet's argument, his coolly elaborate rhetoric, is a dance of indifference that borders on insult. Laertes seems wrong-footed by it, making a nice, but improbable distinction between nature and honour:

I am satisfied in nature,
whose motive, in this case, should stir me most
to my revenge. But in my terms of honour
I stand aloof; and will no reconcilement,
till by some elder masters of known honour
I have a voice and precedent of peace
to keep my name ungor'd. But all that time,
I do receive your offer'd love like love,
and will not wrong it.

He is, of course, committed to a dishonourable revenge, and not concerned to win an abject apology; the public nature of the occasion demands he accept Hamlet's offer, while his concealed intent demands that he withhold it; the pair are perfectly matched in their insincerity. But Laertes' ear is well-attuned to the note of derision in Hamlet's –

> I'll be your foil, Laertes. In mine ignorance
> your skill shall, like a star i' the darkest night,
> stick fiery off indeed.

– and he rightly protests at it:

> You mock me, sir.
>
> HAMLET. No, by this hand.

– a hint towards the more sceptical reading of Hamlet's behaviour in this sequence.

In the final moments of the play 'Hamlet the Dane' at last becomes the avenger:

> Here, thou incestuous, damned Dane,
> drink of this potion. Is thy union here?

And his last thoughts are not for his mother, or for Ophelia, or for the state of Denmark – which he bequeaths to a vain and strutting militarist – but for his own reputation:

> O God, Horatio, what a wounded name,
> things standing thus unknown, shall live behind me.
> If thou didst ever hold me in thy heart
> absent thee from felicity awhile,
> and in this harsh world draw thy breath in pain,
> to tell my story.

None of this should suggest that I lose sympathy for Hamlet; quite the opposite. Hamlet is damaged goods, and the damage has been done by Denmark. It is, indeed, a prison of the mind, in which fear of the human suffocates and debases the human. The law of diminishing returns is evident everywhere. Claudius cannot repent the deed which has brought him his crown and his queen, but he can delight in neither. Gertrude, who has not enjoyed a moment of happiness in our vision, would escape her own prison, first in a wilful fantasy that her son is harmlessly deranged –

> This is mere madness:
> and this awhile the fit will work on him.
> Anon, as patient as the female dove,
> when that her golden couplets are disclos'd,
> his silence will sit drooping.[18]

Act 5 Scene 1

– and then by drinking poison – possibly knowingly[19] – from the cup Claudius has prepared for her son. Laertes suffers the violent death of both father and sister, and then is used by Claudius as an agent to rid him of his dangerous nephew. Ophelia, her teenage spirit crushed by both father and brother, loses her mind when her controlling wires are cut. And in the last moments the English Ambassadors arrive to report the cruel deaths of Rosencrantz and Guildenstern. The only character who remains aloof from this tide of waste – Horatio – has been powerless to exert any significant influence on it.

It is another very bleak vision on Shakespeare's part, one that production history has contrived to present most commonly as a romantic tragedy, in which the vivid personality of the Hamlet-actor himself, and to a far lesser extent the Ophelia, completely eclipse those around them. We are invited to censure or even loathe Claudius, to deride Polonius, to feel pity for Gertrude (or sometimes to deride her too, as a shallow and brainless woman), all the while identifying uncritically with the 'melancholy Dane' whose happier destination will be in the next world with Romeo and Juliet, Thomas Chatterton, and Chekhov's Konstantin Gavrilovich.

The true fabric of the play is much harder-edged, and far, far more complex. But Shakespeare's audience, familiar with Senecan revenge tragedy, and very possibly with the earlier version of the play, be it the 'Ur' text or Q1, were probably better placed than we are to recognise and appreciate Shakespeare's sometimes subtle transformations.

With this play we must acknowledge that there are three versions at variance with each other and although tradition has favoured Q2, authorial validation is absent and choices have to be made. Indeed, they are exciting choices, for multiple versions are freeing to the imagination; and even where the intention is only to bring the play down to a manageable length, this will involve interpretative decisions; to keep this element in, to cut that one out. Cutting is rarely – and certainly not in this case – a matter of even-handedly thinning every element; it changes the play. And directors, in particular, have to take responsibility for that.

My own cuts – and my preference for the Q1 sequence in Act Two – are testimony to my own distrust of Q2. But while I cannot regard a text that is so impossibly long and contains so many apparent anomalies as unimpeachable, let alone an example of master craftsmanship, I do – for all that I disagree with many interpretations laid upon it – trust absolutely the passionate, flaming life of the central character. The Prince alone justifies the play's place among Shakespeare's finest works.

To orientate oneself within Q2's vast text does require some cognisance of the play's complex provenance. There is no need to come down on one side or another in the Q1 debate; that is for academia to argue out. But there are things to be learned at the interfaces between Belleforest, Q1 and Q2; because Q2, whether it postdates or predates Q1, repeatedly deepens the drift of those cruder texts, and takes the play into psychological and moral territory that makes Q1, although produceable, seem such a relatively shallow vehicle. By doing so, Shakespeare may be composing a critique of revenge drama itself. It still amazes me that so many commentators focus their attention on the mystery of Hamlet's 'delay' in spilling Claudius' guts – even express their frustration at it – when drama as far back as Aeschylus has expressed what a cruel and morally bankrupt cul-de-sac revenge justice is.

Can we not see the Ghost for what he is – a malevolent spirit – and stop urging Hamlet on to fulfil his indefensible demand? Can we not question this imaginative, intelligent, vulnerable and ultimately despoiled young man as we might question ourselves? And question his world as we might question our own? Shakespeare always sees beyond both the theatrical conventions of his time, and the fictive moralities that underpin them. Until Hamlet succumbs to Elsinore, and comes to collaborate with it after the murder of Polonius, he stands in opposition to it and to the play of Elsinore that Shakespeare inherited. T.S. Eliot rightly remarked[20] that Shakespeare's *Hamlet* 'is a stratification... superposed upon much cruder material which persists even in the final form.' For Eliot, this led to his famous judgement that the play is 'most certainly an artistic failure... full of some stuff that the writer could not drag to light, contemplate, or manipulate into art', Shakespeare failing to find an 'objective correlative', 'a set of objects, a situation, a chain of events which shall be the formula of that *particular* emotion'. For all my own cavils about the play's construction, I part from Eliot on this. I find the chain of events fully capable of explaining Hamlet's emotions and behaviour; though I find this only when he is presented as on that crucial threshold – of growth and change – between youth and maturity. A thirty- or even forty-year-old man bullying a vulnerable teenager in that angry, abusive 'nunnery' scene might provide infinite fodder for psychiatrists, but it actually diminishes the play. A much younger man, little more than a boy, in huge distress and confusion about his father's death and his mother's adulterous and incestuous remarriage, wanting both to protect Ophelia and to punish her – that is fit material for the theatre and addresses our common humanity, the chaos that can come with sexual awakening and sexual betrayal.

The historic habits of casting have taken the play into territory I suspect Shakespeare did not intend, for all that his friend Burbage was the first among so many mature Hamlets; but the play is clearly capable of this, and the theatre will continue to explore all possibilities and, no doubt, continue to cast charismatic stars in early middle age as the Prince whose 'crescent nature' 'does not grow alone in thews and bulk'.

Production Note

Alan Mahon as Hamlet and Alan Coveney as Horatio, photo © Mark Douet 2016

Horatio: Horatio is one of the play's incidental puzzles. In the first scene he is introduced as a man brought to the battlements to lend a scholar's witness to the apparition, and who then serves as expositor by being better informed than Marcellus and Barnardo of the political situation and the occasion of the preparations for war. But in Scene 2 Hamlet is pleased but surprised to see him, a stray, as it were, from his true place at university in Wittenberg. He 'came to see your father's funeral', but was evidently not of sufficient status to make himself known to Hamlet on that occasion. His subsequent appearance in the play scene – when he seems to materialise from nowhere – goes unremarked by any other character than Hamlet himself; and throughout the play he exchanges not a single word with

Rosencrantz and Guildenstern, with Polonius, Ophelia, Osric, or even the Sexton. In fact, there are times when he seems to be Hamlet's private familiar spirit rather than a flesh-and-blood presence; but then he appears, surprisingly, as an adviser to Gertrude in Act 4 Scene 4, in Q2 warning her, a little heavily, that she ought to speak to the distressed Ophelia:

> 'Twere good she were spoken with; for she may strew
> dangerous conjectures in ill-breeding minds.

In the Folio these lines are spoken by Gertrude herself, but Horatio is still present, awarded the ten lines of description of Ophelia's state which precede that thought, which in Q2 are given to an unnamed gentleman. Horatio is then addressed, somewhat familiarly, by Claudius in the graveyard scene as 'good Horatio'. And at the end of the play, he acts as spokesman for what remains of the Danish court, to the extent of instructing Fortinbras in what to do with the bodies, and appointing himself as spokesman to the people. So, when back home from Wittenberg, is Horatio a high status courtier, very much of its inner circle, or what?

In 2016 I decided to ask Alan Coveney, a member of the company in his sixties, to play the part, thinking of him more as Hamlet's tutor than his fellow student, and so a more striking contrast to Rosencrantz and Guildenstern. He became something of a father-figure, and his statement that 'I knew your father' carried a little more weight than the most basic sense that he knew him by sight. Perhaps he had fought with Old Hamlet; he certainly knew how the old king was dressed when 'he smote the sledded Polack on the ice'; and Hamlet's tribute to him in Act 3 Scene 2 –

> Since my dear soul was mistress of her choice
> and could of men distinguish her election,
> sh'ath seal'd thee for herself; for thou hast been
> as one, in suffering all, that suffers nothing,
> a man that Fortune's buffets and rewards
> hast ta'en with equal thanks...

– speaks of a life fully lived, with many a setback. But Hamlet has also asked:

> For what advancement may I hope from thee
> that no revenue hast but thy good spirits,
> to feed and clothe thee? Why should the poor be flatter'd?

which makes his appearance as a courtier at the Queen's side all the more curious.

Evidently Horatio answers various, not entirely compatible, narrative needs – as expositor, as loyal confidant and sounding-board – and he achieves these as a shadowy presence in the royal court that it seems need not be challenged. It is around those hard facts that the actor must weave a character. The choice of an older Horatio – with its implication that he had a history at Elsinore – somehow validated his presence there, but also gave him a gravitas and seniority that made him invulnerable to being recruited by Claudius alongside Rosencrantz and Guildenstern. It was by no means an innovative choice; Philip Locke played him at the NT in 1976, already grey-haired in his late forties, and there have been other such castings; but with one emendation – the removal of the one inexplicable and jarring note, his brief Act Four encounter with Gertrude – the strategy worked beautifully and I recommend it.

The text of my edition of the play is available on my website.

1.   Sadly, an academic consensus seems to be hardening that Shakespeare wrote 'Innogen', which to the modern ear makes her sound like a green utility company.

2.   Cambridge University Press, 1995.

3.   Scholarly editions of Q1 are available from Cambridge University Press (edited by Kathleen O. Irace) and in the Arden series (*Hamlet: The Texts of 1603 and 1623*, edited by Ann Thompson and Neil Taylor). The plain text of the play in modern spelling, together with Shakespeare's sources, is also available on my website.

4.   Cambridge University Press, 1941.

5.   François de Belleforest's 'The Hystorie of Hamblet' is a French work of 1576, contained in his *Les Histoires Tragiques*. It is based on a story in *Historiae Danicae*, which was written in Latin in about 1200 by the Danish poet Saxo Grammaticus, and published in Paris in 1514. No English translation of 'The Hystorie of Hamblet' is known before 1608, but the case for it being Shakespeare's main source is powerful.

6.   *1599* again.

7.   University entry in England had only to await puberty, though that was commonly late by modern standards, even as late as seventeen or eighteen.

8.   In 'Hamlet', an essay of 1919.

9.   In *Thinking with Shakespeare* (University of Chicago Press, 2011).

10. The occasion seems to be a meeting of the Privy Council.

11. There is an implicit Roman Catholicism in that the Ghost appears to come from Purgatory, a concept banished by the Reformation, and Denmark was famously Protestant, and England at least formally so. Such a ghost also begs a question: in Catholic theology spirits seek the prayers of the living to shorten the time they must endure purgation before being admitted to Heaven, certainly not to incite the living to revenge. The only interpretation of the Ghost acceptable to conforming Protestants would have been that he was the Devil, as Hamlet later says of him, 'abus[ing] me to damn me'.

12. Though see my comments later on the beginning of the 'nunnery' scene.

13. It is true that Voltemand and Cornelius could hardly have got to Norway and back overnight; but there could have been alternative ways of handling that thread, as also with the timing of the summons to Rosencrantz and Guildenstern.

14. Hamlet is somewhat in awe of his father, but we see no evidence of a familiarity between them; a distant parent, perhaps, caught up in politics and war?

15. The Folio corrects this – probably rightly – to 'loneliness'.

16. The latter-day Romantic, John Dover Wilson, remarks in utter contrast: 'the ranting insincerity of Laertes has become commonplace and contemptible beside the agony of this great and tortured spirit'.

17. In his introduction to the RSC edition of the play (Macmillan, 2008).

18. Her "a weeps for what is done' [the Polonius murder] has been similarly interpreted – as a wilful fantasy. But, in contrast to her words quoted here, that was a bald statement that we should at least consider to be one of bald fact. This speech is very different and seems to bear little relation to truth. It is improbably attributed in both Q1 and the Folios to the King, only in Q2 to Gertrude.

19. Gertrude's 'I will, my lord, I pray you pardon me', in response to Claudius' 'Gertrude, do not drink', is absent from Q1.

20. Citing J.M. Robertson's *The Problem of Hamlet* (George Allen and Unwin, 1919).

Afterword

On Cuts, Emendations and Additions

You may be thoroughly confused. Here is a director who advocates the most scrupulous attention to Shakespeare's language, and yet cheerfully admits to changing words and phrases, making cuts, reordering scenes, even to inviting a playwright to add new material.

Such interventions *are* questionable, and although most of ours have passed without comment, a number of them have caused trenchant criticism; among them, some of the cuts and the change in the Act Two sequence in *Hamlet*, and the staging of the midnight tryst in *Measure for Measure*. And there have been more new scenes in plays not treated in this book, most notably in *The Two Gentlemen of Verona* and *All's Well That Ends Well*, that have also raised an eyebrow or two.

But the more one works on Shakespeare, the clearer the distinctions become between areas of text which have engaged the full power of his imagination, and those that that are merely workmanlike playmaking, unfinished business or rough draft. Or, in a very collaborative industry,[1] the work of a lesser hand; does anyone really still believe that the Hecate scenes in *Macbeth*, for all that Heminges and Condell included them in their great Folio, are Shakespeare's own work, or that they are worthy of inclusion in any serious production?

Most of the language that I have analysed in this book belongs in the first category, and is so perfectly pitched, so profoundly imagined and articulated, that to interfere with it would be the utmost folly. As I said of 'screw your courage to the sticking-place', though its literal meaning has puzzled editors for centuries, only the cloth-eared would seek to amend it.

But our key task in Shakespeare theatre is to enable the audience to listen as well as to watch. Language that has lost its clarity over time, and plotting that bewilders, militate against acute, but relaxed listening; in fact, any area of uncertainty in meaning or action is alienating and breaks concentration. The physical management of the Elizabethan playscript – farming a single manuscript out to paid scribes for them to produce the cue-scripts for the actors, possibly act by act, or even scene by scene – would be to a twenty-first-century writer an alarming discipline. Changes of mind necessitating new fair copies would be expensive; time constraints might make them impossible. So a development late in the play that contradicted an element an act or two earlier might just have to stand – or might be corrected informally 'on the hoof', but never find its way into the text that has been handed down.

So we should never be shy of noting Shakespeare's dramaturgical shortcomings, or of trying to repair them. None of those shortcomings can dent his unmatchable reputation, and no repair will have lasting currency, since every new production will begin with the received text, not with a production prompt copy gathering dust in some theatre archive – even one made available on websites like my own. We all try to get to grips with a Shakespeare play afresh, which is just as it should be. Our work will be soon forgotten, while the great Quartos and Folios will live on and on.

*

To add just one qualification to that, but about a non-Shakespeare play, Middleton and Rowley's *The Changeling*, which I directed in our 2004 season, and which transferred successfully with *Macbeth* for a five-week run at the Barbican Pit. For me, this account of the beautiful, privileged Beatrice-Joanna's journey into murder and adultery is the most interesting, and potentially the best, of all the non-Shakespeare tragedies of the period. Its main plot has a Racinian purity of focus and a lean, driving language that lifts the hairs on the back of the neck. It also, in its extensive use of the 'aside', explores the disjunctions between inner self and presented self to a degree that has never been matched in theatre, before or since.

But while the play is widely admired as a text, it is relatively rarely performed. There can be little doubt that this is because of the shortcomings in its comic subplot (set in Bedlam), which not only asks the modern audience to enjoy a rich but sometimes obscure diet of classical and bawdy reference, but increasingly fails to mirror the action of the main plot, and finally fades away without even resolving its own narrative.

Dominic Power's version of this play (again, see my website for the full text) repairs these shortcomings, to my mind magnificently, and does deserve to be revived, even to become a standard. There are a number of tweaks and clarifications to the subplot, including the phoney madman, Franciscus, presenting himself as dumb as well as deranged (frenetically scribbling his love poems to Isabella, before his ruse is discovered by Lollio), but its key development is an entirely new – penultimate – scene in which the rivalry between Franciscus and Antonio climaxes in a potentially lethal duel. This is interrupted by the arrival in the madhouse of Beatrice's father, Vermandero, to arrest the two young men (mistakenly) for the murder of Alonzo de Piracquo; in this way the two worlds of the play are finally brought together.

Gyuri Sarossy (Franciscus) and Jamie Ballard (Antonio) fight it out in the new subplot scene at the Barbican Pit, photo © Graham Wyles 2004

There is a brief account of the version in the Introduction to the most recent New Mermaid edition, edited by Michael Neill.[2]

Lyn Gardner wrote of it:

> Love is a madness in Middleton and Rowley's 1622 drama, a
> piece that often feels like two plays stuck together with 17th-
> century sticky tape, but which here is unusually whole.
> (*Guardian*, 23 March 2004)

And Susannah Clapp:

> ... you get, as if newly minted, the free-floating madness of
> Middleton and Rowley's play – whose high points include the
> substitution of maid for mistress in a bridegroom's bed, the
> trial of an early pregnancy-testing kit, and the triumphant
> severing of a dead man's finger. Most of all, you get the sense of
> personality in flux. (*Observer*, 4 April 2004)

'Personality in flux' has been the main burden of this book. It is
fundamental to our continuing connection with Shakespeare's characters
over the gap of four centuries; the excitement, the joy and the horror of
human potential, of the choices we make, hour by hour, day by day, as we
peer, nervously but hopefully, into what lies 'behind'.

1. See Stanley Wells' wonderful book, *Shakespeare and Co.* (Penguin Books, 2007).
2. Methuen Drama, 2019.

Shakespeare at the Tobacco Factory: Production History, 2000–2017

All productions directed by Andrew Hilton, with the exceptions of the 2008 *Hamlet*, directed by Jonathan Miller, the 2015 *Romeo and Juliet* by Polina Kalinina, and the 2017 *Othello* by Richard Twyman.

Tobacco Factory	Spring 2000	*King Lear*
		A Midsummer Night's Dream
	Spring 2001	*Measure for Measure*
		Coriolanus
	Spring 2002	*The Winter's Tale*
		Twelfth Night
	Spring 2003	*Troilus and Cressida*
		As You Like It
	Spring 2004	*Macbeth*
		The Changeling
Barbican Pit	Autumn 2004	*Macbeth*
		The Changeling
Tobacco Factory	Spring 2005	*Pericles*
		Three Sisters
	Spring 2006	*Titus Andronicus*
		Love's Labours Lost
	Spring 2007	*Othello*
		Much Ado About Nothing

	Spring 2008	*The Taming of the Shrew*
		Hamlet
	Spring 2009	*Julius Caesar*
		Antony and Cleopatra
Bristol Theatre Royal	Autumn 2009	*Uncle Vanya*
		(**stf**/Bristol Old Vic
		Co-Production)
Tobacco Factory	Spring 2010	*A Midsummer Night's Dream*
		The Tempest
Galway Festival	Summer 2010	*Uncle Vanya*
Bristol Theatre Royal	Autumn 2010	*The Misanthrope*
		(**stf**/Bristol Old Vic
		Co-Production)
Tobacco Factory	Spring 2011	*Richard II*
		The Comedy of Errors
		(also the Exeter Northcott)
	Spring 2012	*King Lear*
		The Cherry Orchard and
		On the Evils of Tobacco
		(both Chekhovs transferred
		to the Kingston Rose)
	Spring 2013	*Richard III*
		Two Gentlemen of Verona
		(also UK tour)
	Spring 2014	*As You Like It*
		(also UK tour)
		Arcadia
University of Bristol	Autumn 2014	*The Conquering Hero*
		(Staged Reading)
Tobacco Factory	Spring 2015	*Romeo and Juliet*
		(also Neuss Festival and
		UK Tour)
		The School for Scandal
	Autumn 2015	*Living Quarters*
		(Lead Producer, Tobacco
		Factory Theatres)
	Spring 2016	*Hamlet*
		(also Craiova Festival and
		UK Tour)
		All's Well That Ends Well
		(also Neuss and UK Tour)

Spring 2017	*Othello* (also Exeter, Wilton's Music Hall and Neuss) *Tartuffe*

Postscript: In 2018 the company lost the economic foundation of its unsubsidised work, its twelve-week spring season at the Tobacco Factory. In its place it secured four weeks at the Factory in the autumn, a run at the Ustinov Theatre in Bath, a week at the Neuss Festival and a short UK tour; and, in 2019, another short run at the Factory and a return visit to Wilton's Music Hall. The plays were *Henry V* and *Much Ado About Nothing*, both directed by Elizabeth Freestone, and both very well received, but they could not pay their way. The company then suffered the common blight of the Covid-19 pandemic and, in October 2021, the Trustees decided the company should cease production, dedicating its remaining funds to a small annual bursary to help theatre arts students struggling to pay for their training.

Index

Andrew Hilton

Andrew Hilton is an actor, director, teacher and playwright. He created Shakespeare at the Tobacco Factory (stf) in Bristol in 1999 and remained its Artistic Director until 2017, directing 39 productions for the company, at the Tobacco Factory, the Bristol Old Vic, the Barbican Pit, and on tour in the UK, the Irish Republic, Germany and Romania.

He began his professional carreer in 1972 as an Assistant, then Associate, to Bernard Miles at the Mermaid Theatre in London, before joining the National Theatre as an actor in 1975. He went from there to play many seasons at the Bristol Old Vic, as well as appearing widely on television and radio.

Making Bristol his home in 1979, he began teaching Shakespeare acting at the Bristol Old Vic Theatre School and joined a co-operative theatre company for whom he directed new plays by James Wilson and Dominic Power, the UK premieres of plays by Brian Friel and Michael Gow, and his first production of *Measure for Measure*.

His Shakespeare productions at the Tobacco Factory have been widely praised; in 2001 Jeremy Kingston in *The Times* called the company 'one of the most exciting in the land'; in 2005 Lyn Gardner of the *Guardian* hailed 'one of the great tellers of Shakespeare'; and in 2013 Susannah Clapp in *The Observer* dubbed it 'the Shakespearean powerhouse'. But he has also been a noted director of Chekhov. His account of his 2009 production of *Uncle Vanya* at the Bristol Old Vic (a BOV/stf co-production) was broadcast by the BBC as part of Radio 3's *The Essay* Series.

As a playwright he has co-authored – with Dominic Power – *Tartuffe*, after Molière (Tobacco Factory, 2017), a stage adaptation of James Hogg's novel *The Private Memoirs and Confessions of a Justified Sinner*, and a piece of music-theatre, *Lady with Dog*, based on the short story by Chekhov.

Andrew was born in Bolton in 1947 and read English at Cambridge, studying Shakespeare at Churchill College under Michael Long. In 2013 he was made an Honorary Doctor of Letters by the University of Bristol for his services to theatre in the city.

He is married to the stage manager and artist Diana Favell, and they have one son.